‖‖‖ ‖‖‖‖‖‖ ‖ ‖ ‖ ‖‖ ‖‖‖‖‖‖‖ ‖‖‖ ‖ ‖‖
W9-AAS-450

WHAT THE CRITICS ARE SAYING ABOUT
HOW TO SURVIVE YOUR FRESHMAN YEAR

Winner - Best Book on Adjusting to College Life.
—*ABOUT.COM READERS CHOICE AWARDS*

"Hidden gem."
—*INGRAM LIBRARY SERVICE*

Recommended Reading.
—*POSITIVE TEENS MAGAZINE*

"Ten Good Books for Grads."
—*DETROIT FREE PRESS*

"*How to Survive Your Freshman Year* provides student viewpoints and expert advice on virtually every topic pertaining to first-year students from moving in to finding meals....After reading this book students will be aware of the realities of college life and be better prepared to shape their own unique college experience.
—*JOURNAL OF COLLEGE ORIENTATION AND TRANSITION*

"A guide full of fantastic advice from hundreds of young scholars who've been there… a quick and fun read."
—*BOSTON HERALD*

"The perfect send-off present for the student who is college bound. The book manages to be hilarious and helpful. As an added bonus, it's refreshingly free of sanctimony."
—*THE POST AND COURIER, CHARLESTON, SOUTH CAROLINA*

"Explains college to the clueless."
—*COLLEGE-BOUND TEEN*

"The advice dispensed is handy, useful, and practical. This book will make great light reading for an incoming freshman."
—*VOYA*

"A great tool for young people beginning an important and often daunting new challenge, with short and funny, real-world tips."
—*WASHINGTON PARENT*

"[A] book that can help that college bound freshman get through that tough first year...Who better to try to help that nervous freshman endure the first year than people who have just recently done it. Laced with different hints and stories, it can be a real help for a student."

—HELLUM

"The book contains more than 1,000 pieces of real-life knowledge from hundreds of students who attended more than 100 colleges across the country."

—MAINSTREET, POWERED BY THESTREET.COM

Visit www.hundredsofheads.com to learn more.

How to Survive Your Freshman Year

WARNING:

This Guide contains differing opinions. Hundreds of Heads will not always agree. Advice taken in combination may cause unwanted side effects. Use your Head when selecting advice.

How to
Survive
Your
Freshman Year
Fifth Edition

SCOTT C. SILVERMAN, ED.D.
FRANCES NORTHCUTT, ED.M.
SPECIAL EDITORS

Created by
MARK W. BERNSTEIN & YADIN KAUFMANN

Hundreds of Heads Books, LLC
ATLANTA, GEORGIA

Copyright © 2013 by Hundreds of Heads Books, LLC, Atlanta, Georgia

All rights reserved. No portion of this book may be reproduced mechanically, electronically, or by any other means, including photocopying without written permission of the publisher.

Trademarks: Hundreds of Heads, Because Hundreds of Heads are Better than One!, and related trade dress are trademarks or registered trademarks of Hundreds of Heads Books, LLC, and may not be used without written permission. All other trademarks are the property of their respective owners. Hundreds of Heads Books, LLC is not associated with any product or vendor mentioned in this book.

Cover photograph Jupiter Images
Cover and book design by Elizabeth Johnsboen

Library of Congress Cataloging-in-Publication Data on file

Limit of Liability/Disclaimer of Warranty: Every effort has been made to accurately present the views expressed by the interviewees quoted herein. The publisher and editors regret any unintentional inaccuracies or omissions, and do not assume responsibility for the opinions of the respondents. Neither the publisher nor the authors of any of the stories herein shall be liable for any loss of profit or any other commercial damages, including but not limited to special, incidental, consequential, or other damages.

HUNDREDS OF HEADS® books are available at special discounts when purchased in bulk for premiums or institutional or educational use. Excerpts and custom editions can be created for specific uses. For more information, please email sales@hundredsofheads.com or write to:

HUNDREDS OF HEADS BOOKS, LLC
info@hundredsofheads.com

ISBN-13: 978-1-933512-61-7

Printed in Canada

0 9 8 7 6 5 4 3 2 1

CONTENTS

THE HEADS EXPLAINED

Look for these special symbols throughout the book:

 Remember this significant story or bit of advice.

 This may be something to explore in more detail.

 Watch out! Be careful!

 We are astounded, thrilled, or delighted by this one.

 Here's something to think about.

—*THE EDITORS
AND HUNDREDS OF HEADS BOOKS*

Introduction

Can you believe it? You've made it! You're in college. You're beginning the best adventure of your life, where amazing opportunities await you around every corner.

If your college experience turns out to be anything like mine, and I hope it does, you are about to make some of the best friends you'll keep for the rest of your life, and have awesome, unique and interesting adventures that you'll be talking about for years to come. Before you know it, you'll graduate and go off to bigger and better things, so enjoy these next few years while they last.

Yes, you are going to pull all-nighters, ace some tests, flunk others, you'll argue with a room-mate or friend, you'll date and break-up and date again, etc. In addition to all of that, you're going to have an absolute blast, and you'll have stories that you're dying to share with others.

Here are a few of my favorite or most memorable undergraduate experiences, as they might have looked in my tweets – if Twitter had existed when I was in college. (Warning: some of these are mistakes I learned from, and some are on my list of proudest achievements:)

> ➢ Loaned my antique 1968 Ford Mustang to a friend, who then had a minor accident…

later that night my car exploded in the campus parking lot. #callTripleA #needaridetoworktomorrow #NeverAgain

➢ Squirted water at people through my door.Also tried a partial flooding. Turns out my dad did the same thing when he was in college. #fatherknowsbest #CollegePranks101

➢ Temporarily convinced my roommate I had a contagious disease. He slept elsewhere for a few nights. Almost got kicked out of the residence hall. #RoomtoMyself #ummJustKidding

➢ Applied to be a Resident Advisor. Didn't get the job, not sure why. #seeabove

➢ Road trip with friends for a team contest, packed 10 people into 1 hotel room, didn't get caught, but also didn't win. #FunTimes #OnABudget

➢ Joined and formed multiple student organizations. Made lots of friends and had lots of cool experiences. #NoTimeForSleep #WoreLotsOfHats

➢ Got towed thru a Drive-Thru while riding a cardboard box.Picked up my food. Then a new sign was posted: 'Vehicled Customers Only'. #TrueStory

➢ Served as a Peer Mentor and helped a number of students survive their freshman year. Some of them became mentors too. #GonnaWriteABookOneDay

➢ I ran for student government, served as Senator (twice), Academic Affairs Director, VP Campus Internal Affairs. Loved it. Met a staff person there whose job included advising/mentoring student leaders, supporting all students. #foundmycalling #achievementunlocked #WhoKnew

➢ Moved into a cheap apartment, with lots of problems. 3 different managers in the time I lived there. #Slumlord #lessonlearned

> ➢ Formed a non-profit organization to fight religious discrimination, served as CEO. #makeadifference
> ➢ Successfully lobbied my peers to vote to build a new Student Union Building with our own funds. Now to help design it. #DreamBig #CampusLife #UsingMyVoice
> ➢ I just delivered the Commencement address, sharing many of the above stories. Got my degree and diploma. #AchievementUnlocked #whatsnext

Now you're probably thinking: "Great, how do I check all of those things off my list? Sign me up," or "Wow, I am so *not* going to do that!" That's ok! I am definitely not recommending that you pull pranks with your friends (I do work for a university, after all), and I'm not saying that there is only one way to be successful in college (you have to do what works best for you). Each university and person is different, but there are some nuances about how college works in general, and some things you can do to improve your chances of success. Reading this book will get you off to a great start.

So take a moment and think about what Facebook posts or Tweets you will be most proud of when *you* graduate. What will your LinkedIn page say about your accomplishments? What skills have you developed and what experiences have you had? Think ahead, to roughly four years from now (give or take a year if you're finishing early or are going to be on the "Bonus Year" plan). Now, while still pretending you're at graduation day and looking back on your college experiences as told via your Social Media pages, what are the highlights? Jot these down here in the book.... over the next year and until you graduate, revisit them and revise as necessary.

The point is, you are going to have stories that are different, but just as entertaining, memorable and remarkable as mine are, you just have

to invest a little time and energy. Get involved
in campus life, attend programs and events, and
join a student organization, just to get a head
start. Study too, of course - but do more than just
study. College is all about learning how to make
the choices that are right for you, gaining skills to
survive in the "real" world, and learning how to be
successful in life.

You're going to encounter lots of advice in this
book, and some of the tips you see from students
or graduates may conflict with others. Here's a
great rule of thumb: There is no one perfect way
to survive your first year of college, or the rest of
college, for that matter. Different tips will work
for different people in different ways, and much
depends on the circumstances. We have included
tips, anecdotes and suggestions that will help you
succeed, as well as some that you obviously won't
want to replicate. We're showing you a true and
authentic look into what college may be like; use
this as a resource, not a manual.

If there's one thing I've learned from the 15+
years I've spent on college campuses, it's this:
Don't be afraid to make mistakes; everyone who
takes risks makes mistakes…but use the opportunity to 'own' your mistakes and learn from them,
and take some risks because the rewards will be
worthwhile.

So read this book and glean everything you
can from it. The tips, resources and advice in here
might be useful for your friends, too – so remember to "Like" our page on Facebook (Facebook.
com/YourFreshmanYear)! Have an amazing
Freshman Year, and a great college experience.

Oh, and next year you're on your own!

Scott C. Silverman, Ed.D.
Associate Director of Student Affairs
University Honors
University of California, Riverside

When we published the first edition of *How to Survive Your Freshman Year* in 2004, we were walking in uncharted territory. We believed—strongly—that kids going off to college would benefit from, and enjoy, a book full of the wisdom and experiences of many hundreds of others who have lived through freshman year and come out with something interesting to say about it. But the enthusiasm with which readers responded surprised even us. The book quickly became the year's best-selling college guide, and it has gone from strength to strength since then.

We've now got 20 books in our Hundreds of Heads® Survival Guide series—including books on getting into college, succeeding in college, and even getting *your kids* into college, as well as marriage, divorce, raising kids, dieting, retirement, and many other wonderful challenges life throws at you.

Other advice books, no matter how smart or expert their authors, are generally limited to the knowledge of only one person. But two heads are better than one, as the old saying goes—and it turns out that hundreds of them are even better. So we interviewed lots – and we do mean lots – of students and graduates from big schools, small schools, Ivies and state universities. Greeks, geeks and jocks weighed in with their college experiences. The results are remarkably universal. From dorm life and roommates to college parties and dating; from choosing your major to implementing helpful study practices; from battling homesickness to avoiding fashion faux pas—it's all here for your educational use. You might even be relieved to know that the things you worry about are, in fact, common concerns among your fellow students.

As you might expect, we heard many different views—and some of those views differed from one another. Are fraternities and sororities a good choice or not? How close should you try to stay with your high school friends? And, of course—to party or not to party? You'll make your own decisions, but you can do it armed with the insights of the people featured on these pages.

And now we're on to the fifth edition of *HTSYFY*, which is even better than its predecessors. The new version of this indispensable guide features not only updated wisdom from college students across the country, but also bicoastal expert advice from Scott Silverman, Associate Director of Student Affairs in the University Honors department at The University of California, Riverside, and Frances Northcutt, an educational consultant and former Honors Advisor at Hunter College at the City University of New York. Scott and Frances – and the many other experts whose advice is featured in these pages – weigh in with invaluable perspective for college freshmen based on their many years of advising students as they go through this wonderful and complex new period in their lives. And be sure to check out the bios of our expert contributors in the back of the book - many of them have included their contact information, in case you want to follow up.

You're embarking on one of the best experiences of your life. Have fun. Study hard. And know that you've got hundreds of friends to show you the way.

Mark W. Bernstein
Yadin Kaufmann

Get Ready: What to Take to College

I t is a universal truth that college freshmen leave packing until the last minute. Why? First, it's a big job and you didn't feel like doing it. Fair enough! Second, you couldn't quite believe that the big day would really come. Oops!

And third, you had a gut sense that leaving home just might be harder than you thought during all those years of high school when you couldn't wait to be out on your own. So your subconscious concocted the perfect plan: instead of getting weepy and emotional during this fraught time, you and your loved ones will be stressed out, irritable, and panicked over the chaos of last-minute packing. Brilliant! Well, sooner or later you've got to do it. Here's some advice on what to take along – and what to leave behind.

A JOURNAL. It's kind of a manic-depressive time, freshman year. There are really big highs and really big lows. During the lows it helps to write it out.

—ANONYMOUS
    YALE UNIVERSITY, SOPHOMORE

MY PHOTOS. THEY KEPT ME GROUNDED.

—HANNAH SMITH
HARVARD
UNIVERSITY, JUNIOR

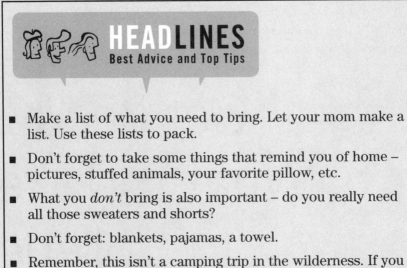

HEADLINES
Best Advice and Top Tips

- Make a list of what you need to bring. Let your mom make a list. Use these lists to pack.

- Don't forget to take some things that remind you of home – pictures, stuffed animals, your favorite pillow, etc.

- What you *don't* bring is also important – do you really need all those sweaters and shorts?

- Don't forget: blankets, pajamas, a towel.

- Remember, this isn't a camping trip in the wilderness. If you forget something like toothpaste, you can always buy some.

Bring your blanket. Make sure it's comfy.

—*Chana Weiner*
Barnard College
Sophomore

Bring some good pajamas. It's uncomfortable sleeping with other people in the same room, but one thing that helps is to have good pajamas that cover most of your body parts. You can lounge around in them without worrying about how you look.

—*S.G.*
Columbia University, Senior

• • • • • • • •

Medicines are key because you don't want to be running around looking for something.

—*David*
Kean University, Junior

• • • • • • • •

Get a frisbee. It will help get you out and hanging out with other people. And that is a great way to find out where people are living and what classes they are taking.

—*David*
Kean University, Junior

BRING LOTS OF BEDDING. Foam "egg crates" are a must. The mattresses at my school are covered in rubber in case you wet the bed or something, so I got a feather bed, and lots of people have foam things. Then you can get a good night's sleep.

> —EDITH ZIMMERMAN
> WESLEYAN UNIVERSITY, SOPHOMORE

A CASE OF NO-DOZ, Pop-Tarts, and several extra room keys.

> —S.L.M.
> INDIANA UNIVERSITY, GRADUATE

AN EXCELLENT PAIR OF STUDIO-GRADE headphones for those times when you want to jam but your room-mate wants to snooze. You cannot get through college without your music.

> —MARGOT CARMICHAEL LESTER
> UNIVERSITY OF NORTH CAROLINA AT CHAPEL HILL, GRADUATE

A TENNIS BALL. It's great to toss around the lounge and in the hallway, and it is a great conversation starter. As you throw the ball around, people come in to toss and the camarade-rie begins.

> —DAVE BANVILLE
> AMERICAN UNIVERSITY, GRADUATE

AIR FRESHENERS; you can make your dingy room smell like apples and cinnamon. When I got to my dorm room it smelled like sweat and smelly socks. Most first-year dorms don't have air conditioning, so be prepared and bring something that smells good.

> —Y.H.
> UNIVERSITY OF VIRGINIA, JUNIOR

Top 10 FRESHMAN FAVORITES

Sleeping bag
Guitar
Headphones
Blender
Blankie
Photos
Organizer
Cell phone
Bible
Toothbrush

A REALLY NICE CHAIR; something you can move, something that folds up. If there are five or six people in a room, everyone is sitting on the floor. But if you bring in your chair, you can keep it for yourself. Or, if there's that girl, give it up to her and you earn bonus points.

—CHRIS PROVENCHER
JAMES MADISON UNIVERSITY, FRESHMAN

66 Communal showers are gross, so bring shower shoes. Everybody wears them, except my roommate. But at least she took showers! 99

—SIERRA
CAL POLY SAN LUIS OBISPO, JUNIOR

A NICE TOWEL IS REALLY IMPORTANT. People see you in your towel and you need to look good. Douglas Adams said the towel is the most important piece of equipment in the universe, because you can do so much with it.

—TIM JOYCE
GEORGETOWN UNIVERSITY, SENIOR

If I could, I'd bring my bed from home.

—CESAR
YALE UNIVERSITY
FRESHMAN

GET A KICK-ASS MOUNTAIN BIKE to ride between classes—and an even more kick-ass lock.

—J.G.
FLORIDA STATE UNIVERSITY, GRADUATE

DON'T FORGET ...

- Detergent and fabric softener
- Laundry basket, hamper, or bag
- Shower caddy
- Shower shoes
- Robe
- First aid kit
- Sewing kit
- Small toolkit
- Hangers
- Extra-long sheets
- Batteries
- Cell phone charger
- Computer cables
- Computer printer
- Desk lamp
- Electric cords
- Flashlight
- Surge protector
- Laptop lock
- Power strip
- Small fan
- Umbrella
- Cup, bowl, plate, silverware
- Can opener
- Fridge and microwave
- Mini-reading light
- Egg crate mattress pad
- Tupperware
- Snacks
- Corkboard/dry erase board
- Acetaminophen, aspirin, ibuprofen
- Band-aids, Neosporin
- Brush and comb
- Cologne/perfume
- Cotton balls
- Cough drops
- Dental floss
- Hair dryer
- Hairstyling products
- Lotion/moisturizer
- Nail clippers, tweezers
- Pepto-Bismol
- Q-Tips
- Razors, shaving cream, aftershave
- Shampoo, conditioner
- Soap
- Toothbrush and toothpaste
- Vitamins

DON'T FORGET THE INTANGIBLES

BRING GOOD JUDGMENT. Having good judgment will help freshmen start off in the right direction.

> —KAMALI BENT
> CORNELL UNIVERSITY, GRADUATE

• • • • • • • •

A SENSE OF SELF: You always have to see where you are and where you want to be in the future. It's something that's always changing.

> —RUTHANN
> MOUNT HOLYOKE COLLEGE, GRADUATE

• • • • • • • •

FRESHMEN SHOULD TAKE a blank slate with them to college; a fresh and clean start. If they did poorly in high school or were nerds, college is the time to change all of that. In college, you determine your future.

> —VIVIAN ORIAKU
> UNIVERSITY OF MIAMI, GRADUATE

• • • • • • • •

IF I COULD BRING ONE THING to college, it would be maturity. But I suppose that's what college is all about . . . living and learning!

> —ANONYMOUS
> INDIANA UNIVERSITY, GRADUATE

• • • • • • • •

I WOULD BRING SLEEP IN A BOTTLE.

> —COLLEEN
> PRINCETON UNIVERSITY, JUNIOR

• • • • • • • •

PATIENCE IS ABSOLUTELY KEY. You will undoubtedly be faced with a variety of people, classes, rules and requirements over the four years of college that will test your patience, so starting off with a healthy dose is good.

> —REBECCA
> HUNTER COLLEGE, SENIOR

FRESHMEN SHOULD BRING a plan for the future, and a positive attitude with them to college. And ... stunna shades! LOL.

—*SHAQUEENA LE'SHAYE LEWIS*
UNIVERSITY OF MIAMI, GRADUATE

* * * * * * * * *

THE MOST IMPORTANT THING any incoming freshman should take with them to college is an identity as a strong individual. Having great organizational skills and a weekly to-do list will cut down on the stress.

—*QUONIAS*
UNIVERSITY OF WEST GEORGIA, SENIOR

* * * * * * * *

BRING THE ABILITY TO FOCUS. Focus on your academics and remember why you're going to college in the first place.

—*J.M.G.*
DUKE UNIVERSITY, GRADUATE

* * * * * * * *

A GROUNDED SENSE OF SELF and an open mind. These two things will keep you optimistic and prepared for the new and exciting journey ahead. You will have a greater confidence and will be able to stay true to yourself in trying situations. These are the best years of your life, so enjoy every minute of them!

—*HAYLEY MASON*
HOWARD UNIVERSITY, SOPHOMORE

MY PLANNER. I didn't use one in high school. But when I got to college, I had so much going on that I couldn't afford NOT to use one. With all the deadlines for papers, applications and tests, no one can keep everything straight in their head. So, to encourage myself to stay organized, I bought a cute, visually appealing planner/calendar that I would want to write in. It is my life! From dates for schoolwork, to clubs, to social activities and even just little notes to myself about things I need to remember to do, my planner has everything I need to know in it.

—MERELISE HARTE ROUZER
GEORGIA INSTITUTE OF TECHNOLOGY, SOPHOMORE

FRESHMAN FIRST-AID KIT

Feeling sick? Accident-prone? Sure, you can go to the Wellness Center (if it's open) or knock on your RA's door (if he's not out that night), or hike over to the local drugstore or 7-Eleven (if the temperature isn't below-freezing) – *or*, you can remember to pack your very own first-aid kit and really be ready for anything!

- Band-Aids
- Antibiotic ointment
- Thermometer
- Pain reliever of your choice (ibuprofen, acetaminophen, etc.)
- Travel-sized containers of any other over-the-counter medicines you use
- Contact information for your doctor(s) back home
- Reusable gel "ice" pack (keep it in your mini-fridge)
- Ace bandage
- Antiseptic soap or wipes
- Tweezers

A TRUNKFUL OF COMFORT

There are many things to fill your old leather trunk with before heading off to college. Comfortable bedding is a must. A soft comforter and a substantial pillow will make your dreams of calculus and Shakespeare that much sweeter. A microwave, some Pyrex, and a few packets of cocoa will help to make cold winter study sessions more bearable. Moreover, a rug or two can help to add a bit of warmth to a dorm room. The greatest things to bring to college, however, won't fit in your trunk. These are things like self-confidence, composure, and respect. Don't be afraid to stick to your guns, hold your morals, and be yourself. College can be a time of becoming someone new, for sure, but that doesn't mean you have to become someone else. If you have respect for yourself, people will have respect for you. Respect for others is also essential.

—DREW HILL
COLBY COLLEGE, JUNIOR

BRING WARM CLOTHES if you go to school up north. I'm from Miami and I didn't know what a winter coat was. Now I have a couple – and an umbrella.

—HILARY TRESS
NEW YORK UNIVERSITY, JUNIOR

MY JOURNAL. It's a companion when you don't have one. It sounds cheesy, but I used mine a lot.

—STEPHANIE
UNIVERSITY OF PENNSYLVANIA, SENIOR

BRING EXTRA LIGHTING for your dorm room and an air mattress in case a friend comes over.

—JESSICA
BARNARD COLLEGE, JUNIOR

FRESHMAN FACTOID
At Stanford University there are roughly 13,000 bicycles on campus on any given day.

Stuffed animals. . . I brought mine!

—*CATHERINE G. BARRETT*
BRYN MAWR
COLLEGE
SOPHOMORE

A BOX FAN of reasonable torque and a bath towel, preferably damp. The fan directed out the dorm window was to create an exhaust vacuum effect while the damp towel, covering the gap at the foot of the door, prevented the escape of any extraneous, ahem, smoke.

—*A.D.*
UNIVERSITY OF NEW HAMPSHIRE

• • • • • • • •

ORANGE-FLAVORED GATORADE. More Gatorade is consumed to relieve hangovers than while playing any sport. And stay with orange, because red can stain when it comes back up.

—*ANONYMOUS*
UNIVERSITY OF FLORIDA, GRADUATE

• • • • • • • •

DO NOT BUY A TRASHCAN WITH A LID, because once it is full you will turn it into a table. You may think you're better than that now, but so did I.

—*BARRY LANGER*
OGLETHORPE UNIVERSITY, JUNIOR

• • • • • • • •

A NICE WATERPROOF BOOK BAG. If it rains, your books get wet and there's not a lot you can do to fix them. It hurts the sell-back value, too.

—*B.M.*
UNIVERSITY OF MARYLAND, JUNIOR

• • • • • • • •

BUY EXTRA UNDERWEAR! Pants don't get dirty that fast... it's always the underwear that needs to be washed first!

—*EMILY*
HARVARD COLLEGE, SENIOR

A MECHANICAL PENCIL WITH A BIG ERASER. If you're like me and you'd rather pay attention in class than do a bunch of reading, a good mechanical pencil is great for taking clean, concise notes.

> —J.S.
> UNIVERSITY OF GEORGIA, GRADUATE

. . . .

EARPLUGS. There's a lot of noise in the dorm.

> —RICK SHILLING
> PENNSYLVANIA STATE UNIVERSITY, GRADUATE

. . . .

A CLIP-ON READING LAMP. Or just a light you can shut off from your bed.

> —AMANDA
> WELLESLEY COLLEGE, SENIOR

. . . .

I WOULD DEFINITELY BRING THAT ONE DVD OR BOOK that you can't live without. Last semester was pretty stressful and being able to curl under the blankets and marathon a favorite show from high school probably kept me from burning all of my papers in a manic bonfire. It sounds silly, but grab onto that DVD or book like it's a lifeboat, because it very well may be (not to be overly dramatic or anything). Plus you can lend it to friends if you want to let them have access to a part of your brain.

Also, socks. You can never have enough socks.

> —SHANNON KELLEY
> KENYON COLLEGE, JUNIOR

Bring your wallet and a lot of money.

—COLIN O'CONNOR
GEORGETOWN
UNIVERSITY, JUNIOR

A GUITAR. It's something that relaxes me, and it helps socially. You can always pull out your guitar and play on the lawn or wherever, and other people will come up and talk.

—*LEAH PRICE*
GEORGETOWN UNIVERSITY, SOPHOMORE

• • • • • • • •

I WOULD BRING MY PILLOW—it smells like my sleep.

—*ANONYMOUS*
UNIVERSITY OF RHODE ISLAND, SOPHOMORE

• • • • • • • •

I HAD A BATTERY-CHARGED, PORTABLE BLENDER. It was super. It cost $50. I was dorm shopping with my dad, and I said, "I need that blender." He was like, "You don't need a portable blender for college." I was like, "No, no, Dad, I need that. Take the comforter out of the cart. I need that." So we got it. And I made everything in it. A blender helps make friends.

—*CASEY*
GEORGETOWN UNIVERSITY, SENIOR

• • • • • • • •

BEST GIFT TO ASK FOR FROM YOUR PARENTS: One really great sleeping bag. You'll use it for everything, from spring break in a hotel room with 20 other people, to backpacking across Europe or the U.S.

—*WENDY W.*
UNIVERSITY OF GEORGIA, GRADUATE

• • • • • • • •

A KAYAK: I am an introvert and I love spending time alone.

—*DENALI*
PRINCETON UNIVERSITY, JUNIOR

A Hot Pot. I hated the food at my college, so every other meal I made Oodles of Noodles. You can make tea, coffee, soup — anything, really — in a Hot Pot.

—*ALYSSA*
JAMES MADISON UNIVERSITY SOPHOMORE

A George Foreman grill. Those grills are so fast and easy, and everything is pretty good, from steak to grilled cheese. No college kid should be without one.

> —*Jeff*
> *Bowling Green State University, Graduate*

• • • • • • • •

Underwear.

> —*Walter*
> *University of Maryland–College Park, Sophomore*

• • • • • • • •

Everyone should bring one book that they really enjoy reading and re-reading. I brought *Ender's Game* by Orson Scott Card, and whenever I was having a really stressful week or just needed a break from the required reading for classes, I read my comfort book.

> —*Sarah*
> *Wellesley College, Sophomore*

• • • • • • • •

Bring your mom's credit card.

—*J.G.*
George Washington University, Senior

A few candles, a pack of cigarettes, and some good poetry.

> —*Anonymous*
> *Calvin College, Graduate*

• • • • • • • •

Bring an umbrella. Yes, it rains at college, too.

> —*Phil*
> *University of Virginia, Senior*

• • • • • • • •

I got a list from the university on what to - and what not to - bring with me. If your college or university offers something like this, make sure you use it.

> —*David*
> *Kean University, Junior*

WHAT *NOT* TO BRING

DORMS ARE SMALL. ESPECIALLY AS A FRESHMAN. Don't buy too much stuff. The checklists at stores like Target and Bed Bath & Beyond are a good start, but you don't want to overbuy and cram yourself into your first college year. Laundry turns into a pain pretty quickly when you're on your own, so a lot of socks and underwear will make your life a lot happier.

> —*MICHAEL CUMMO*
> *BOSTON UNIVERSITY, SENIOR*

I JUST DIDN'T KNOW WHAT TO BRING, so I kept packing every little thing I might need or want to have with me. I would have brought my bathroom and bed, too! When I got to school I had no place to put anything. I ended up bringing back as much stuff as I could each time I went home. After break, I came back up with only the things I really needed.

> —*ILANA COOPERSMITH*
> *RUTGERS UNIVERSITY, GRADUATE*

DON'T BRING YOUR HIGH SCHOOL YEARBOOK with you. Yes, I missed high school but I was so busy that I did not even open the book. It is a major dust collector and you have to be the one to clean it off.

> —*DAVID*
> *KEAN UNIVERSITY, JUNIOR*

DON'T BE THE ONLY PERSON IN YOUR DORM with a car, and if you are, don't let other people borrow it. If you do, there will be trouble.

> —*HANNAH*
> *EMORY UNIVERSITY, JUNIOR*

I CAME HERE WITH MY DAD'S STATION WAGON and a minivan filled with my stuff. About a week ago, my parents came back and we packed the station wagon back up and sent stuff back home. It was too much. I brought my notes from my classes in high school. I brought my books from home. I didn't even want to look at a book or notes unless it was from a current class.

—*H.D. BALLARD*
UNIVERSITY OF VIRGINIA, FRESHMAN

THERE'S NOT ENOUGH SPACE to keep your stuff, so don't bring a lot of stuff.

—*MARINNA FADOR*
BOSTON COLLEGE, FRESHMAN

TOP FIVE THINGS *NOT* TO BRING

1. **Ice hockey gear:** You'll be home again before it gets cold enough to use it. And if your goal is to impress potential dates, hang a medal on the wall or put up a photo of you and your team with a trophy—packs the same punch but takes up much less space.

2. **Your jewelry collection:** You don't need it all, and you definitely don't need the stress of making sure it doesn't get stolen. And you don't have the space.

3. **Your favorite books:** If you have them lying around, you may end up reading when you should be out meeting people.

4. **Romantic candles (or any other kind):** They're against the rules. Don't go down in history as "that *@#%& freshman who burned down our dorm." Besides, you can buy electric candles nowadays for those special occasions when mood lighting is in order.

5. **Inspirational posters of any kind:** If you need a reminder to "Hang in there," put it in your planner—not on your wall, where it'll hang your social life.

MY FAN. There are many things that you will need assistance in airing out. A lot. Fans make this easier. In the same vein, having a hairdryer can really help with this too. Just some kind of thing to move air.

—*BARRY LANGER*
OGLETHORPE UNIVERSITY, JUNIOR

• • • • • • • •

A FOLDOUT CHAIR. Visitors will constantly be stopping by your dorm room. Plus, the chair can double as seating for a tailgate!

—*LINDSEY WILLIAMSON*
VANDERBILT UNIVERSITY, GRADUATE

• • • • • • • •

" Buy a sturdy, roomy backpack. You'll need it to hold thick, heavy textbooks for courses like English, political science, biology, algebra, etc. "

—*BRIAN TURNER*
UNIVERSITY OF GEORGIA, GRADUATE

• • • • • • • •

HAVING A PRINTER in my room is really helpful. I can print in my room without going to the computer center or waiting until the next day.

—*ANNIE THOMAS*
UNIVERSITY OF MICHIGAN, SENIOR

CLASSIC ROCK 101

We don't want to tell you what music to listen to while you're in college. Every generation has its tastes, after all. But there are *some* albums that deserve consideration by everyone who attends college – if not a class dedicated to the record (covering its meaning, social effect and place in history, etc.), then at least a really good listen (or 50) while attending classes and doing all the extra-curricular things that college students do. Here, in no particular order, are 25 socially vital albums that are well worth your time. We're not saying these are the best albums of all time – or even the best albums by the particular performer or band that created them. But they have entertained, moved, enlightened, and inspired millions – and we hope they do the same for you.

Bob Dylan, *Highway 61Revisited*

Neutral Milk Hotel, *Into the Aeroplane Over the Sea*

Pink Floyd, *The Wall*

Nirvana, *Nevermind*

2Pac, *Me Against the World*

Joni Mitchell, *Blue*

U2, *Joshua Tree*

Neil Young, *Harvest*

The Rolling Stones, *Exile on Main Street*

Marvin Gaye, *What's Going On*

The Beastie Boys, *Paul's Boutique*

Carol King, *Tapestry*

Led Zeppelin, *Led Zeppelin*

Bob Marley and the Wailers, *Legend*

Radiohead, *OK Computer*

Ramones, *Ramones*

Liz Phair, *Exile In Guyville*

The Beatles, *Abbey Road*

Grateful Dead, *Workingman's Dead*

Johnny Cash, *At Folsom Prison*

Notorious B.I.G., *Ready to Die*

The Clash, *London Calling*

Jimi Hendrix, *Are You Experienced?*

R.E.M., *Murmur*

The Beach Boys, *Pet Sounds*

The Editors

A PORTABLE CALENDAR. The one thing that has saved me from being completely overwhelmed with all the classes, activities, and various other happenings in my life is my calendar, in which I write EVERYTHING down. My days are much more manageable when I have a good idea of what I'm doing and when.

—*SETH*
OGLETHORPE UNIVERSITY, FRESHMAN

Get Set: Leaving Home

Leaving home can be scary, exciting, stressful, joyful, time-consuming, hilarious, tragic, and tough. Rest assured, almost no one manages to get from home to college with perfect dignity and grace. You may think you're just fine with going away (until the moment arrives, that is). Or, you may fear the event for weeks in advance. Either way, you're probably in for a surprise; departing for school is never as bad, nor as easy, as you think.

Here's some advice on getting mentally set to go: Stay busy, spending plenty of time with friends and family; make sure absolutely everyone has your cell phone number and mailing address at school; and swap worrying about the future for enjoying the present.

DON'T FREAK OUT ABOUT saying goodbye. Keep in mind that you will see them again soon, probably in just a few months. You can call, email, write, and get care packages to stay in touch.

—*ELIZABETH*
CORNELL COLLEGE, FRESHMAN

SAY GOODBYE, KISS THEM, AND MAKE THEM DRIVE AWAY QUICKLY.

—*C.H.*
UNIVERSITY OF VIRGINIA, FRESHMAN

HEADLINES
Best Advice and Top Tips

- Leaving home is harder than you think.
- Say goodbye to your parents quickly—it will be easier on all of you.
- Once you adjust to the shock of being away from home, you'll have a great time.
- It can be harder to leave your friends than your family—you know you'll see your family again.

A FEW DAYS AFTER MY DAD DROPPED ME OFF at college, I found out that he had mailed me a letter telling me everything that I'm assuming that most parents tell their children when they leave them at college. It was really nice because I now have a physical reminder of my dad, in his handwriting, and it let him give me advice without the drama of the big college good-bye.

—LIZZIE
BOWDOIN COLLEGE, FRESHMAN

· · · · · · · · ·

DON'T BE AFRAID TO LEAVE HOME, no matter what. When it was time for me to start college, leaving my mom while she was fighting breast cancer was one of the hardest things I ever had to do. But if I had stayed home, I wouldn't have met my husband, whom I am still gaga over after six years of courtship and three years of marriage. And Mom was the prettiest breast cancer survivor and mother of the bride ever.

—ERICA LANGE-HENNESEY
TEXAS STATE UNIVERSITY, SENIOR

LEAVING FAMILY IS A BIG ADJUSTMENT. I got lonely my first year and my parents were pretty strict about keeping me at school until I got over it. It was very hard but I grew from it. When I joined the football team, they came up for games, which was great. But the way I fought it mostly was by keeping busy; that's the best way. It's still hard.

—*RYAN SMITH*
CARNEGIE MELLON UNIVERSITY, JUNIOR

" I was sadder to leave my friends than my parents. I'll see my parents again and they won't change. But leaving all my high school friends . . . everyone's going to be different, because they all went to different schools. "

—*BAYLESS PARSLEY*
UNIVERSITY OF VIRGINIA, FRESHMAN

I LEFT GUAM AND FLEW to Georgia by myself, and stayed with my extended family before school started. It was tough leaving my family, and there definitely were tears and lots of hugs. Saying goodbye to your parents is going to be tough no matter what, especially if you are close to your family. But before leaving home, it's important to be open with your parents and let them know how much you'll miss them, and how often you plan to call them. It's a tough time for them, too.

—*MICHELLE Y. LEE*
EMORY UNIVERSITY, SENIOR

I thought I'd be the most homesick person on this campus, but it wasn't that bad. You just have to make it quick.

—*C.H.*
UNIVERSITY OF VIRGINIA, FRESHMAN

WHEN MY PARENTS MOVED me to college, the dorm didn't have elevators, so they helped me carry my stuff up four floors. After that, we went back to the hotel where they were staying and I burst into tears. I said, "Please take me with you. I want to go home. I'll go to school there." My dad looked at me and said, "I would take you, but I just moved all of your stuff up four flights of stairs. Stay a semester and then see what you think." That was great advice.

—*ERIN*
CENTRAL BIBLE COLLEGE, GRADUATE

• • • • • • • • •

LEAVING HOME IS ALL ABOUT you and your parents each having more sex, more frequently and more easily. C'mon—the 'rents act all weepy to see their little chick flying the coop, when in reality they can't wait to turn their bedroom into a steamy den of *coitus parentalis.* And you feign maturity, eager to take on the responsibilities of living on your own and furthering your education, when in reality you are ecstatic that at the end of a night, instead of having to do it in the back of your car in the school parking lot, you can finally take a special someone home to the (relative) privacy of your dorm room.

—*JOHN*
UNIVERSITY OF WISCONSIN AT MADISON, GRADUATE

HAPPIEST COLLEGE STUDENTS

1. Rice University, Houston, TX
2. Bowdoin College, Brunswick, ME
3. University of California, Santa Barbara, CA
4. Clemson University, Clemson, SC
5. Vanderbilt University, Nashville, TN

MY FAMILY LIVES IN OMAN, so it was hard for my mom: when she dropped me off, she knew I wouldn't be back for Thanksgiving. It's hard to leave your parents: You're used to the family environment so much more.

—*NATASHA PIRZADA*
GEORGETOWN UNIVERSITY, SOPHOMORE

* * * * * * * *

" It's better going to a college far, far away, because when you need something done, or you miss your family, you have to stick through it. When you're at a college close by, it's hard because your parents still think you're in high school and want to see you every day. "

—*KATIE HOLDEN*
RUTGERS UNIVERSITY, FRESHMAN

* * * * * * * *

I HAD A REALLY GOOD TIME after I committed myself. I think it's all a matter of making the decision that you want to be there and you want to be doing what you're doing. People spent a lot of time choosing the college they want to go to. It makes a big difference if you're excited about where you end up.

—*ANNE*
GEORGE WASHINGTON UNIVERSITY, SENIOR

WHAT'S IN A NAME?

It makes little difference when you're an upperclassman (Ah! That sounds nice.) but when you're just starting out, wouldn't it be nice to be addressed with some respect? Go ahead and set the standard by calling yourself what you'd like others to call you.

- **Freshman:** classic, traditional. Also somewhat sexist.

- **Frosh:** short, convenient, and gender-neutral; unfortunately, ugly.

- **First Year or First-Year Student:** also gender-neutral, but sounds a lot better.

I WAS EXPECTING MY MOM to be sadder. She was like, "All right, see ya." I was like, "Is that it? That's all I get?" But I was the third one to get dropped off. They were sad the first time.
—*M.A.S.*
UNIVERSITY OF VIRGINIA, GRADUATE

• • • • • • • •

I THOUGHT I WAS GOING TO HATE COLLEGE. My parents dropped me off my first day and were leaving me there, and I looked at them and said, "I don't think this is going to work out. Can I just come back to the hotel with you guys?" They were just like, "Nope, sorry." My mom got in the car and started crying. And my dad was like, "She'll figure it out." I stayed and I ended up having a great time in school.
—*J. DEVEREUX*
GEORGETOWN UNIVERSITY, GRADUATE

LIVING **WITHOUT YOUR PARENTS** for the first time is a bigger deal than many of us want to admit. It didn't hit me that I was leaving my parents for good until they were driving away after dropping me off at the dorms. For the first few weeks of school I was calling them every day, just to make sure everything was going smoothly at home since my departure. After I got settled in, the phone calls reduced to a couple a week. Maintaining a close relationship with your parents is vital to succeeding freshman year. You're going to experience a lot of ups and downs, and it's always nice to have your parents' support through the good and the bad.

—*I*LAN *G*LUCK
*U*NIVERSITY OF *M*ARYLAND, *J*UNIOR

SAYING **GOODBYE TO MY PARENTS** was really hard. My mom, dad and sister brought me up to school and we all spent the day setting up my dorm room and decorating it. At the University of Michigan, we have a new student ceremony that all new students go to. I went with my hall and by the time I came back my parents were gone. We had said goodbye before I left for the ceremony, but it really set in when I came back and they weren't there. My sister left me a really cute note about how she was going to miss me and I could come home soon. That's when the tears started.

Being sad about your parents leaving is totally natural. I think many students have a lonely feeling the first couple of hours after they leave, but do something to get your mind off of it. Open your door and keep setting up your room. Wander down your hall to see if anyone needs help, or call someone you know. The feeling will pass really quickly and you will get into the groove of your new college life.

—*A*NNIE *T*HOMAS
*U*NIVERSITY OF *M*ICHIGAN, *S*ENIOR

TALKING BEFORE THE TRANSITION

Before you head off to college, it's probably a good idea to cover these important transition topics with your parents:

"How often will you be coming home?"
Maybe you're counting on home-cooked meals and free laundry service every weekend – but your parents are assuming you're saying goodbye until Thanksgiving. Or maybe it's the other way around, and while you can't wait to be on your own, your parents feel a more gradual 'letting go' would be good for everyone. Try to discuss this openly and make a plan now. (You can reassess later if you need to.)

Chores
If your family home is in New Jersey and you're headed to college in Florida, this may be a quick conversation. But what if it's geographically feasible for you to keep up with some of the contributions you've (no doubt) been making to the family: caring for younger siblings, mowing the lawn, driving grandparents to medical appointments, etc.? Talk to your parents about what level of home involvement will still let you settle in, make connections on campus, and become accustomed to new academic expectations.

Working
Try to get on the same page with your parents about how much you should work during your freshman year. Many freshmen (and their parents) aren't aware of how much studying they'll need to do, and sign up for too many hours working on campus or off. An over-committed first semester can saddle you with low grades that jeopardize your financial aid and academic progress. Use a good schedule planning tool (like the ones we have in this book) and calculate how many free hours you *really* will have each week.

A, B, C, and the rest of the alphabet...

Your parents won't be getting report cards in the mail, and professors won't be calling them if and when you get into academic trouble. Before the first quiz, exam, paper, or presentation, figure out how you are going to communicate with your parents about grades.

Options you may want to consider include a check-in every other week, or once a month. Alternately, you might update your parents whenever you get a grade on a major assignment. Academic advisors recommend that students combine assignment and assessment deadlines for all classes into one easy-to-read list. If you do this, you can give your parents a copy and they can follow along as the semester progresses. But be prepared to hear, "Hey, October 20th is coming up -- are you ready for your biology midterm?"

Troubleshooting

You don't want to let your parents down, and it may not be easy for you to tell them if something is going wrong. Students hide flunked exams, alarming credit card bills, crushing loneliness and other difficulties from even the most caring and supportive families. Make communication easier by agreeing on a signal. If you can start with a simple text of "Mayday!" (or whatever you come up with together), there's a better chance you'll feel like initiating what could be a very important conversation.

Frances Northcutt

As SOMEONE WHO IS very close to my parents, I had a pit in my stomach at the thought of saying goodbye to mom and dad. But once they left and I ran off to the next orientation activity, I realized that I felt as though a weight had been lifted off my shoulders! That being said - don't make a big deal of saying goodbye and make sure you have plans for right after. Not only does the distraction take your mind off of homesickness, but some-times the anticipation of the goodbye is more painful than the real thing!

—STEPHANIE DREIFUSS
DUKE UNIVERSITY, SENIOR

• • • • • • • •

MY FRESHMAN YEAR, I STRUGGLED being away from home. The thought of going home only on Thanksgiving and Christmas made me sad. I can remember the day my family dropped me off at my dorm my freshman year. I cried, and became slightly depressed. I was so down I didn't make the attempt to get to know my roommate. Although it is hard transitioning to a new environ-ment, I learned to remind myself why I am here in college. I came to realize that although I am sad and would rather be home with my family, col-lege is a once-in-a-lifetime experience. Yes, you miss your family and they miss you. But I had to remember I wanted to make my family proud. As a senior in college, I look back and have to admit, all the pain and struggles I dealt with when I came to college were worth it.

—CHARLINDA HAUDLEY
UNIVERSITY OF ARIZONA, SENIOR

3 Go: Starting Out

You're dealing with all the emotions that go along with leaving home. You're attempting to cope with all your hopes and fears about college. You have a to-do list three pages long, and your college's orientation program will have you busy from 7 a.m. till midnight for what seems like the next month. And in the midst of all this chaos, people keep telling you that these are the best years of your life! You really hope they're wrong.

Would it help to know that fun and adventure will eventually worm their way in through the insanity? They will. Would it help to know that your college years can be some of the best years of your life, but that they can also serve to open doors to even greater experiences? They can.

So take a deep breath, hold onto your to-do list, and jump in. And read on to hear how other students successfully swam to the other side.

DON'T BE TOO SHY to ask for help. A lot of people are confused, but if you're lost together, there's more chance of getting it right.

—ALFIE WILLIAMS
GEORGIA INSTITUTE OF TECHNOLOGY, SOPHOMORE

STARTING OUT, EVERYBODY IS BASICALLY LOST.

—JOHNNY
GEORGETOWN UNIVERSITY, JUNIOR

HEADLINES
Best Advice and Top Tips

- Arrive on campus early to learn the layout of the campus before classes start.
- Freshmen tend to travel in packs; try to walk with just one or two other people.
- The first few days can be overwhelming, but the adjustment comes quickly.
- Be outgoing, meet as many people as you can those first few weeks of school.

THE LIVING IS COMPLETELY DIFFERENT. At home, my parents took care of everything. It's a big adjustment: doing laundry, cleaning dishes, going out and getting food. I get back to school from a vacation and I forget—I'm kind of expecting my friends to be making food.

—MATT MONACO
GEORGE WASHINGTON UNIVERSITY, FRESHMAN

. . . .

I MADE MOST OF MY FRIENDS IN THE BEGINNING.
You start off hanging out in a big group and then you realize whom you relate to, and those are the people you spend your time with.

—ANDREW KARELITZ
UNIVERSITY OF PENNSYLVANIA, FRESHMAN

. . . .

DON'T TRY TO FIND A GROUP OF FRIENDS. First, meet as many people as possible and wait until later to find your group.

—JENNIFER A. SICKLICK
GEORGE WASHINGTON UNIVERSITY, FRESHMAN

Smile. it helps.

—CASEY
GEORGETOWN
UNIVERSITY, SENIOR

I **REMEMBER WALKING** into my first lecture hall and saying, "Wow!" There were 700 people in one room and I was shocked. Then the kid behind me whispered, "Aww, freshman." It only took one class for me to get used to the atmosphere. It wasn't so bad!

—*ORLY COBLENS*
UNIVERSITY OF MICHIGAN, FRESHMAN

Don't be afraid to go up to people and introduce yourself.

—*MANI*
UNIVERSITY OF MARYLAND FRESHMAN

IT'S NOT WORTH TRYING TO SAVE TIME by buying your books early. My friend and I were told that the first days of college are really crazy, and the advice was to "buy all your books right away to avoid lines!" We bought $400 worth of books (each), including a hardcover dictionary. We realized we had done it all wrong the next day, when we looked at our schedule, which needed some revisions. Make sure your classes are totally lined up before buying your books.

—*JANNA HAROWITZ*
McGILL UNIVERSITY, GRADUATE

COLLEGE WAS AT FIRST a horrific and strange experience for me because the world was larger than I thought it was. But everyone has to start somewhere. Don't feel scared or inferior, because everyone around you had to start out where you are!

—*K. HARMA*
WESTERN WASHINGTON UNIVERSITY, GRADUATE

DON'T TRAVEL IN HERDS THE FIRST WEEK. For example, when attending the obligatory frat parties and keggers, don't travel to and from with your entire dorm. Everyone will know you are a freshman. Choose a couple of people to go with and try to blend in.

—*ANONYMOUS*

THE HARDEST THING ABOUT LEAVING HOME was getting used to the freedom. I went from a setting where everything was controlled by my parents to one where I could do whatever I wanted. You have to balance things; have fun, but don't go crazy!

—CANDACE LA PAN
UNIVERSITY OF NORTH CAROLINA AT GREENSBORO, SOPHOMORE

The teachers are going to try to scare you the first week or two and you'll feel overwhelmed. But just keep on track.

—GREG
JAMES MADISON UNIVERSITY, JUNIOR

THE FIRST DAY, MOST FRESHMEN HAD NO IDEA how to get from their dorm rooms to their classes. They were pitifully obvious, standing around the bus stops, trying to read the bus route maps inconspicuously. The worst cases were the poor geeks tracing the routes with their fingers. So arrive on campus early. The week before classes start, just get on the main bus route near your dorm. Ride the entire route—learn where it goes. Then do the same for each of the other routes. That way, when classes start, you won't be late, lost, or an obvious neophyte.

—TONYA SMITH
UNIVERSITY OF GEORGIA, GRADUATE

WHEN YOU MOVE INTO YOUR NEW ROOM, choose the bed where people will see you when the door is open. While you are moving in, people will walk by and see you setting up your room and will stop and say hi.

—B.K.
CORNELL UNIVERSITY, GRADUATE

THAT FIRST DAY OF COLLEGE felt like a grown-up version of summer camp. Some of us hadn't realized that kids really did grow up in these far-away places. It was not odd to hear, "No really, c'mon; Iowa?" or, "Kalamazoo is a *real* place?!"

—MICHAEL
GRADUATE

DON'T EVEN THINK ABOUT IT

DO NOT show up with mono and bronchitis. When you arrive at school all you'll want to do is smoke tons of dope and kiss the ladies, both of which are contraindicated treatments for your affliction.

DO NOT think that the type of mono and bronchitis you have won't be contracted by the young lady with whom you spend your first few days at school kissing and smoking dope.

DO NOT think that it's perfectly acceptable to kiss the roommate of the young lady you've been kissing, just because it's late and you and the roommate have been drinking in a dark room alone, smoking tons of dope, and her breasts seem oh so lovely.

DO NOT think that either one of the roommates will accept your proposals to go on kissing both of them behind the back of the other roommate.

DO NOT think that the roommates will not share stories and commiserate and call you a philandering bastard behind your back, especially once they figure out they both have mono.

DO NOT think that it's just fine to smoke even a tiny bit of dope at this point.

And when you're in the hospital with double viral pneumonia for two weeks, **DO NOT** expect that either of the roommates will come visit you.

—LEE KLEIN
  OBERLIN COLLEGE, GRADUATE

BEFORE YOU START, talk to a current student or recent grad and ask for advice. It may be worthless, but it may help you avoid some pitfalls.

—*ANONYMOUS*
UNION COLLEGE

• • • • • • • •

BEFORE CLASSES START, take a walk through campus and get acquainted with the buildings. That way, you can recognize some of the buildings and sites later, through the chaos. On my first day, there were so many people running around that it was fairly intimidating for me, and it was difficult to find my classes.

—*MICHAEL ALBERT PAOLI*
UNIVERSITY OF TORONTO, GRADUATE

• • • • • • • •

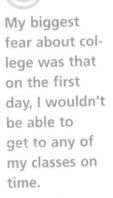

ONE OF THE BIGGEST CHALLENGES I've encountered is finding time to eat at the dining hall. The first week I was here, I hardly ate at all because I didn't know when to go and didn't have enough people to go with. I hate going there alone. You walk in and you don't know which table to sit at. You can sit with anyone and they'll probably be nice about it. But you feel like you have to go with someone, just for security.

—*C.H.*
UNIVERSITY OF VIRGINIA, FRESHMAN

• • • • • • • •

SCOPE OUT THE LOCATION of your classes prior to the first day. Those kids who walk into class fifteen minutes late looking stressed out and out of breath? No one wants to be that.

—*AMANDA*
UNIVERSITY OF COLORADO AT COLORADO SPRINGS, SOPHOMORE

> My biggest fear about college was that on the first day, I wouldn't be able to get to any of my classes on time.
>
> —*KEVISHA ITSON*
> *NORTHERN ILLINOIS UNIVERSITY FRESHMAN*

CAN YOU HANDLE THIS?

Our friends at Knox College have a tradition called the Pump Handle, which has been around since 1885. On the first day of classes each year, the president leads a welcoming line, shaking each person's hand in turn. After that, everyone shakes the hands of those who have gone before, and the line grows, snaking around the campus. If that wasn't crazy enough, many students and staff members come dressed in wacky costumes.

THE FIRST DAYS OF COLLEGE ARE THE BEST: For a few brief drunken moments, there are no cliques, no caste, no class, and no classes. It's a big, egalitarian, drunken orgy. At least, that's the way I partially remember it; I could be wrong.

—*JOHN*
UNIVERSITY OF WISCONSIN AT MADISON, GRADUATE

THE FIRST FEW DAYS OF COLLEGE ARE WEIRD; you're bombarded by cheesy campus groups and pressured to commit to a thousand things that aren't even cool. Take time to relax. Don't worry about jumping into anything too soon.

—*KATIE MCAFEE*
BAYLOR UNIVERSITY, JUNIOR

JUST GIVE IT TIME. At first, I would call or message some of my old buddies from high school, talking with old friends. It was good to have some close friends as a sounding board for the things I was going through.

—*WONNIE RYU*
EMORY UNIVERSITY, SENIOR

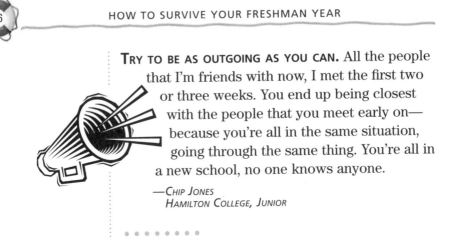

TRY TO BE AS OUTGOING AS YOU CAN. All the people that I'm friends with now, I met the first two or three weeks. You end up being closest with the people that you meet early on—because you're all in the same situation, going through the same thing. You're all in a new school, no one knows anyone.

—CHIP JONES
HAMILTON COLLEGE, JUNIOR

. . . .

" Find a campus map. The weekend before classes begin, figure out where all your classes are. You'll feel much more at ease on the first day. "

—SIERRA
CAL POLY SAN LUIS OBISPO, JUNIOR

. . . .

I DID A PRE-ORIENTATION PROGRAM on the arts. I'm glad I did it. I made some great friends, and it was great to be on campus early. But I don't think that the content of the program was that important. It was just great to have people that I recognized once school started, and any of the programs would have been good for that.

—CATIE
HARVARD COLLEGE, SENIOR

CAN I GET SOME CREDIT HERE?

You may be starting college with a few credits already under your belt. Don't forget to follow these steps to make that credit official!

- **Advanced Placement:** If you took any AP exams, check to see whether your college will give you academic credit for them. Most colleges have a handy chart indicating exactly how many credits and which course requirements you can get based on your score. Hint: this chart can usually be found on the Admissions website. Last but not least, don't forget to have your scores sent to your college!

- **International Baccalaureate:** Many colleges are willing to award credit for IB work as well. Alas, handy charts are rare when it comes to IB; IB credit is usually evaluated by an expert on campus. Ask at Admissions or consult your academic advisor.

- **A-Levels:** If you're coming from an international school run on the British system, you may have A-Level credits. These can make you eligible for more advanced coursework. Before you register for classes, check in with an academic advisor.

- **Prior College Credit:** Be sure to have your official transcripts sent from the Registrar's Office of your previous college to your new college. If you think your credit might affect your course choices for your first semester, be sure to review an unofficial copy of your transcript with an academic advisor.

Frances Northcutt

3 ESSENTIAL TO-DO'S ON THE DAY BEFORE CLASSES BEGIN

1. Walk to your classes. With your schedule and a campus map in hand, start at your dorm and walk to all of your classes. Head to your first class first – you need to know how long it will take you to make your way from your dorm across campus. If you get lost on your walk-through, just be thankful it's not a 'real' day.

2. Write down a weekly schedule – classes, study time, free time. The truth is, you have no idea what your schedule will be like even two weeks from now. But creating a schedule now will make it easier to update it later. Consider your schedule a draft that constantly evolves throughout the semester and school year.

3. Relax. Watch a movie with your new dorm mates. Walk around your dorm and say hello to people. Eat a good meal. Get some rest. College starts tomorrow!

Frances Northcutt

THINGS WON'T BE PERFECT AT THE BEGINNING. You're going to have a couple of rough months when you're trying to find your niche and remember why on earth you came to college. But give yourself time to integrate, to decide how you want to spend your time, who you want to spend your time with, and what kind of people will complement those objectives. You can drive yourself crazy trying to do everything with all sorts of people or you can try to figure out what makes you happy and whom you're comfortable with. But that won't happen immediately. It takes at least a year, maybe a little longer.

—*ANONYMOUS*
UNIVERSITY OF VIRGINIA, SENIOR

THE FIRST FEW WEEKS, freshmen move around in packs. Try to make friends with some upperclassmen. You're more likely to get into parties without a herd of freshmen around you.

—*KEVIN WALSH*
GEORGETOWN UNIVERSITY, SOPHOMORE

Keep your Social Security number handy for the first several days.

—*BRIAN TURNER*
UNIVERSITY OF GEORGIA, GRADUATE

BE SURE TO GET THERE EARLY on the first day. When I got to school, it took us over four hours to get everything moved in. My room was on the 14th floor, so we couldn't just walk stuff up the stairs. It took forever to wait for the elevator.

—*SARAH TIPPY*
WESTERN ILLINOIS UNIVERSITY, SENIOR

IF YOU COME FROM A SCHOOL that sends a lot of kids to your university, it is okay to hang out with them for the first few weeks of school. A lot of times, people are really concerned with branching out immediately. But if you have a few people that you know, it is much easier to make new friends. Not only that, but the group that you know will always bring along people you don't know, and vice versa.

—*ANNIE THOMAS*
UNIVERSITY OF MICHIGAN, SENIOR

DON'T SETTLE DOWN TOO FAST with your friends. It's great to make some friends off the bat, but don't let that limit you during the course of the year; you have a lot of time to get to know a lot of people, so keep making friends beyond the first couple of days.

—*CATIE*
HARVARD COLLEGE, SENIOR

JUST DO IT: ORIENTATION

SOME EVENTS DURING ORIENTATION week might seem lame or silly, but I encourage freshmen to participate in them. Three years later, I still recall that one girl who thought she was Britney Spears during a hypnotist performance during orientation week. She's my friend's roommate, and we still laugh about it.

—*MICHELLE Y. LEE*
EMORY UNIVERSITY, SENIOR

ORIENTATION IS WHEN THE SCHOOL tells you things that they really told you previously in tours and in the pounds of literature that they send to you in the mail – but with more detail and a little bit more application of how you can use it.

—*BARRY LANGER*
OGLETHORPE UNIVERSITY, JUNIOR

PARTICIPATE IN YOUR ORIENTATION. It may seem lame and you might think you know everything about the school, but it helps you get set up for classes. When they have you run around the campus eight times in one day, you learn it and you get familiar and more comfortable with your new home. You also meet a lot of people. The more people you meet, the more resources you know about, and the more you can help yourself in college.

—*ELIZABETH*
CORNELL COLLEGE, FRESHMAN

I SKIPPED ALL THE ORIENTATIONS. My sister told me I didn't have to go to them if I didn't want to. So I took that as, "Go to the bar instead." But that's not the best advice. That way, all you meet are bar people. I never knew the other three-quarters of our class that didn't go to bars.

—*CASEY*
GEORGETOWN UNIVERSITY, SENIOR

ORIENTATION IS A SCARY TIME and an awkward time. It is too short to get really comfortable, but enough time to get an introduction to the school. It is important to be really outgoing during orientation and try to meet at least a couple of people. This way, you have two or three people to call during welcome week to go out with, grab lunch, explore campus or get books. You will feel a lot more confident if you tackle the first couple of days with a friend rather than by yourself!

—ANNIE THOMAS
UNIVERSITY OF MICHIGAN, SENIOR

ENJOY ORIENTATION, because there will be no experience like it for the rest of your undergraduate career. First of all, it's more like summer camp than school – every day is full of activities, BBQs, music, and entertainment. Second, at no other time will everyone be so open to new people. Take advantage of this friendly climate by stepping out of your comfort zone. Say "hi" to a stranger, go get dinner with random people from your dorm, and go to as many of the events offered as you can (even though some will sound lame). It's funny how the people you meet during orientation turn out to be your best friends when you graduate. At that point, you can look back and reminisce about the mildly embarrassing things you did or said when you first got to college!

—STEPHANIE DREIFUSS
DUKE UNIVERSITY, SENIOR

MAKE AS MANY NEW FRIENDS AS POSSIBLE. There is no better time to meet people than when everybody is a complete stranger to everybody else. We had to do a freshman-wide community service project, attend at least 9 or 10 different seminars, and we had a dance. It was all very scheduled, but it provided time for the students to mingle and casually integrate with each other.

—SETH
OGLETHORPE UNIVERSITY, FRESHMAN

Be brave; be the one to initiate the conversation.

—*ALEKSANDR AKULOV*
HUNTER COLLEGE
SOPHOMORE

GET TO THE DORMS EARLY on the first day! I was in a triple my freshman year, and by the time I got to my dorm at 7:30 a.m. (it supposedly was not going to open until 8 a.m.), a local girl was already there and had claimed the best spot. It all worked out fine, though. My roommates and I arranged our room in a way that gave us all some individual space.

—*MAYA NEWMAN*
COLUMBIA UNIVERSITY AND
THE JEWISH THEOLOGICAL SEMINARY, GRADUATE

• • • • • • • •

THE FIRST WEEK IS all about saying and doing whatever the hell you feel like saying and doing. It's the wrong time to be self-conscious, since literally everyone else is in the exact same boat you're in. If you're you, you will have no trouble at all finding people that you will naturally feel at ease spending time with.

—*J.V.*
THE COLLEGE OF WILLIAM & MARY, GRADUATE

• • • • • • • •

IF YOU LIVE CLOSE TO SCHOOL, don't go home. Be as outgoing as possible and leave the door to your dorm room open. People will walk by and say hi. Guaranteed. It will be awkward and uncomfortable, but after a week or so it will be so much better. Just remember that everyone feels the same way that you do.

—*ANNIE THOMAS*
UNIVERSITY OF MICHIGAN, SENIOR

• • • • • • • •

I JUST GO UP TO PEOPLE I don't know and try to make friends. It's a lot different from high school, where everyone knows you, and you're friends with everybody.

—*KEVIN BUSHEY*
GEORGIA STATE UNIVERSITY, FRESHMAN

THE FIRST WEEKEND OF ORIENTATION, I felt really homesick. Not because I'd been away from home for long—obviously!—but because I felt out of place. My floor was entirely made up of freshmen and many of them, to me, seemed to have found their "group" right off the bat. I'd met a ton of nice people, but it takes me a little while to open up, and I felt like I had no real connections yet. After calling up my older brother crying, he told me that no matter what it seemed like, no one had found a "group" yet. It turned out he was right. The people who seemed to be best friends the first week didn't necessarily stay that way. And people who I thought I had no connection with eventually become some of my best friends at college (e.g., my roommate!).

So don't worry if you don't feel like you have a best friend the first or second or even third week at school. Everyone feels that way, whether they show it or not. The friends that matter take time to find.

—*EMMA*
HAMILTON COLLEGE, JUNIOR

. . . .

IF YOU'RE NERVOUS ABOUT THE FIRST DAY, take a walk around the campus a day or two before and find your classes. Some campuses are huge; mine was actually divided into two campuses with a highway running through the middle. I went to the entirely wrong side of campus on day one, so a lot of time was lost.

—*COREY*
SAN DIEGO STATE UNIVERSITY, JUNIOR

. . . .

AS CORNY AS IT SOUNDS - BE YOURSELF. You'll never be happy if you're trying to please other people.

—*AMANDA*
UNIVERSITY OF MIAMI, JUNIOR

GET ORIENTED - OUTDOORS!

"I can't imagine starting my college career without this program. Without it, I would have felt less prepared. Not only is it a valuable learning experience, it is an incredible experience I will remember all my life."

What program changed this student's life? Was it an academic skills course, a research project, a pizza party with a hypnotist? No, this student, and thousands of others around the U.S., started college by camping with his peers on what's known as an outdoor orientation or wilderness orientation program. In these pre-orientation programs, students get to know a small group of their classmates during several days of outdoor activities.

I have been researching the impact of these programs for more than a decade, and I would advise anyone attending a college that offers such a program to participate, whether you're a tent-owning, fleece-wearing outdoorsperson or a city slicker with no appetite for dirt. My research shows that while many students approach such programs with fear and resistance, nearly all are grateful to have participated. At one college, 93% of the students who went on the outdoor orientation program said it was the best experience of the first year. These programs are offered at about 20% of the traditional four-year, residential colleges in the US.

Students who participate in outdoor orientation programs report that they adjust more easily to college life, thanks largely to the support of the small group of peers they get to know very, very well during the trip. But perhaps the most compelling reason to participate is that they're *fun*. Going on such a trip will ensure that you start your college career laughing, learning, and probably singing some silly songs.

One student I surveyed summed it up best: "There is only one thing that I could possibly say about [the program], and that is, that it was the most fun I have ever had in my entire life. I made friends that I feel will last forever and will always be there for me no matter what."

Brent J. Bell, Ph.D.
Associate Professor of Outdoor Education
University of New Hampshire

I DID A SUMMER SESSION which was about a month and a half before freshman year and I took three courses; it was mostly just to get you adjusted to school. It was probably the best thing I could have asked for -- I got a head start, I learned all about my school, things like where everything was. I figured it out before most people got to school, so I didn't feel as much like a new kid on the first day of freshman year. I definitely suggest doing that if it's available.

—TAYLOR WHITNEY PETTIS
BLOOMSBURG UNIVERSITY, JUNIOR

• • • • • • • •

THE FIRST FEW MONTHS WERE EASIER than I thought they would be. But everyone I knew hit a patch right before they went home, after they'd been here for a couple of months. It was easy to come here, but after a couple of months you start to miss the security of home. Especially when the tests start.

—D.F.
NEW YORK UNIVERSITY, SENIOR

MY SCHOOL PUT ME IN A 'GROUP' for orientation. It was made up of a bunch of people in my residence hall and we went to all the week's activities together. As the start of classes loomed closer and closer, we decided to explore the campus for cool study places. Definitely one of the smartest things we could have done to prepare for school! In high school, I studied in the same place all the time: my bedroom. It worked, because my homework time lasted from early to late evening.

—*EMMA*
HAMILTON COLLEGE, JUNIOR

• • • • • • • •

BE WARY OF BECOMING That Freshman Who Friends Everyone. Yep, every class has one, and yes, I promise you that you will be remembered that way for your entire college career. Wait until you actually have conversations with people until you go on a friending spree.

—*SOPHIE STONE*
FRANKLIN AND MARSHALL COLLEGE, JUNIOR

• • • • • • • •

YOU SHOULD ALWAYS TALK TO RANDOM PEOPLE everywhere you go. I met everyone that way freshman year. In my orientation group I met the bassist and the keyboardist from one of the bands I play in now. Most people think freshman orientation stuff is annoying and just blow it off - but I made really good friends there.

—*PETER STONE*
TUFTS UNIVERSITY, SOPHOMORE

Expectations: College Dreams & Campus Reality

C omplete these two sentences: "The best thing that could happen to me this semester would be ..."; and (you guessed it), "The worst thing that could happen to me this semester would be ..."! Now compare your answers with those of your classmates: the odds are good that you'll share the same, or similar, hopes and fears. Is the work too hard (or too easy)? The dorm crowd too crazy (or not crazy enough)? The food inedible (or unidentifiable)? Well, whatever the scenario, chances are you'll figure out how to deal with it. And college professionals are there to help you. Here's more guidance for when college realities pay you a visit.

HIGH SCHOOL SUCKS. College is awesome. Freshman year is really awesome.

—J.V.
THE COLLEGE OF WILLIAM & MARY, GRADUATE

BE PREPARED FOR CHANGE.

—MICHAEL A. FEKULA
UNIVERSITY OF MARYLAND, GRADUATE

Best Advice and Top Tips

- Sometimes it takes a while to find your group of friends. Be patient.
- The constant need to define yourself can be very stressful.
- If you feel like transferring, hang on. Try harder to join groups and meet more people before making any big decisions.
- Lots of students worry about adapting to a very different culture when going to a school in a different region of the country, not to mention a different country altogether.

I WAS CONCERNED ABOUT adapting to a southern school and its culture, since I came from San Francisco. But I soon realized that while the culture might be preppy and southern, the minds of the students are more progressive. Professors are also just as open, so I felt more at ease as my freshman year went on. At first you might feel alienated, judging by the cliques around the students and the huge presence of Greek life. Regardless of your personality, you'll find your own group of friends who share the same interests.

—ANONYMOUS
UNIVERSITY OF VIRGINIA, JUNIOR

MY NUMBER ONE WORRY was gaining the "freshman 15." So I went to the gym three times a week, I joined the dance team, and I became a vegetarian. That's a lot of stuff, but it worked.

—M.T.
GEORGIA STATE UNIVERSITY, SENIOR

GETTING THE MOST OUT OF YOUR PEER MENTOR

Peer mentor programs are trendy. University administrators think it's a wonderful idea to match up freshmen with older, wiser students who can show you the ropes and make you feel at home. Unfortunately, too many initial meetings between peer mentors and mentees go like this:

> *"Okay, so do you have any questions?"*
> *"Uh, not right now."*
> *"Oh, okay."*
> (Mentor and mentee sit in awkward silence.)

If you are at risk for "mentor meeting discomfort," don't just sit there—memorize these useful questions, and you'll be all set! Your mentor will feel wise and helpful, and you may actually learn something.

- What was the most helpful thing anyone ever told you about college?

- What scared you the most about starting college? How did you cope?

- What's the best way to make close friends?

- Did you make any big mistakes your freshman year? What would you do differently?

- What was the best thing that happened to you freshman year?

Frances Northcutt

My biggest worry when I was a freshman was that I would be broke all of the time ... and I was.

—CECILIE
PARSONS SCHOOL OF
DESIGN, JUNIOR

MY BIGGEST MISCONCEPTION about college was that I would be one-hundred-percent free of parents, and I definitely wasn't. I had to force myself to become more independent by getting a job and not calling home every day.

—CHIDIMMA UCHE ETO
DUKE UNIVERSITY, GRADUATE

• • • • • • • •

EVERYONE TALKS ABOUT how college is an opportunity to start over ... but no one ever mentions how to recover from horrendous first impressions. What if I came off as completely socially inept? How could I recover from that? I felt a little "off" in terms of language. I'd been used to speaking a mixture of Chinese and English—Chinglish, if you will—so suddenly switching to pure English was an adjustment. I'd often be talking and have to wave my hands around trying to translate a word into English. I don't think my fears ever turned into reality, since I have a fair amount of friends now. Chalk that one up to worrying way too much about a new, unknown situation.

—MEL
UNIVERSITY OF VIRGINIA, SOPHOMORE

• • • • • • • •

Consider

I'M NOT TOO BIG on the drug/alcohol thing: in fact, I abstain from both altogether. My biggest fear for college was that I wouldn't fit in: that people would find me "lame"; that I wouldn't make friends, being an abstainer and all. However, I found that other kids were really not as shallow as I thought. I had no problem making friends. Drinkers, non-drinkers, math nerds, ice-climbers, Trekkies ... you name 'em, I befriended 'em. As clichéd as it sounds, people liked me for who I was.

—DREW HILL
COLBY COLLEGE, JUNIOR

IN THE BEGINNING

THE MOST DIFFICULT THING freshman year was the constant need to define yourself in every conversation, in every new person you meet, and in every class you attend. You're in a totally new environment and no one knows who you are. That was kind of unnerving. It took me a while to embrace it, but I found my best friends in the middle of my first semester, and that helped me. I found them when I was rappelling off the football stadium. I found my niche. Here I get to be the crazy hippy outdoorsy rock-climbing adventure-racing person, which is really great.

—*DENALI*
PRINCETON UNIVERSITY, JUNIOR

THE BEST PART ABOUT FRESHMAN YEAR was having the independence away from home and getting to choose my classes and what I was going to do with my time.

—*ELIZABETH ROTH*
UNIVERSITY OF PENNSYLVANIA, SENIOR

IT'S FUNNY; I think if I'm not in class I must be late for something or missing something. I'm so used to being in school eight hours a day!

—*TOBIAS*
HARVARD COLLEGE, FRESHMAN

IN THE BEGINNING OF FRESHMAN YEAR, everybody is looking for the party and making friends as fast and easily as possible. You get sucked into doing things that you might not want to do, like, you're hanging out with a crowd during orientation and they want to go to some frat party, and you might not really want to do that. You have to not be afraid to stand apart and not participate in something that you don't really want to do. That way, you find the friends who are really like you. The people who are not doing the things that you don't want to be doing are waiting to meet people just like you.

—*MOLLY*
BROWN UNIVERSITY, SOPHOMORE

GETTING STARTED WITH DISABILITY SERVICES

If you have a learning, physical, psychological, or other disability, you may be able to receive special 'auxiliary aids' or accommodations to help you live up to your potential in college.

What kind of accommodations might you be granted? Students with mobility problems who are attending a large campus could be assigned an early registration appointment so that they can choose classes with plenty of travel time in between. Deaf or hard of hearing students could benefit from sign language interpreting or note-taking services. Students with learning or psychological disabilities are sometimes given extended time on exams or the opportunity to take them in a quiet, distraction-free location. Many forms of assistive technology are available as well.

There is a very important difference between the process of receiving accommodations at the college level and what you may have been used to in high school: help is available, but you have to seek it out. And since that process can take a while, don't delay -- get the ball rolling as soon as you have accepted the college's offer of admission.

Start by reaching out to the right people on your campus. Different colleges have different names for the office that helps students with special conditions succeed. Some colleges go with a fairly obvious moniker such as Disabilities Services. Others choose a more technical name, such as ADA Accommodations or Section 504 Compliance. (Names like these come from the Americans with Disabilities Act and its instructions for postsecondary institutions.) Others are more creative -- for example, Hunter College in New York City has an Office of AccessABILITY. If you can't find what you're looking for in your admissions packet or on the college website, call student services or the campus operator.

Once the disability services office has your basic information, they will ask you for documentation. To receive accommodations for a learning disability, you'll have to get a full evaluation performed by a learning disabilities expert. Most colleges do not keep these evaluation experts on staff, but can make a referral. (Warning: These evaluations can be expensive.) If you have a physical or psychological disability, you'll need to get a letter from your doctor or other medical professional.

After your records have been examined and the office has determined the appropriate accommodations, you, your professors, and the office will work together to implement them. It's up to you to talk with your professors at the beginning of each semester, making them aware that you are registered with the disability services office and are planning ahead for each approved accommodation.

Frances Northcutt

THINGS ARE LESS STRUCTURED IN COLLEGE. Professors don't bother taking attendance at most lectures, you don't have the same class (or sleep) schedule every day, and you can have breakfast for dinner. With all of this increased flexibility, you will find that you have more responsibilities – keeping up with class material, maintaining healthy sleeping/ eating habits, and budgeting your time appropriately. Getting used to college life is all about understanding and fulfilling these responsibilities, while still enjoying yourself!
—*STEPHANIE DREIFUSS*
  DUKE UNIVERSITY, SENIOR

THE OTHER SIDE OF THE DESK: THE CASE OF THE MISSING FRESHMAN

Colleges measure success in many ways, but one of the most important is retention: how many students who start out at the college actually stay, persist, and eventually graduate. In order to make retention numbers as high as possible, college administrators are always looking at what helps students stay and what causes students to leave. We know that the students who aren't connected to anyone—peers, resident advisors, faculty, student life, staff— are more likely to struggle academically and socially, which can lead to dropping out or being expelled. As a result, when college administrators get together for meetings, we often talk about the "disconnected" freshmen: the students who aren't showing up for class, who don't come to dorm meetings, who sit alone in the dining hall, who don't make eye contact when they're walking across campus. Those students may *feel* invisible, but they aren't. College staff and faculty usually notice if a student is isolated from others, and we do want to help.

Frances Northcutt

ONE PARTICULAR FEAR that I had coming into Rice was that I would no longer stand out in the classroom or in extracurricular, since practically everyone who comes to Rice was a standout in her high school. I thought everyone might be really competitive in classes or cutthroat about getting leadership positions. My first few years I applied for jobs, internships, and leadership positions and was rejected for practically all of them. Rather than get discouraged and give up, I just kept trying and continued to develop good relationships with supportive members of the faculty.

—EMILIA
RICE UNIVERSITY, JUNIOR

MY NUMBER ONE WORRY was being away from my mom. Luckily, my school was only an hour and 45 minutes away, so I went home every weekend. We also had a really good mobile-to-mobile plan where we could talk as much as we wanted to for free.

—*QUONIAS*
UNIVERSITY OF WEST GEORGIA, SENIOR

COLLEGE ISN'T LIKE HIGH SCHOOL; you have to actually try to get good grades. When I was a freshman I would write a paper with no thesis and think that I would still get an A on it (which happened in high school). Then you get the paper back and you get a B-minus and it says, "You don't have a thesis." It's hard to slip things by professors; they know the tricks, especially in freshman classes. You have to try that extra bit harder.

—*KIM KAPLAN*
STANFORD UNIVERSITY, SENIOR

ASK THE ADVISER

College just started, but I really don't like it here. Should I transfer?

Lots of students have a tough first week, month, or even semester, but that doesn't necessarily mean that things won't get better. In fact, if you stick around, you may find out that this college is the right one for you after all.

So why do you feel so out of place now? Starting college is a huge adjustment, and it's rare for that adjustment to go 100-percent smoothly. If you give up now and stop trying to make friends, enjoy your classes, and get involved on campus, you'll never know what might have been.

Frances Northcutt

ARE YOU FOLLOWING THE RULES?

Do you even know what the rules are? Your college's policies and regulations are available to you from several sources - and you obviously need to check those to see what applies to your school. Here's a general overview to get you started and to help put things into perspective.

FINANCIAL POLICIES

Pay special attention to policies that pertain to registration and tuition and fees. In general, students may register and add or drop courses without penalties before the first day of classes. However, most institutions hold registered students responsible for percentages of tuition and/or fees once the semester has started - even if they never attended a class. On the other hand, after a certain point in the semester, students may be restricted from officially withdrawing from a class. Thus, you should always consult an academic advisor before deciding not to continue with courses.

Financial aid, too, may be affected if you add or drop courses, as the level of aid generally depends on the number of credits you take per semester. You also may need to maintain a certain GPA in order to continue receiving aid.

Make sure to pay any and all outstanding tuition and fees by your college's deadlines, since students are routinely dropped for non-payment. Should this occur, you may find it difficult to secure your original course load or to register for a subsequent semester.

BEHAVIORAL POLICIES

The Student Code of Conduct primarily addresses behavioral concerns. These concerns go far beyond lying, cheating, or stealing. Certain institutions formulate a Code of Conduct to generate a unified message against inappropriate behaviors within the community. The code almost always discusses academic integrity issues. Academic integrity is a term used to describe to ethically sound behavior that relates to educational endeavors. The most notable academic integrity issues pertain to plagiarism and to cheating on exams. Colleges focus on developing policies that will help foster ethically sound students.

RESIDENTIAL POLICIES

Residential campuses normally develop policy manuals with focused policies. This helps to establish parameters for circumstances that relate directly to living in the residence halls. Topics covered may include prohibitions such as unauthorized guests, drugs, and other banned substances. Some campuses restrict overnight guests, while others may permit overnight guests only over a weekend. While it may seem like common knowledge to steer clear of drugs and alcohol, some campuses even ban drug-related paraphernalia or imagery. Could you imagine getting dismissed from the halls because you had a particular picture of Bob Marley on the wall, although you truly loved his music?

ACADEMIC POLICIES

Your academic program may have its own academically related policies, and your professors will certainly have their own policies as stated in the course syllabus. Familiarize yourself with the most important policies before you begin your studies. If this time has passed, consult with the appropriate departments before making serious decisions.

Where can you find these policies? On your college's website, or within the respective department. Here are the most relevant sources:

- The Student Handbook or webpage
- The Academic Policies and webpage
- The Course Catalog
- Residence Life Handbook and webpage
- The Office of Financial Aid
- The Office of the Bursar
- The Office of the Registrar

Tatum Soo Kim, M.S.Ed.
Director of Academic Services
New York University-SCPS
Division of Programs in Business

COLLEGE INVOLVEMENT 101

Research shows that the more engaged students are during college, the higher their level of success throughout college and in their careers. Engaging in campus activities will help you build skills and experiences, and make you a well-rounded candidate for jobs once you graduate. Your involvement also supports your college and makes it a better place to go to school.

Things To Do During Your First Year on Campus

- ☐ Find one or two student organizations that interest you, and join them.
- ☐ Attend at least two big campus events: This is one of the coolest things about college that you won't get anywhere else in life: Convocation, Welcome Week, Homecoming, or a Fall Festival/Block Party/Spring Splash events, etc.
- ☐ Attend a sporting event for at least two different sports.
- ☐ Go to a professor's or TA's office hours and ask a question.
- ☐ Buy some cool college merchandise from your campus store and wear it regularly.
- ☐ Explore your college town with roommates and hall mates.
- ☐ Take a picture with your university's mascot. Maybe later you can try out to be the mascot.
- ☐ Explore some of the hidden gems of your campus – a botanic garden or a courtyard that's tucked away.
- ☐ Read your campus newspaper. If you want, you can try to write for it.
- ☐ Listen to your campus radio station.
- ☐ Attend at least one meeting of your student government. You may really enjoy the topics discussed and get motivated to help create positive change on campus.
- ☐ If you have the opportunity to meet someone important, influential or famous on campus, do so.

Grades are important, of course - for future employers, grad schools, etc. But even more important, perhaps, will be what you say when they ask you what you did in college, what you learned, to share a story about your college experience, etc. Getting involved on campus will help you best answer those questions - and that probably means a lot more than simply getting great grades....

Scott C. Silverman

BIGGEST DIFFERENCE BETWEEN high school and college: Freedom and the ability to do what you want, when you want. For someone who can manage their time, college is a great time to have fun, meet people and do new things. But for those that lack time management, they find it is gone all too soon.

—*G.I.*
GEORGE WASHINGTON UNIVERSITY, SENIOR

. . . .

EXPECT ANYTHING AND EVERYTHING! Expect toiletries to go missing, especially if kept in the public bathroom. Expect to find random fliers for a hundred different clubs under your door every day of the first week. Expect to have R.A.s that care, and those who don't even know your name. But above all, expect to be sick at least once during your first year in a dorm, no matter if you were healthy as a horse in high school. Just make sure to have the basic medicines with you so if you can't go home easily, you can at least take care of yourself without having to leave your room.

—*MERELISE HARTE ROUZER*
GEORGIA INSTITUTE OF TECHNOLOGY, SOPHOMORE

WELCOME HOME!
TIPS FOR VETERANS

As a veteran who may have spent time away from friends and family in highly challenging circumstances, the perspective and experience you bring to campus is vastly different from that of most other first-year college students. Your college experience is likely to be different from that of your peers in certain ways, too. Here are some success strategies:

- **Access your GI Benefits:** Your tuition can be substantially reduced with GI benefits, but these benefits are not granted automatically. You have to apply for them. Check out http://gibill.va.gov/apply-for-benefits/.

- **Apply for Financial Aid and Scholarships:** There are scholarships specifically created to support veterans.

- **Find your campus office to support student veterans:** There may be even more resources specifically available to you on campus than you thought possible – including (occasionally) priority registration.

- **Complete the College Level Examination Program (CLEP):** Taking these exams will help you to potentially get credits for some introductory and breadth courses based on everything you learned during your service. For more information, check out http://clep.collegeboard.org/.

- **Remember, you are not alone:** With the growing number of veterans returning home and going to college, some of your peers may be going through some of the same things that you are. Find them by asking around, checking for a student veterans organization, or even forming one on your own. http://www.studentveterans.org is a great resource to check out as well.

- **Political viewpoints and perspectives about the military may differ widely from your own:** This could be frustrating and at times agonizing, particularly if one of your peers is quite vocal. It's important for you to be able to understand their views and concerns, as well as to be able to articulate your own.

- **Be patient and understanding:** This applies not only to your interactions with others, but you also need to give yourself time during this transition back to civilian life. Depending on your experiences during active duty, you might also have to deal with post-traumatic stress or anxiety. Campus resources may be able to help.

Scott C. Silverman

MANY PEOPLE LOOK DOWN on community college. But the classes at community colleges are often harder than you would think. I also had a lot of the teachers who were retired from the larger state university nearby and were recycling the exact same coursework at a discounted rate. I know community college is a mixed bag, and that it's easy to get lost or lose focus. But if you stay dedicated, it's a good way to save money and still get a good education.

—COREY
SAN DIEGO STATE UNIVERSITY, JUNIOR

MY BIGGEST FEAR before starting school was moving to another city, especially one like Atlanta. I thought I was going to be living in the Deep South and I was afraid of being completely bored with Atlanta. I coped with this by concentrating my time on finding the good in moving and seeing the move as an opportunity to explore a completely new place. I ended up enjoying what Atlanta has to offer.

—*ALEX*
EMORY UNIVERSITY, SOPHOMORE

THE THING THAT STANDS OUT THE MOST about my freshman year is the fact that I was completely responsible for my learning. No one cared if I came to class or not; no one cared if I took notes or studied for a test. I remember thinking that it was wonderful to have so much freedom, and if the professors didn't care, why should I? I took full advantage of having no attendance phone calls, no conduct grades, no authoritarian instructors. By the time I figured out that I was wasting my time (and my parents' money) and that I had to take responsibility for my education, it wasn't too late, but my GPA never fully recovered.

—*S.A.S.*
UNIVERSITY OF SOUTH FLORIDA, GRADUATE

MOST BEAUTIFUL COLLEGE CAMPUSES

1. Florida Southern College, Lakeland, FL
2. Princeton University, Princeton, NJ
3. Sweet Briar College, Sweet Briar, VA
4. University of Mississippi, University, MS
5. Lewis and Clark College, Portland, OR

3 DIFFERENCES BETWEEN HIGH SCHOOL AND COLLEGE

1. You have to rely on yourself.
2. You learn to become self-sufficient pretty fast.
3. Your time is less scheduled. Managing your time is key in college.

—LINDSEY WILLIAMSON
VANDERBILT UNIVERSITY, GRADUATE

IN COLLEGE, no one will ever call you out on skipping class, being uninvolved, going crazy on weekends, etc. I'd heard this, but it didn't really sink in until I got here and I realized that nobody cared if I didn't attend EVERY orientation event. If I thought it was better that I went to sleep rather than attending the social events that lasted until midnight, then it was my decision. However, most events (especially classes) are important enough that you're cheating yourself if you don't go. In college, you have to be entirely self-motivated rather than relying on requirements to get you involved.

—LIZZIE
BOWDOIN COLLEGE, FRESHMAN

THE BIGGEST DIFFERENCE, undoubtedly, is the independence students have in college. It's a great feeling knowing that you are free to go anywhere, sleep anytime, and eat as much as you would like. Just make sure that you schedule time for studying.

—JONATHAN LIU
UNIVERSITY OF TENNESSEE - KNOXVILLE, FRESHMAN

GET A MENTOR!

Of course you're excited to be in college, but the newness can also be intimidating or confusing at times: the way classes are scheduled, for example – or how to decide which classes to take. How do professors grade? What is *really* expected of you? Is the syllabus important or will the professor tell you when to study and what to read? The questions go on and on; college is very different from high school.

One way to get your questions answered and to feel more confident about the transition, is to get a mentor. A mentor, in this context, is someone with first-hand knowledge of the college experience, the expectations of college, and how to be an effective student on the campus. The mentor is someone you can feel comfortable asking questions of, and have the confidence to know that s/he can either give you the correct answer, or point you in the direction of someone who can. A mentor will give you advice and will be there to listen to you and help you clarify your goals, and also help you find solutions to challenges that arise. A mentor is someone who wants you to succeed and will help you do just that. When all else fails, you are confused, or just want guidance and support, the mentor is the one you turn to.

So where do you find a mentor? Anywhere, really: on campus, in your community, at your place of worship, or at your place of employment. A mentor can be a helpful professor or counselor at the school or a more experienced student on campus. The key is to choose someone who has first-hand knowledge about college, and how to be a good college student. Does s/he know how to study? Can s/he give you advice about social life on campus, financial aid, life issues that may arise, etc.? Choose a person who is easy to talk to…someone you feel comfortable asking questions of, and someone you trust and think you can look up to. Is that person in the career that you would like to be in? Is that person a model student? Has that person been to college, and was s/he successful?

After you decide on someone you think would be an appropriate mentor, it's as simple as asking that person to help you with your college experience. People are usually very willing to help when they can.

Once you get a knowledgeable mentor, your college experience will never be the same; it'll be smoother and more interesting with a trusted advisor to help you navigate college life!

Michelle T. Williams, Ed.D.
Director, JobTrakPA, Community College of Philadelphia
Adjunct Lecturer, Neumann University

DON'T EXPECT COLLEGE TO MEET YOUR EXPECTATIONS. But embrace everything that college gives you. I expected college to be this 'holy grail' experience, completely crazy, and I did do amazing things, but it was not necessarily what I thought it was going to be. Try not to have crazy expectations, and to just go with the flow.
—MATT
TUFTS UNIVERSITY, SOPHOMORE

• • • • • • • •

STRICT PARENTING EQUALS NOT DOING WELL in college. Strict parenting doesn't prepare kids for the overload of freedom they will experience in college. Relaxed parents bring up kids who can balance school work and social life. Don't expect to go to college to have fun. Do the work first and enjoy yourself later.
—DAVID
KEAN UNIVERSITY, JUNIOR

FREEDOM!

YOU ARE FREE TO BE who you want to be, and you don't have to be the prom queen or band geek that you were in high school. It's a time to explore who you are, what you want in your life, and what path you will take. You're free from conforming to what your group of friends is interested in; if you don't want to be in a theater class or an economics class, you don't have to be. In the end, everyone in college is working toward life after college, whether that means business school, pre-med, or liberal arts.

—*MICHELLE Y. LEE*
EMORY UNIVERSITY, SENIOR

THIS IS THE SINGLE MOST CLICHÉD DIFFERENCE, but it really is the freedom. You have so much more available time and so many options to do what you wanted that you did not have in high school because you were spending roughly eight hours a day in the school building. Now you have a lot more available time to invest how you choose. Invest it wisely, though, or it will come back to bite you.

—*BARRY LANGER*
OGLETHORPE UNIVERSITY, JUNIOR

IN HIGH SCHOOL, the school you attend, your friends, and your parents primarily dictate your direction in life. College is a time when you can do WHATEVER YOU WANT! Take classes that interest you. Join clubs that seem interesting. Work out when you want and get drunk when you want. It's up to you whether you sink or swim.

—*ILAN GLUCK*
UNIVERSITY OF MARYLAND, JUNIOR

THE BIGGEST DIFFERENCE between high school and college is basic: You are on your own. You can do whatever you want, whenever you want, however you want. If you want to stay up until 3 a.m. for three weeks in a row, that's fine. But you need to learn what plan and schedule works best for you. (I promise that eating pizza, drunk, at 2 a.m. every weekend, isn't best for anyone.)

—ANNIE THOMAS
UNIVERSITY OF MICHIGAN, SENIOR

UNLIKE HIGH SCHOOL, where most of the homework is due the next day, the workload in college comes in waves. Some weeks there will only be some reading and other times you might have two papers and a test in the same week.

—KANU
HUNTER COLLEGE, SOPHOMORE

• • • • • • • • •

MY FRIENDS AND I WERE HORRIBLE at managing our time to meet our class requirements. This was a whole new experience for us and we tackled the situation just as we did in high school: We waited until the last minute before actually doing the required work. The problem with that: Last minute in high school meant the day the assignment was given; last minute in college meant a month after it was given. There's not enough time to accomplish a month's worth of work in just a few days. Freshmen need to learn that they must schedule their own academic calendar. This is one of the most crucial adjustments to be made by freshmen.

—RAJ MATHEW
MACAULAY HONORS COLLEGE AT CUNY HUNTER, JUNIOR

FIRST-GENERATION COLLEGE STUDENTS

How do you talk to your family members about college? As the first in your family to go to college, how to you know how to succeed on campus? Most of the tips in this book apply to you just as they apply to any other student. Here are a few that are especially relevant for the "first-generation" college experience:

1) **Attend New Student Orientation:** You'll learn more about your campus resources, get a thorough tour, make a four-year course plan and register for your first term of classes. You'll get your bearings and figure out how best to tap into resources available to you on campus and in the community. Plus, you'll make your first new college friends!

2) **Tap into campus resources:** Your campus has a lot of resources available to you, and most, if not all, of them are covered by your tuition fees. Your campus should even have a suite of programs and guides specifically geared towards first generation college students.

3) **Involve your family:** your family will be proud that you are in college and will want to celebrate every success with you. Some parents of first-generation students may not understand that you have to dedicate so much time to college, so you may have to convince your family that the resources and tips you are getting from campus will help you thrive. Many of the pages in this book are things you can share with them as well.

4) **Find a mentor:** Upper division students or peer mentors will be a great help, particularly if they, too, are first-generation college students.

5) **Communicate your feelings and experiences:** It helps to talk to others about how you are experiencing college, whether it's friends, family members or staff. Some of what you may experience can include:

   a. Pride – you did it, you're here!
   b. Guilt – you made it to college, other relatives and friends did not.
   c. Confusion – you may feel out of the loop.
   d. Responsibility – not only for your own education and helping improve the situation in your family, but also sending money home to help the family and a feeling that you need to be home to help take care of younger siblings, for example.
   e. Isolation – you are not alone, but feeling like you are may lead to embarrassment over your socioeconomic status, or being unfamiliar with college lingo. Let's be honest though – none of your classmates has ever gone to college before, either. Don't stress about it, just learn to adapt.
   f. Excitement – often mixed with a dose of anxiety, about what college means to you and your family, now and in the future.

6) **Some family tips:** The more connected your family is to your university, and the more you share with them about what you are experiencing, the less likely they are to pressure you. If they know that for the week before final exams, going home is not an option (and you will make it up to them by being home for Winter Break), then they will feel as though they are contributing to your college success. Have them come visit too, and introduce them to some of your friends, your RA and others you've gotten to know on campus. If there is a family orientation, bring them to it.

Check out this website for other resources:
   http://www.firstinthefamily.org/collegeyears/

Scott C. Silverman

ASK THE ADVISER

I'm having a few problems, and not just with my classes. It's not like I can't handle it, but it would be nice to just talk to someone and not have them tell me all the things I should be doing differently.

The staff at the counseling center are trained to listen, and not to tell you what to do. You are an adult, and can make your own decisions, but sometimes it helps to talk through your experiences with someone objective. Counseling sessions are confidential, so you can be upfront and honest about whatever's on your mind without worrying about it getting back to your professors, your friends, or your family.

Frances Northcutt

THE BIGGEST DIFFERENCE BETWEEN high school and college is that professors do not treat you like babies. They rarely give "busy" homework on a daily basis. Instead, there are only a few papers to write, in which you must demonstrate what you have learned in class or how extensively you researched.

—KANU
HUNTER COLLEGE, SOPHOMORE

• • • • • • • •

I WASN'T EXPECTING TO SPEND as much time sitting up and talking to people, going to people's dorms and talking until 3 am. That was pretty cool. It didn't help with sleep habits or work habits but it was definitely worth it, looking back.

—EMILY
HARVARD COLLEGE, SENIOR

Dorms: The Good Life?

Your parents tell you that your dorm is a hundred times fancier than the dorms they had when they were college students— you just wish they could see what your hall looks like on Sunday mornings. And even at the very best of times, five minutes after the custodial staff tunneled their way through, there are still plenty of interpersonal adventures to face: The neighbor who steams broccoli every single night at 6:45. The neighbor who stays in shape by kicking a soccer ball against the wall for hours. And then there's you—wanting to have fun and hang out, but sometimes craving just one moment of peace and privacy. Read on to see what else you might be in for—and what to do about it!

GROW ACCUSTOMED TO SEEING some things in the bathroom that you just wouldn't at home. You will learn to cherish personal space and privacy in ways you never could before.

—J.V.
THE COLLEGE OF WILLIAM & MARY, GRADUATE

LEARNING TO LIVE WITH OTHER PEOPLE IS AN IMPORTANT SKILL TO HAVE.

—MELISSA K. BYRNES
AMHERST COLLEGE GRADUATE

HEADLINES
Best Advice and Top Tips

- Be respectful of your roommates and clean up after yourself.
- Set a monthly cleaning schedule with your roommates, and stick to it.
- Try to meet all the people on your floor—it makes sharing a bathroom easier.
- Dorm life means adjusting to living with a lot of other people in a small space.

Dorms are a good place if you can deal with living in a box with another person.

—*K.M.*
NORTHWESTERN UNIVERSITY GRADUATE

I LIVED IN DORMS FOR THE FIRST TWO YEARS.
I lived in an all-girl dorm, and for the first two weeks, everyone was happy. But then we all started getting our periods at the same time, and everyone became bitchy all together. It was terrible. And the dorm was filthy. You'd think an all-girl dorm would be clean, but girls are definitely dirtier than guys. Our bathroom was disgusting. And the end of the year was ridiculous—we had garbage cans spilling into the hallways. Living off campus now is like a slice of heaven.

—*SUSAN LIPPERT*
EMORY UNIVERSITY, JUNIOR

· · · · · · · · ·

SET MONTHLY CLEANUP TIMES and stick to them. Failure to do so might result in an infestation of dust bunnies.

—*KHALIL SULLIVAN*
PRINCETON UNIVERSITY, JUNIOR

WHENEVER YOU LEAVE YOUR DORM ROOM, bring your key with you. My friend woke up late one day and half-unconsciously took a shower in the dorm bathrooms. He only had a towel on, and flip-flops. After his shower he returned to his dorm room to find it locked; he was locked out. Everyone was in class, even his RA. He had to run to the other side of campus in his towel to our friend's laundry room to borrow some clothes so that he could go to lunch and to class.

> —E.F.
> CLAREMONT MCKENNA COLLEGE, SOPHOMORE

Dorm life is an essential experience.

> —MELISSA K. BYRNES
> AMHERST COLLEGE
> GRADUATE

• • • • • • • • •

LIVE IN THE DORMS WITH FRESHMEN in small ratty rooms. It doesn't sound right, I know, but it's what I wish I had done. My school had a variety of dorms that ran from old, predominantly freshman dorms with tiny, two-person rooms, to newly renovated, upper classman dorms that were like six-person apartments. I chose the middle of the road; a mostly upperclassman dorm with large rooms. Big mistake. These types of dorms aren't conducive to meeting lots of people, which is what freshman year is all about.

Through a classmate in one of the older dorms with tiny rooms, I discovered a social wonderland. Everyone in the building was a freshman, everyone kept their doors open, and everyone wandered around meeting and greeting. There was pretty much a family or little town atmosphere; everyone hung out and did lots of stuff together. This is what the freshman experience was supposed to be.

> —JEFF
> BOWLING GREEN STATE UNIVERSITY, GRADUATE

If you put a thousand freshmen into a building, anything can and will happen.

—B.
GEORGE WASHINGTON UNIVERSITY, SENIOR

MAKE FRIENDS WITH PEOPLE who are not on your hall. That way, when you need a break from your dorm or your roommate, you can call those people and say, "I need to get out of here, I'm coming over!" I would usually completely leave my dorm during the day. I wouldn't return to my room until the evening. That way my life didn't revolve around my hall. Find something to do by yourself outside your dorm, like biking, running, or singing; whatever it is that will get you out.

—SUMMER J.
UNIVERSITY OF VIRGINIA, SENIOR

• • • • • • • •

IF YOU'RE GOING TO LIVE IN THE DORM, I hope you like noise. Dorms are what they are advertised to be: a place to meet people and have lots of fun. Some of my best friends to this day are people I met and bonded with while trying to survive dorm life. So, if you opt for living in the dorms, expect a lot of fun and interesting experiences; just don't count on getting a lot of studying or sleep.

—K. HARMA
WESTERN WASHINGTON UNIVERSITY, GRADUATE

• • • • • • • •

I WISH I'D BEEN MORE SOCIABLE. I wish I'd met more people, because now I don't really know that many people, except for my close friends. Now that everyone has gone their separate ways I don't really know any casual acquaintances or anything on campus. You form bonds in your freshman dorm and when everyone moves out and goes to other dorms, you can go see them and visit and that kind of stuff. It's kind of like a network that you can use throughout your college career. And I don't really do that.

—T.
STANFORD UNIVERSITY, SENIOR

OFF-CAMPUS FOLLIES

I thought living in a dorm would be stifling and stupid, so I got an apartment next to campus with three other roommates. Now *that* was stupid. Friends from the dorms—and their friends—considered our place Party Central, since they had no other place to go and were too young to get into bars. There was a parade of people in and out of  the place almost every night—not to mention an abundance of alcohol and drugs. The police came four different times, warning us to quiet down. Regulars included the entire trumpet section of the marching band, a five-piece rock band of bare-chested guys, a torch-juggling pharmacy student, and a cross-dresser named Phil. The apartment was trashed and I was always afraid of getting in big legal trouble. I tried to kick everyone out, but my roommates refused to back me up. At the end of the year, I packed up my stuff and moved into the dorms.

—W.
UNIVERSITY OF GEORGIA, GRADUATE

If you're missing your room at home, try and personalize your side of the dorm room. Within a few weeks, you'll feel like it's where you belong. What's weird, though, is when I went home for a few days, I felt like I wasn't home, and I wanted to go back to my dorm room. I've talked to multiple people about this, and lots of other freshmen have this same feeling.

—JONATHAN LIU
UNIVERSITY OF TENNESSEE - KNOXVILLE, FRESHMAN

ADVICE FROM A FORMER R.A.

- **MAKE FRIENDS WITH YOUR RESIDENT ASSISTANTS.** They know most of the professors and staff on campus and can put you in touch with people a lot more easily than if you had to just walk in or cold-call an office.

- **IF YOU HAVE ROOMMATE PROBLEMS,** handle them right away. If you wait, you might get stuck with someone who already had a roommate move out, so you'll probably end up with a worse roommate.

- **IF YOU DRINK UNDERAGE,** use cans, not bottles, and be quiet. You're far less likely to get caught if you're quiet.

- **IF YOU SMOKE POT,** don't do it in your room. It is very easily smelled and tracked down.

- **IF YOU DAMAGE YOUR ROOM,** report it immediately. The staff likes students who are up-front and appear apologetic. If we find it when you move out, you will definitely get a bigger bill, and your parents will be mad.

- **FIND OUT THE DORM RULES UP FRONT.** Some schools can call your parents for offenses, some schools can revoke your housing for getting in trouble, and so on. You don't want to have to explain to your parents mid-semester that you got kicked out for playing your stereo too loud.

- **DO ANYTHING YOU CAN TO MOVE IN EARLY.** Moving in with everyone else is a nightmare.

- **YOUR RESIDENCE DIRECTOR CAN ALSO BE A GOOD RESOURCE** to talk to about classes, professors, what to take and what to avoid, and other campus tips. Many students avoid the hall staff, but if you drop by on occasion, they will go out of their way to give you good information and help you.

—*MELISSA*
GRADUATE

I MET MY FIRST TRUE COLLEGE FRIEND when my best friend from high school came up to visit me on Welcome Weekend. We sat with my bedroom door open and played our guitars. A girl who played guitar heard us and came by to talk. She became my first college friend.
—*AMY FORBES*
MISSISSIPPI STATE UNIVERSITY, GRADUATE

• • • • • • • •

I'M AN ONLY CHILD and I lived with three girls in one big room. It was a pretty big adjustment the first semester. I remember being kind of miserable. You don't get much sleep and there's a lot of work to do. But you get through it.
—*ANNE*
GEORGE WASHINGTON UNIVERSITY, SENIOR

• • • • • • • •

TRY TO GET PLACED IN THE FRESHMAN DORMS. Even though the long elevator wait and community bathrooms seem horrible—and they are— you won't meet anyone if you live in the smaller, nicer dorms.
—*ASHLEY LEAVELL*
BOSTON UNIVERSITY, SENIOR

It's much more fun living with other people than living by yourself.
—*MATT LACKNER*
PRINCETON UNIVERSITY GRADUATE

THE BARE FACTS: REMEMBER THIS NAME

George William Crump. According to our sources (Wikipedia), he gets credit as the first college student to be arrested for streaking. It happened in 1804 at Washington and Lee. Crump, by the way, went on to become a U.S. Congressman and Ambassador to Chile.

LIVE IN A DORM and get the freshman experience. You don't have the amenities that you have in an apartment, but you have the experience; sharing the hall, sharing space with roommates.

—JESSICA
UNIVERSITY OF PENNSYLVANIA, JUNIOR

" No matter how nice your R.A. is, don't date him. It always turns out to be a bad thing. "

—KYM
SAN JOSE STATE UNIVERSITY, SOPHOMORE

Make sure you have good music coming out of your room, since that's a good conversation starter.

—B.K.
CORNELL UNIVERSITY
GRADUATE

CONSIDER RENTING A FURNISHED APARTMENT. I did that when I first started at a community college. It was awesome, and the price difference was very small. I didn't have to put in any money to buy my own gear, and when it came time to move, I didn't have to worry about selling my stuff or putting it out on the street corner. Sometimes the furniture inside the apartment was a bit cheap; my bed had these horrible wooden planks keeping the mattress up, and if I shifted too much the planks would fall and the bed would sag. I still felt like it was a good way to save some money, and it was nice to just have everything there.

—COREY
SAN DIEGO STATE UNIVERSITY, JUNIOR

MY FRESHMAN YEAR WAS THE BEST YEAR of my life. Within two days of arriving I had made some of the best friends I've ever had. I lived in a freshman dorm, which I recommend very highly. Everyone is going through the same things you are, and they're all looking to make friends, so it makes for a tight-knit community. In the mixed dorms there are a lot of people who already have their friends, so they just aren't as outgoing.

—T.P.
STANFORD UNIVERSITY, SENIOR

RESPECT YOUR ROOMMATE and don't leave pizza in the room for a week. It's not your roommate's job to throw it out. The room stinks; it's not livable. People don't want to come in your room because it stinks. And don't try to blame the bad smell on the fact that your roommate's clothes are on the floor. That is not what's causing the nasty, rotten smell in your room. That would be the pizza box that you left there for a week.

—ANONYMOUS
UNIVERSITY OF VIRGINIA, SOPHOMORE

THE REMEDY

TO BATTLE HOMESICKNESS:

1. Keep busy. Go to campus events.
2. Decorate your dorm room; that can definitely make it feel more homey. A comfy bed with lots of padding and sheets will be your best friend.
3. Call home. It's OK to call multiple times a day, especially when you just want to hear Mom or Dad's voice. I still do it as a sophomore.

By second semester, you'll be calling the dorms your home.

—SHEILA CRAWFORD
NORTH CAROLINA STATE UNIVERSITY, SOPHOMORE

MAKE IT A POINT to get to know everyone on your floor at the dorm. Invite everyone to a weekly pre-dinner cocktail party. Play some icebreaker games so that everyone gets to know everyone else. Without their old high school cliques and social circles to fall back on, most people are truly eager to meet new people and make new connections. My dorm years were phenomenal, thanks to all my fantastic floor mates.

—*LAURA WOLTER*
UNIVERSITY OF TEXAS AT AUSTIN, GRADUATE

• • • • • • • •

Seek out the people on your floor who have installed bars in the bedrooms. They will be fun to hang out with.

—*AMY FORBES*
MISSISSIPPI STATE UNIVERSITY GRADUATE

ONE OF THE MOST IMPORTANT THINGS about surviving freshman year is that if you live in coed dorms like I did, you're going to see people in all states of life. You're going to see them on the can, you're going to see them before they've painted their face on, and you're going to have to get over the shock.

I've met long-term friends in the dorms. Everyone bonds in a totally different way when you live there. People go through difficult times—separation from family, separation from friends—and you all have that in common.

—*ZACH FRIEND*
UNIVERSITY OF CALIFORNIA AT SANTA CRUZ, GRADUATE

• • • • • • • •

REACH OUT IMMEDIATELY to people living on your floor. It didn't thrill me to know that I would have to share a bathroom with 40 other girls. But I ended up having the most fun. Bonding with my roommates and floor mates, going to floor events, and even playing pranks were all memories to be cherished.

—*RAE LYNN RUCKER*
BIOLA UNIVERSITY, GRADUATE

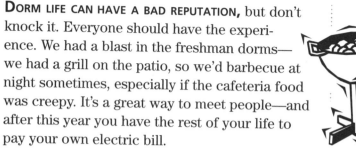

DORM LIFE CAN HAVE A BAD REPUTATION, but don't knock it. Everyone should have the experience. We had a blast in the freshman dorms— we had a grill on the patio, so we'd barbecue at night sometimes, especially if the cafeteria food was creepy. It's a great way to meet people—and after this year you have the rest of your life to pay your own electric bill.

—*J.I.*
SONOMA STATE UNIVERSITY, JUNIOR

• • • • • • • •

GET A ROOM NEAR THE SHOWERS. My dorm was always so cold in the mornings, especially in the winter. I hated that long walk down the hall while I was practically naked.

—*ANONYMOUS*
YOUNGSTOWN STATE UNIVERSITY, SENIOR

FIVE REASONS TO JOIN YOUR DORM COUNCIL

1. It's the fastest way to learn the names of everyone in your dorm.

2. You'll always have an excuse to talk to the cutie down the hall... "As your dorm representative, I just wanted to see if you had any requests or concerns concerning dorm life? Any requests at all?"

3. You can put it on your résumé.

4. Actually make dorm living conditions better!

5. It's one of the very few organized student activities you can participate in without putting on shoes.

DECORATING TIPS: A WORLD OF INTERIORS

MAKE SURE TO TALK TO YOUR ROOMMATE to see what you need to bring and what you don't. I talked to my roommate before I moved in but we did not discuss everything and ended up having doubles of some things, and then there were many things we forgot to bring so we had to go out and buy them. And, get a rug—it's a good investment for a dorm. The floors are usually dirty and a rug at least looks cleaner.

> —*E.M.G.*
> *UNIVERSITY OF SOUTH FLORIDA, JUNIOR*

GUYS, KEEP YOUR ROOMS CLEAN, because there will be girls in your room and they'll be turned off if you have disgusting rooms.

> —*REID ATTAWAY*
> *JAMES MADISON UNIVERSITY, SOPHOMORE*

KNOW YOUR SPACE before you pack up and arrive. One family came with a U-Haul full of stuff—a bed, desk, everything—and saw there was no room for any of it. They turned around and drove it right back home.

> —*TOM SABRAM*
> *CARNEGIE MELLON UNIVERSITY, SOPHOMORE*

IF YOU'RE GOING TO STEAL FURNITURE for your dorm room, steal it from the lounge. They won't find it until they spray for bugs over spring break—then you only have a few weeks of classes left anyway.

> —*J.G.*
> *FLORIDA STATE UNIVERSITY, GRADUATE*

GO NUTS ON THE DECORATING. Be tacky, be shocking. This is the only time in your life you can get away with hanging a beer sign in your window or assembling a Buddha shrine in your bathroom. I actually had an Elvis shrine in my bathroom.

—*WENDY W.*
UNIVERSITY OF GEORGIA, GRADUATE

SPEND TIME MAKING YOUR ROOM a place you would want to hang out in and study in. If you don't feel comfortable in your room, which is basically your college home, where are you going to feel comfortable?

—*JULIE*
PRINCETON UNIVERSITY, SOPHOMORE

HIGH-CLASS DORMS

College freshmen and their parents spent an average of $929 - more than other college students - on dorm furnishings, electronics, apparel, and supplies.

College students are increasingly decking out stark dorm rooms with designer-quality décor and the latest consumer electronics. Social media, design apps and shopping sites have been making it easier to share ideas and make purchases with roommates from afar. Some retailers' online tools let students create their own virtual room and share it via Facebook, Pinterest or email.

DORM ADVENTURES

WE HAD MICE. We had a sewer pipe break in our building, and all these little mice were running around. So we set traps. Our hall worked together to catch them; it was teamwork.
>   —*LAUREN WEBSTER*
>   *BARNARD COLLEGE, JUNIOR*

GIVE YOURSELF UP TO THE CABIN FEVER that sometimes comes with dorm life. Never again will you have the opportunity to run around in your pajamas, darting into the open doors that line the halls. Once, when it was snowing, my roommate and I opened our door, blasted music, ran to every one of our friends' rooms, did a little dance, then moved on to the next. It's one of the goofiest memories I have of my freshman year.
>   —*ALLISON GRECO*
>   *MONTCLAIR STATE UNIVERSITY, GRADUATE*

WE WOULD ALWAYS PLAY JOKES on each other. We had a suite mate who had really bad vision. One time, my roommate took her glasses off when she was washing her face and she couldn't find them. She was panicking. But we got my roommate back by taking all her clothes and towels while she took a shower. And when she came out, we were waiting outside with a camera. She was pissed! She was not a good sport about it.
>   —*S.R.I.*
>   *CORNELL UNIVERSITY, GRADUATE*

ONE OF MY FRIENDS LIVED above a group of guys who would blare music until one or two in the morning. She would go down in her pajamas and ask them to turn the music down, but they never did. So one morning when she got up at six, she opened up her windows and blared country music until she could hear them stirring and cursing.
>   —*ANONYMOUS*
>   *WESTERN WASHINGTON UNIVERSITY, GRADUATE*

UNUSUAL HOUSING OPTIONS

- Schiller International University (Florida) has university-owned and -operated hotels.
- Springfield College (Massachusetts) has an 81-acre "campground and outdoor adventure area."
- Southern Vermont College boasts a 27-room Edwardian mansion.
- Taylor University (Indiana) has a "NASA-approved clean room" for the neat freaks.
- University of Chicago is said to be the college campus most like Hogwarts.

“ You have to be conscious of everyone around you. And also, living in the dorm, everyone knows about everyone else. If you do something dumb, everyone knows about it. ”

—*MAUREEN SULLIVAN*
GEORGETOWN UNIVERSITY, SOPHOMORE

LEAVE THE DOOR OPEN to your dorm room. Prop it open with a chair if it won't stay open on its own. People will wander by, and if you're doing something fun—like watching a movie, playing a video game, or eating candy—they'll stop to see what's up. I met a lot of people this way.

—*LAUREN TAYLOR*
UNIVERSITY OF GEORGIA, GRADUATE

MY DORM ROOM WAS WRECKED. It was an absolute mess. I chose a dorm room where we had our own bathroom; that was a huge mistake. It got destroyed. You have a roommate and you think, "Well, maybe I'll wait for him to clean it up." But it never happens. By the end of the year, I didn't even go in there.

—*JOHNNY*
GEORGETOWN UNIVERSITY, JUNIOR

• • • • • • • •

Don't be shy. Go up to people in your building and introduce yourself.

—*KELLI*
UNIVERSITY OF DELAWARE SOPHOMORE

WHEN I CAME TO SCHOOL, I KNEW NO ONE. I entered an all-male dorm and everyone thought we were dirty, stinky guys—and we were. With no girls around, there was no need to really focus on hygiene. But because we were so isolated, we bonded super tight and have great friendships for life. We have the last laugh: Now we can bathe, but the other folks don't have our strong friendships. All-male dorms are a good idea.

—*JUSTIN PEABODY*
CARNEGIE MELLON UNIVERSITY, JUNIOR

• • • • • • • •

I LIVED IN A MIXED DORM my freshman year. I was sad because I wanted to live in an all-freshman dorm, but there were these two senior guys on my hall whom I became close with. It's wonderful because they graduated and they stayed in the Bay Area; if I ever have problems or want to talk about something, they're in the real world and have a little more perspective. They influenced what classes I took as a freshman and what major I picked. I think it's important to take advantage of those resources and not be afraid to seek them out and talk to them about classes and stuff.

—*JULIE TORRES*
STANFORD UNIVERSITY, SENIOR

FRESHMAN DORMS ARE LIKE A BIG, happy family. Once you get to know everyone, you'll have people you can rely on for anything you need. Broken computer? Your trusty technology genius is just upstairs. Can't sleep? There are always a few dorm night owls in the common room. Wondering about a class for next semester? Chances are you'll find someone who already took it. Be ready for people to count on you for something, too! By earning a reputation as a master stain remover, I subjected myself to an entire year of removing people's unconquerable stains.

—*STEPHANIE DREIFUSS*
DUKE UNIVERSITY, SENIOR

I TRY TO HAVE A "low impact" on the room - meaning, I try to keep the volume down on music or television when my roommate's clearly doing work or sleeping, and I generally clean up after myself.

—*MANNY*
GEORGE WASHINGTON UNIVERSITY, SENIOR

MAKE FRIENDS WITH SOMEONE WHO HAS A CAR. Without transportation, it's hard to get snacks or even toiletries, especially if the dorms are far from town. Sometimes you just need to go to Walgreens. It's also nice to have someone to take you on an In-N-Out Burger run at midnight when the dining halls aren't an option and you're hungry.

—*ANDREW*
UCLA, SENIOR

DON'T TRY THESE AT HOME, PART 1

ONE OF MY BEST FRIENDS from college played a hilarious prank in her residence hall in freshman year. She and a group of her hallmates put conditioner in condoms and left them all around bathrooms in their hall. The RAs were furious, but it made for a great story.

—MICHELLE Y. LEE
EMORY UNIVERSITY, SENIOR

• • • • • • • •

MY ROOMMATE SECRETLY RECORDED my cacophonous shower singing and played it for our hall. The two of us also schemed to pour cold water on a neighbor while she was in the shower. One time, my friend hid under my bed making scratching noises until I was terrified that I had mice.

—STEPHANIE DREIFUSS
DUKE UNIVERSITY, SENIOR

• • • • • • • •

DURING FINALS WEEK, I was studying in the common area of my floor. The elevator opened and I saw that the elevator had been fully furnished with a chest of drawers, a few books sitting on its top (along with a vase of fake flowers), a chair, a bookshelf, a bowl of popcorn (which I found to be the most odd), and a few posters that were hastily taped to the wall.

—REBECCA
HUNTER COLLEGE, SENIOR

• • • • • • • •

BUY A LOT OF DAWN or dishwashing soap (the Costco-size bottles) and pour them down the drain of a water fountain that people use. Let the soap bubbles begin! The fountain turns into a bubble bath.

—G.L.
GEORGE WASHINGTON UNIVERSITY, SENIOR

THE DEFAULT PRANK IS just stealing something from someone else's room and waiting for them to notice/come storming into your room. That's always hilarious.

—*ANONYMOUS*
UNIVERSITY OF CALIFORNIA AT BERKELEY, FRESHMAN

DON'T TRY THESE AT HOME, PART 2

1. One of the most basic things you should become acquainted with: knowing the location of your hall's fuse box. Learn where your room is (so that you don't accidentally turn your lights off when you're trying to mess with someone else's.)
2. If you really don't like someone, penny-lock them in their room, shut off the power, and launch "water" (insert other fluids) balloons at them through the drop ceiling. This is likely to cause a ruckus you won't want to miss.
3. If you have any means of getting a hold of sand, find a way into your victim's room and cover everything with sand. If there is a container, fill it with sand. If there is a sink, fill it with sand. Having a beach-themed dorm room might sound sweet. But there is nothing more time-consuming and irritating to get rid of than sand. Water turns it to mud, and you will never be able to vacuum it all up.
4. One prank that is rather time-consuming but very simple to pull off – fill up several hundred solo cups with water, start at the edge of the room farthest from the door, and work your way towards the door, covering every square inch of the room with solo cups filled with water. There is no other way for the poor bastard to get into his/her room without first removing every cup from the room, maximum two at a time.

—*J.V.*
THE COLLEGE OF WILLIAM & MARY, GRADUATE

DORM LIFE IS CRAMPED. Don't expect to be spending too much time there, especially if you want to study. Also, get ready for it to be loud on Friday and Saturday nights; the halls will undoubtedly be filled with giggly, obnoxious drunk people getting ready to go to frat parties.

—*HANNAH*
UNIVERSITY OF CALIFORNIA AT BERKELEY, FRESHMAN

THE MOST IMPORTANT THING I LEARNED was to keep my dorm room door open. I had a single, so not only did this make my room seem bigger, but people would stop by all the time to say hi or come to hang out. The people who always kept their door closed were cut off from the openness and friendliness of our floor, and we barely ever saw them.

—*ANNIE THOMAS*
UNIVERSITY OF MICHIGAN, SENIOR

CHEM FREE?

IF YOU LIVE IN A NORMAL DORM, you can expect drinking – in the dorm, in your room, and probably a lot. I personally don't drink, but all of my roommates and everyone on my floor do. While I haven't felt any pressure to imbibe (and most people respect my decision), I do have to deal with everyone else when they're drunk and rowdy. This means a little extra cleaning and having to be patient with noises, distractions, and occasionally having the whole floor smell like beer. For the most part, this is fine with me because I'm getting the "college experience" and my roommates' crazy stories without personally getting drunk. But if you have any moral problems with alcohol or simply don't want to deal with it, chem-free is the only way to go.

—*LIZZIE*
BOWDOIN COLLEGE, FRESHMAN

AT THE END OF MY FRESHMAN YEAR, the carpets literally had to be pulled up and replaced. We wrecked them. It happens if you plan on being the social center of your building.

—*BARRY LANGER*
OGLETHORPE UNIVERSITY, JUNIOR

I HAD TO SHARE A BATHROOM with about 20 girls and a kitchen with about 40 girls. That took a bit of an adjustment; there were some "whoa" moments. But I feel that is part of the college experience. Just be as clean and polite as possible.

—*REBECCA*
HUNTER COLLEGE, SENIOR

YOU WILL LEARN THAT there are two kinds of people when it comes to food and drink– the moochers and the moochees. Moochees get the respect, but moochers eat and get drunk at their expense.

—*J.V.*
THE COLLEGE OF WILLIAM & MARY, GRADUATE

IT'S IMPORTANT TO FIND TIME to be by yourself in your room. Living in the dorms is always hectic. We all need time to relax alone, and this is often hard to come by in the dorms. Don't be afraid to shut your door and relax alone.

—*ILAN GLUCK*
UNIVERSITY OF MARYLAND, JUNIOR

EXPECT TO LIVE IN a diverse environment. Expect to be independent. Expect to have a lot of fun. Expect to procrastinate, but learn to prioritize.

—*ALEKSANDR AKULOV*
HUNTER COLLEGE, SOPHOMORE

TIPS FOR COMMUTERS

So you've decided not to live on campus…maybe your parents want you close to home, or you have to help take care of younger siblings or keep expenses low. That's ok; a lot of students choose to live off campus. Whether you live in an apartment off-campus, or live with your family an hour away; whether you drive, bike, skateboard or walk to campus, you're a commuter student. And your college experience will be different from that of your peers who live on campus. Here are some tips that may help you succeed:

1. **Get a job on campus:** If you're going to work while you study, you might as well work on campus. On-campus employers understand how difficult it is to be a student and to work a lot of hours at the same time. They often will be more flexible with your schedule and let you work around your class schedule. During midterms and finals you can adjust your hours as needed to prepare and study.

2. **Schedule your classes to maximize your time efficiency:** Maybe you want to take all of your classes back-to-back, or fit all of them in fewer than 5 days a week, to reduce your commuting days. You won't always be able to make your schedule work out as smoothly as you want, but that's ok, too. Having breaks between classes allows you to participate in on-campus activities and gain valuable co-curricular experiences.

3. **Take advantage of your "down time":** Commuter students can find great things to do on campus in between classes – beyond just going back to your car to take a nap between classes. You can spend that time reviewing your notes for the next class, working on assignments or preparing for that upcoming exam. Make sure you find a way to access computer files you may need while you're on campus.

4. **Utilize your campus resources:** When you're on campus, take advantage of your university resources - many of which are free. The Career Center can review your résumé and job interview skills (or even get you a job on campus!), the Recreation Center and Health Center offer wellness and fitness options, and you can connect to a peer mentor through a variety of programs.

5. **Connect to other commuter students:** Many universities have recognized that commuting to campus is harder than living on campus, both logistically and in terms of transitioning into and through college. There may be get-togethers of other commuter students, a lounge on campus where commuter students can hang out and interact, and specific programs to support commuter students.

6. **Transportation tips:** If you drive to campus, leave plenty of time to get to campus and find parking. You can't use traffic or a lack of parking spaces as an excuse for being late to class or exams. Carpool or rideshare whenever possible – you'll save gas money and car repair bills, and on the days you're not the driver, you can sleep or study.
   If you bike to campus, register your bike with campus police in case it ever gets stolen (and get a great lock to reduce that possibility).
   If you walk, pay attention to your surroundings and don't walk with your earphones in... Finally, however you commute, plan ahead so you can run your errands on the way home rather than making separate trips.

7. **Make friends with people living on campus:** It's going to happen: There will be a late-night program on campus that you really want to attend, and if you have a friend on campus, you can go to the event with them, and hang out afterwards. It keeps you off the freeway late at night when you're tired, and builds your social circle. Having friends who live on campus, and others who live off-campus, will give you a variety of people to interact with.

8. **Get involved on campus:** You'll learn organizational and management skills, develop new talents and experiences, and be exposed to a variety of people and circumstances that will benefit you throughout college and later in your career. College is all about what you make of it. Yes, you might be working full time, helping out your family or just spending a lot of time on the road, but you should also explore new opportunities, attend campus events, join student organizations and take on leadership roles. College is as much about making great stories out of the experiences you have and the lessons you learn from those experiences, as it is about completing your degree.

Scott C. Silverman

I LIVED IN A CO-OP MY FIRST YEAR, so I wasn't pampered by the dorms. It's chaos 100 percent of the time, but it's worth it. It's about self-sufficiency. We don't go to the army after high school, like they do in Israel. Here we go to college, so here is where we need to learn independence, develop a thick skin, and learn how to balance life.

—KATE LEFKOWITZ
UNIVERSITY OF CALIFORNIA AT BERKELEY, JUNIOR

TAKING THE TIME TO DECORATE your room and make it homey is extremely important, especially freshman year. Bring a stuffed animal, or set up curtains in your room. Things like that make your room feel more like a home. Having a plant in your room is a huge bonus, potted plants or flowers... It's nice to have something to care for and look after! Getting a carpet and changing the curtains made my room so much homier and really changed the feel of the room completely.

—CATIE
HARVARD COLLEGE, SENIOR

. . . .

I JUST MOVED OFF-CAMPUS into an apartment after being on-campus for two years. There's a lot of annoying things about being on-campus here - like their strict guest policy. That can be a really good thing to think about when you're choosing to live on-campus or off. But I'd definitely recommend living on-campus at least your first year so that you can get used to college before having to pay bills and stuff!

—NINA
TEMPLE UNIVERSITY, JUNIOR

. . . .

DEFINITELY GO THE DORM ROUTE your freshman year. That's where I met all of my friends, including the girl I live with now! You meet the most people by sharing the bathroom, waiting for a shower stall or while brushing your teeth. My friends and I would have shower parties! We'd all make a plan to meet at 9 pm, bring in a radio and blast the music while singing in the shower. I think establishing a clique your freshman year is really important, and the dorm is the place to do it. Stay longer than one year if you can.

—JESSICA DOSHNA
UCLA, GRADUATE

LIVING IN THE DORMS is a great way to meet people, but don't limit yourself to just those people, either. I regret that I didn't join any clubs my first year. I didn't realize the importance of making a variety of friends, and it's a lot harder to meet people as you get deeper into college because people have already formed core groups.

—*ANDREW*
   UCLA, SENIOR

Talking to Strangers: Your Roommate & You

T he gods smile upon you and you score a single dorm room. Privacy!
Space! Peace and quiet! You're so lucky—or are you? Hear all that
laughter and great music coming from the triple down the hall? That's
where the fun is. That's where you're not.

And that's the roommate dilemma: On the one hand, cheek-by-jowl (or
worse) with a total stranger (or worse); on the other hand, a passport to
adventure! A best friend for life! With luck, sensitivity, and some negotiating,
you can achieve that precious middle ground. And if not, well, just knock
on the door of that triple down the hall; the party's still going on.

IT'S HARD TO TELL YOU WHAT TO EXPECT after filling
out the roommate survey – half the kids who say
they like neat rooms actually do like neat rooms,
and the other half only say that in order to snag a
neat roommate who will do all the cleaning.

—J.V.
THE COLLEGE OF WILLIAM & MARY, GRADUATE

FEEL FREE TO
AVOID YOUR
ROOMMATE IF
YOU NEED TO.

—JOHN BENTLEY
TRINITY UNIVERSITY
GRADUATE

HEADLINES
Best Advice and Top Tips

- Be honest on your roommate form or you may end up with someone you don't get along with.
- Don't live with your high school friends; meet new people.
- Having a roommate you click with can be the best part of college life.
- If you and your roommate are at odds, don't be afraid to request a room change.

YOU CAN BE INDIFFERENT TO PEOPLE you pass on your walks around campus, but if you're indifferent to your roommate, silence turns into coldness, and coldness turns into animosity, which might turn into hatred. So continue to cultivate your relationship with your roommates. Also, if you know that you are a naturally introverted person, go for a single. Many upperclassmen choose to have singles, so they must know something.

—*SEAN CAMERON*
PRINCETON UNIVERSITY, SOPHOMORE

● ● ● ● ● ● ● ●

BE REALLY HONEST ON YOUR ROOMMATE FORM or you might end up with somebody you don't get along with. It's hard to share your personal space with someone else. The space tends to be really small.

—*RUTH FEINBLUM*
BRYN MAWR COLLEGE, JUNIOR

DURING MY FRESHMAN YEAR I lived with an Orthodox Jew, a practicing Seventh-Day Adventist, and an atheist/agnostic. We survived—in a room made for two people, with four beds and four alarm clocks—by learning to leave G-d out of it!

—BRIAN ROSEN
PRINCETON UNIVERSITY, GRADUATE

- - - - - - - -

DON'T BE ROOMMATES with your old high-school friends because then you just bond together and you don't meet other people. But if you live with a new person she'll introduce you to a whole bunch of other aspects of life. She'll open you up to a whole world you wouldn't have expected. It worked for me. It was a good experience with my roommate and I learned a lot.

—KYM
SAN JOSE STATE UNIVERSITY, SOPHOMORE

- - - - - - - -

YOUR ROOMMATE IS THE FIRST PERSON you really get to know. After going to bed, my roommate and I would talk for about 45 minutes about the most random things. It's the person you meet first and know the best first. You branch out from there and get to know the whole floor.

—BRYAN
GEORGETOWN UNIVERSITY, SOPHOMORE

- - - - - - - -

I LOVE MY ROOMMATE. She's my closest friend here. We talked the day after we got the rooming information and we clicked on the phone. Don't come on too strong with your roommate, and don't think you have to be friends right away. But if you do, that's great.

—M.D.
BOSTON COLLEGE, FRESHMAN

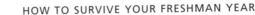
DON'T WORRY IF YOUR ROOMMATE is from a different world. I moved in with a gal from small-town Ontario, Canada, who had never met a Jewish person. When she found out I was Jewish, she asked me all sorts of funny questions. On one occasion, when I explained that Lay's potato chips were kosher, she worried that she'd be converting to Judaism by eating a bag! We never became close friends, but she was a perfect roommate for me. We kept the place clean, were respectful of each other's stuff, and had a perfectly nice relationship.

—A.S.
QUEENS UNIVERSITY, GRADUATE

. . . .

I'M IN A TRIPLE. What happens in a triple is that two people combine and go off together. And that's what happened with me; I'm the odd one out. But I don't feel bad about it because they're not my kind of people.

—AMY HOFFBERG
UNIVERSITY OF DELAWARE, FRESHMAN

. . . .

Some people
make great
friends, and
some people
make great
roommates.

—YALDA A.
UNIVERSITY OF
CALIFORNIA AT
BERKELEY
GRADUATE

CHECK UNDER YOUR ROOMMATE'S BED for old, moldy food. For two weeks our room completely stunk. People were avoiding my room and I was wondering, "What's going on?" I never thought to look under my roommate's bed. When I did I found an old can of salsa and moldy bread.

—SIERRA
CAL POLY SAN LUIS OBISPO, JUNIOR

. . . .

IF YOU HAVE A ROOMMATE WHO'S PSYCHO, don't be afraid to leave. Just go to the R.A. and get reassigned. It's a hassle, but it's better than living with a psycho.

—S.G.
COLUMBIA UNIVERSITY, SENIOR

FRESHMAN YEAR WAS CRAZY. It was tough to get adjusted to school life; there was a lot of partying and a lot of girls. Just say no—to everything. And if your roommate can't say no, change roommates. My roommate couldn't say no, and I couldn't say no; we just played off each other. It wasn't good.

—KENTON
UNIVERSITY OF VIRGINIA, SENIOR

• • • • • • • •

MY FIRST ROOMMATE HAD MADE OTHER PLANS. But I got a new roommate, and it was a great experience. Sometimes you click and get along with someone. We didn't argue, and we had a lot of fun. We each had our own separate lives; our boyfriends got along. It was a great roommate setup. The lesson: If your first roommate doesn't work out for whatever reason, there's probably someone else out there who will become one of your best friends.

—GINGER M. BRODTMAN
SPRING HILL COLLEGE, GRADUATE

• • • • • • • •

I ENDED UP ABSOLUTELY ADORING my roommate's personality. But her tidiness, on the other hand, was an issue. My friends would joke that you couldn't even see my side of the room because of her stuff overflowing onto it, and my parents were horrified at the mess. But she turned out to be one of my best friends, so the best thing I could do was joke about it and try to give subtle hints. It wasn't even close to the worst scenario possible for a random roommate, but it was a challenge! I'm proud to say that we're still friends to this day.

—MERELISE HARTE ROUZER
GEORGIA INSTITUTE OF TECHNOLOGY, SOPHOMORE

When in doubt, put on a movie and watch it with your roommates. It promotes bonding and seems to make any problems fade away.

—RAE LYNN RUCKER
BIOLA UNIVERSITY
GRADUATE

THERE'S ONE IN EVERY CROWD

Hope for the best, but expect the worst. When I moved into the dorms, I was expecting that the college would pair me up with someone who shared my interests, and who would become my new best friend. Boy, was I in for a surprise! I had *five* other roommates:

- A slightly overweight girl from San Diego who was some kind of singer. She would sing constantly . . . and I mean *constantly*. She was extremely bossy, annoying, and required a lot of attention.

- A Goth lesbian. She would sit on the patio, smoke a pack of cigarettes an hour, and cry about how some girl had screwed her over.

- A girl who wore black lipstick and drawn-in eyebrows. We only saw her when she answered the door for her homeys (who all looked like they belonged on the streets of L.A.), and then they would lock themselves in her room and smoke pot for days on end.

- An Asian girl who told her father she was living in the dorms, but was actually living with her boyfriend. I think I saw her six times in the whole year (one of those times, she asked to borrow a pair of my underwear!).

- And Julia. She was the roommate I needed. She was like me and she became my best friend.

Ultimately, I learned to accept people for who they are; you will find that there is something to love about each of them. My roommates opened my eyes (and heart) to diversity.

—HEATHER POLLOCK
CALIFORNIA STATE UNIVERSITY, GRADUATE

I LIVED WITH MY BEST FRIEND and it was the worst thing I did my freshman year. We didn't speak for a year after that. It was like a competition, rather than a partnership, always seeing who could make plans to do something cool, seeing how high the dishes could stack up. At first, we did everything together, but then learned we didn't like each other's company that much and almost never talked. That's not easy when you live with someone. When the year was finally over, it was a relief. We'd had enough of each other; there was no reason to hang out.

—IRVING BURNS RAMSOWER III
UNIVERSITY OF FLORIDA, GRADUATE

. . . .

" If your roommate is not good— for instance, if the person steals your food, throws dirty laundry on your bed, etc.—get out as soon as possible because your life will be hell. And it's easy to do that, too; just go to your R.A. "

—K.
NORTHWESTERN UNIVERSITY, GRADUATE

. . . .

THE WORST THING THAT HAPPENED with my roommate: She decided to tap dance at 7 a.m. to get back at me because I kept her up at night.

—MELANIE
PENNSYLVANIA STATE UNIVERSITY, SOPHOMORE

THE ROOMMATE-SELECTION SURVEYS never ask questions that are meaningful enough to give you insight into how it's really going to be like to live with someone. So just expect the unexpected and get ready to be flexible. According to the survey, my freshman-year roommate appeared to be a conservative who liked country music. She turned out to be a very dynamic and wild gal who kept me laughing throughout the year.

—K. HARMA
WESTERN WASHINGTON UNIVERSITY, GRADUATE

· · · · · · · ·

I HAD A ROOMMATE WHO HAD SEX in the room while I was sleeping. I thought they were just lying there; I would hear whispering and I thought they were just talking. Nope, they were porking. They told me later, when they were drunk. That's all right though, I'm OK with that.

—SEIJI YAMAMOTO
STANFORD UNIVERSITY, GRADUATE

· · · · · · · ·

DON'T LET PEOPLE'S FLAWS GET TO YOU. Everyone has flaws. If your roommate is messy, discuss it. One friend's roommate was a total slob. She would make macaroni and cheese, eat half of it, and let the other half sit for a week. I saw lemon juice curdle in her room. It was gross!

—KEISHA
EMORY UNIVERSITY, SENIOR

· · · · · · · ·

MY ROOMMATE THINKS I'M MESSY and I think she's too neat. We argue over that. And we have a division going down the middle of the room; her stuff on one side and mine on the other.

—WHITNEY
YALE UNIVERSITY, FRESHMAN

I HAD A ROOMMATE WHO SNORED and I had to go to the study lounge to sleep. I would take my blanket and comforter and sleep on a couch or chair at two in the morning. I got out the second semester. I didn't have the heart to tell him. Other than the snoring, we got along great.

—RICK SHILLING
PENNSYLVANIA STATE UNIVERSITY, GRADUATE

• • • • • • • •

" Set up ground rules with your roommate. I walked in on my roommate and her boyfriend having sex in the middle of our floor. Another time, they did it in the room when they thought I was asleep. Not cool! "

—CHAVON MITCHELL
XAVIER UNIVERSITY, GRADUATE

• • • • • • • •

I WOULD ARGUE with my roommate. She would tell me that I'm an obsessive-compulsive and she couldn't deal with it anymore. And I would be like, "What are you talking about, you psycho." So, I spent a lot of time in the library, which is a good thing.

—S.
UNIVERSITY OF VIRGINIA, SOPHOMORE

LESSON: TALK ABOUT IT

My roommate was a very sweet girl, but she had the most bizarre sleep schedule and work schedule ever. We lived in a one-room double, and she liked to go to bed at 5 a.m. and then wake up at 8 a.m. and do more work. Then she would go to class until 3 p.m. and then sleep in our room until 9 p.m. I felt like I could never enter the room without disturbing her. I let it bother me for a lot longer than I should have: I didn't say to her, early on, "Can you do your work somewhere else at four in the morning?" As soon as I did talk to her about it she was really understanding.

—*MACKENZIE LUZZI*
PRINCETON UNIVERSITY, SOPHOMORE

IN ORDER TO DEAL WITH MY ROOMMATE and the guy with whom she was cheating on her boyfriend, I found ways to vent my frustration, like blow-drying my hair in the middle of the room at 8 a.m. while they were still asleep, or coming back to the room unexpectedly to catch them at awkward times. These things were pretty harmless but they made me feel somewhat better.

—*ALLISON GRECO*
MONTCLAIR STATE UNIVERSITY, GRADUATE

• • • • • • • • •

LEARN HOW TO SLEEP THROUGH ALARMS. My roommate got up every morning at five o'clock to go to basketball practice. Her alarm woke me every morning for a good two months. Get some sort of system, where you put a pillow over your head, and then you take the pillow off after your roommate leaves so you can hear your own alarm.

—*CATE*
BROWN UNIVERSITY, JUNIOR

THE SCHOOL ASSIGNED ME A ROOMMATE, and we didn't get along at all. She was completely my opposite—she smoked, she swore, she was messy. It was very uncomfortable anytime we were in the room together. Eventually we avoided that situation, except to sleep. As soon as the semester was over she asked for a transfer, and I was never happier.

—*JENNY PRISUTA*
YOUNGSTOWN STATE UNIVERSITY, SENIOR

• • • • • • • •

DON'T BRING ANY PRECONCEIVED NOTIONS about what your roommate will be like. You might be disappointed, or you might go into the situation not being as open as you could when you realize the person is completely different than you imagined.

—*DANIELLE*
DUKE UNIVERSITY, GRADUATE

• • • • • • • •

MY ROOMMATE AND I TALKED via email before we came to school. We realized we had a lot in common. We both play guitar and we were both bringing acoustic guitars. Then we got here and we realized we both have completely different tastes in music. But we get along really well. We compromise really well. If it's time to clean the room, we don't fight about it. One of us volunteers and it gets done.

—*REID ATTAWAY*
JAMES MADISON UNIVERSITY, FRESHMAN

• • • • • • • •

MY ROOMMATE IS MY TWIN SISTER. I get along with her. We know how to live together; my sister does the laundry and I clean the room.

—*MANI*
UNIVERSITY OF MARYLAND, FRESHMAN

I have a terrible roommate. He plays video games all the time. He stays up until six in the morning. Needless to say, I lose a lot of sleep.

—*ANONYMOUS*
ST. JOHN'S UNIVERSITY FRESHMAN

IN ORDER TO SURVIVE YOUR ROOMMATES, you have to be friendly and considerate. If you are nice, you will get treated the same way (and if you don't, then you have a reason to be treated like a jerk). Some people like living alone in singles, but I enjoy a crowd. Sure, it makes hooking up tricky (and hilarious) sometimes, but it also expands your social circle, and gives you lifelong friends—or enemies! It all depends on what kind of person you are.

—*PETE*
PRINCETON UNIVERSITY, SOPHOMORE

. . . .

" I talked to my roommate on the phone and I was totally convinced that I wasn't going to like her. She sounded like a person who was very different from me, but now she's one of my best friends. "

—*SIERRA*
CAL POLY SAN LUIS OBISPO, JUNIOR

. . . .

MY ROOMMATE AND I have a big difference in music tastes. I listen to rock and alternative, and she listens to this really bad R&B all the time. Whoever gets to the room first gets to choose the radio; sometimes it's a dash from class back to the room.

—*ANONYMOUS*
YALE UNIVERSITY, SOPHOMORE

I WALKED INTO MY ROOM for the first time freshman year to see that my roommate had decorated my side of the room with posters, a hanging thing over my bed, and the quote "G-d is dead" on the eraser board. That night I took everything down because I wanted to put up my own stuff. That was the start of our amazing roommate relationship. Oh, and the fact that her boyfriend lived in my room. My survival was pledging a sorority, so I was never there.

—M.
    AMERICAN UNIVERSITY, FRESHMAN

Give your roommate his space, and he should give you yours.

—DANIEL RUSK
UNIVERSITY OF
MARYLAND
SOPHOMORE

• • • • • • • •

I WENT FROM NEVER HAVING TO SHARE anything in my whole life, including my bedroom, to moving into a triple with two girls who were my complete opposite. How did I manage to survive? Flexibility and compromise.

—RAE LYNN RUCKER
    BIOLA UNIVERSITY, GRADUATE

FIVE THINGS NOT TO SAY TO YOUR ROOMMATE

1. "I just know we're going to be best friends." (Pressure!)

2. "Sure, I don't mind if your boyfriend/girlfriend sleeps here." (You'll regret it later.)

3. "We're so alike ... do you mind if I tell people we're twins?" (Creepy!)

4. "Borrow whatever you want." (Don't say it if you don't really mean it.)

5. "You want to major in WHAT?"

Schedule monthly outings with all of your roommates.

—*KHALIL SULLIVAN PRINCETON UNIVERSITY, JUNIOR*

I WOULDN'T WANT TO GO BACK to the living conditions I was in freshman year. You can learn a lot, but it's aggravating when you have to deal with someone who doesn't blend with your personality. For instance, I'm not real neat, but my roommate freshman year was a real neat freak. We had our problems there. Don't bend over backwards for your roommate, but there are sacrifices you have to make. When you say "compromise," it sounds like you have to lose something to make the other person happy. Instead, you find a way to make it a win-win situation.

—*BRIAN JAMES MADISON UNIVERSITY, JUNIOR*

CLASSIC COLLEGE COMEDIES

One of the great traditions of college is watching movies about college – specifically, movies that glorify partying in college and make the whole experience out to be a hilarious, R-rated romp. Below is a list of some classics in this vein. But maintain perspective: College is more than a gratuitous comedy.

National Lampoon's Animal House	1978
Porky's	1982
Revenge of the Nerds	1984
Back to School	1986
PCU	1994
How High	2001
National Lampoon's Van Wilder	2002
Old School	2003
American Pie Presents: Beta House	2007
Road Trip: Beer Pong	2009
Adventureland	2009

My ROOMMATES AND I SAT DOWN in the beginning of the year and talked through all of our habits, which was really helpful; both of my roommates were very quiet so I'm not sure if I would have known how they felt about having guests staying over (male and female!), doing chores, and that kind of thing, otherwise. And then we also talked about it again halfway through the year, because at that point we could re-evaluate how things were going and if something came up that's upsetting, there's a place to talk about it without making a really big deal out of it.

—EMILY
HARVARD COLLEGE, SENIOR

ONE OF MY ROOMMATES was very conservative, very traditional. The other was this vegan lesbian. They were both wonderful people, but it was interesting to be occasionally mediating between the two.

—MELISSA K. BYRNES
AMHERST COLLEGE, GRADUATE

FIND OUT WHO YOUR ROOMMATE IS before you come—and check him out. If he is not a good fit, get out of it. If you complain loud enough, they will swap him for you. This is great advice.

—DEREK LI
CARNEGIE MELLON UNIVERSITY, JUNIOR

Consider

IT'S HARD BEING SICK WITH A ROOMMATE. You have to share this really small space. I once had this health-nut roommate who was a germophobe. That was really bad. Every time I got sick, she would open doors with a Kleenex. What was I supposed to do? I couldn't go home.

—KAIT DUNTON
UNIVERSITY OF VIRGINIA, JUNIOR

USE YOUR INGENUITY to get a good roommate. When you are listing what you are like in the application for roommates, be honest. I know a guy who pretended to be a "stay in and study" kind of guy, and he got stuck with a roomie who never left the room and had a sleeping disorder. If he had been honest and said he liked to party, this would not have happened. If you get a bad roommate, get out of it before it gets worse. The longer you wait, the harder it is.

—JUDSON KROH
CARNEGIE MELLON UNIVERSITY, JUNIOR

• • • • • • • •

I WAS TOLD I would have just one roommate my freshman year. Little did I know I'd have a permanent visitor: my roommate's boyfriend. He was like "the guy on the couch"; he would stay Friday to Wednesday, always on the couch, on my computer, or even on my bed when I came home from class. Although I was open to guests, I had to tell my roommate I was sick of having a dude in my space all the time. It didn't go down well. Soon she moved down the hall into a single; she set up her very own love nest.

—LISA G.
NEW YORK UNIVERSITY, JUNIOR

• • • • • • • •

THE OTHER DAY, my roommate asked me to leave the room. I asked why. He said, "You know." He wanted to be alone, if you know what I mean. So I left, for like an hour. That's one of the things you have to put up with when you have a roommate.

—C.
COLUMBIA UNIVERSITY, JUNIOR

ASK THE ADVISER

Why won't Res Life let me switch roommates?

It's not because they want you to be miserable. And it's not because they don't care, either. But while some housing offices will process change requests with no questions asked, others are far more interested in helping students learn to *work through* their differences. Your dorm experience is part of the college mission to expose you to new ideas, new cultures, and new ways of interacting with the world. So be prepared to sit down with your roommate and your RA for some mediated sharing and negotiation. "I" statements are favored (rather than blaming your roommate): "I have trouble sleeping when music is playing at 4 a.m." "I'm curious about the occult symbols that have been appearing on the ceiling over my bed." "I have a very sensitive nose and strong odors are a problem for me..."

Frances Northcutt

I AM A MESSY PERSON. Mess just doesn't bother me! But most of my roommates were not like that. The best advice I have is to just keep your mess to yourself! Be as messy as you want in your room, but do your best to keep the communal areas clean. I know it can be hard (it certainly was for me!), but it will help your relationships with your roommates. If you are a clean person, it is important to realize that you might live with a messy person! Be patient, as cleaning and being clean might not come naturally to your roommate.

—ELIZABETH
UNIVERSITY OF ILLINOIS AT URBANA-CHAMPAIGN, GRADUATE

MY ROOMMATES WERE ALL from the deep South. One of them was the daughter of an Episcopalian minister. We got into some clashes. She told me that I was going to hell, in all seriousness. She was concerned for my soul. So, I didn't have anyone to talk to about that. But other than that it was fine. I had some friends who went to a bigger college nearby, and I would drive an hour and a half to hang out with them there.

—HANNAH SMITH
HARVARD UNIVERSITY, JUNIOR

Become good friends with your R.A. He or she could be nice, and may one day help you lock your horrible roommate into the room with pennies.

—ANONYMOUS
MICHIGAN TECHNOLOGICAL UNIVERSITY GRADUATE

• • • • • • • •

MY ROOMMATE CAME WITH ONE BAG to school, he didn't have any sheets for his bed, and he had this long beard that he used to cut in the sink and it got everywhere. He was a wreck. He couldn't be more different from me and the other guys in our suite. I tried to be friends with him, but it became clear that we were opposite personalities. So we agreed to disagree. He wasn't so bad that I couldn't live there, but I spent a lot of time out with my friends and every once in a while showed up there to sleep.

—JOHN BENTLEY
TRINITY UNIVERSITY, GRADUATE

• • • • • • • •

Consider

I HAD ARRANGED TO BE ROOMMATES with a high school friend—and the adage that you don't know someone until you live with them really applies. They may do things that you find bothersome, and if you weren't living with them, these characteristics may not have been revealed. So I recommend not rooming with someone you've known previously.

—YALDA A.
UNIVERSITY OF CALIFORNIA AT BERKELEY, GRADUATE

NEAT NERDS WELCOME

My roommate smoked Dunhills all day. There were piles of ashes under his bed; it was disgusting. He left stuff strewn about, so I was always kicking stuff back to his side of the room. At first appearance he seemed cool, like someone I would get along with. He was a wrestler, really into writing, but he was a dud and really unmotivated to do well—or do anything—in school. I tried not to confront him, but there were times when he'd be up late—making noise or smoking—and I was the one who would be getting up for class in the morning. I do recall one run-in, where there was a little pushing involved. Beware of kids who taunt you and don't respect your privacy. You may not appreciate it on day one, but you'll be happy with a soft-spoken, class-attending roommate. It's tough to find someone in sync with you. You may think you want to room with someone who on paper appears to be like you, but it could be misery living with him or her.

—J.
COLUMBIA UNIVERSITY, GRADUATE

DON'T GET "SEX-ILED"; set ground rules with your roommate right away. One month into freshman year, my roommate's 26-year-old boyfriend moved in, and I found myself sex-iled for an entire week. When I tried to get into my room to get some books, it was locked. These kinds of situations can be avoided by talking about the possibility in advance.

—LAURA TRUBIANO
HAMILTON COLLEGE, JUNIOR

THE MORAL: HE SURVIVED

My freshman year roommate was a genuinely awful person to have to live with. He walked around without a shirt on 95 percent of the time and had the most horrible-looking man-nipples. He woke up for crew at 4 a.m. and blew his hair dry after showering. He shaved his pubes in our sink twice a week. He never said anything even remotely funny that didn't end up also making people horrendously uncomfortable. And all he contributed to the room was a fridge.

While this was a key and essential item to someone like me that liked to host pre-game parties four nights a week, I hated having one that he'd purchased. He was of the opinion that because the fridge was his, he could eat or drink anything inside of it, despite the fact that he never bought anything. Ever.

He claimed he couldn't buy alcohol because his parents would see it on their credit card statement, but he never threw in cash to help. He would bring the most awkward friends to the room. They also helped themselves to all the food and drink, without asking. Usually, I would tell you that the best way to deal with such a person would be to drink. Having done this myself, know that it will only aggravate the situation (especially when he/she is sober).

—J.V.
THE COLLEGE OF WILLIAM & MARY, GRADUATE

THE KEY TO HAVING A GOOD RELATIONSHIP with your roommate is the first two weeks of school. You will have to judge if you think this person has the potential to be one of your closest friends, or your complete opposite. If you think you will have a rough time being friends with your roommate, there is no need to force the issue. Obviously, you should be courteous, but if you are not the greatest friends you can still have a livable situation.

—ANDREW OSTROWSKY
PENNSYLVANIA STATE UNIVERSITY, JUNIOR

A GOOD ROOMMATE IS DIFFERENT from a good friend. He or she should have about the same sleep schedule as you do, practice good hygiene, and not be too messy. I rarely talk to my roommate outside of the dorm room, but he's a great roommate who always makes the room smell nice.

—*JONATHAN LIU*
UNIVERSITY OF TENNESSEE - KNOXVILLE, FRESHMAN

Consider

WE HAD A ROOMMATE IN MY SUITE my freshman year that we ended up asking to leave. It was not an easy thing to do, especially because the three of us that were asking him to go just did not want to initiate the confrontation. We asked for advice from one of the heads of student affairs, and then approached him one night about it. We had our laundry list of reasons ready, and it makes it much more effective if you have that set up and ready before you approach them about it.

—*BARRY LANGER*
OGLETHORPE UNIVERSITY, JUNIOR

LET'S CLEAR THE AIR

I had a terrible roommate experience. Our personalities clashed, we came from completely different backgrounds and had different values. But one thing that bothered the most: She would fart all the time. I tried using Febreze, perfuming my side of the room, leaving the window open, asking her to excuse herself outside. It got to the point where I was never in the room during waking hours, and the library became my best friend. Moral of the story: Expect the unexpected. My roommate's bowel problem wasn't even on my list of things to worry about college life.

—*MICHELLE Y. LEE*
EMORY UNIVERSITY, SENIOR

SOME PEOPLE THINK IT'S BETTER to live with someone who's just like them. But I learned that's not always the case. During my freshman year, I was paired with someone who was like me: a "clean freak." We got along fine, but surprisingly enough, we never became close friends. After she moved out at the end of the first semester, I moved in with Veronica. I knew she was a little more cluttered and messy than I was, but we became best friends. She is easy to talk to, and living together was a blessing.

—EMILY TUCK
CALIFORNIA STATE UNIVERSITY, GRADUATE

• • • • • • • •

I HAD HAD ROOMMATES BEFORE at camps and summer courses at colleges and I was really excited about it. I lived in a walk-through room that was bigger but had less privacy. I didn't think I'd miss the privacy so I was happy to take a bigger room. But my roommate and I had completely different sleep schedules. This was fine at night because my roommate would go to sleep first, but then she'd wake up 3 hours earlier than I did, and she was super clumsy and would accidentally knock things over and wake me up... I wish I had thought more about privacy when choosing rooms.

—HALEY
HARVARD COLLEGE, SENIOR

• • • • • • • •

TRY TO HAVE AN OPEN MIND about your roommate. It makes a difference.

—DAVID
KEAN UNIVERSITY, JUNIOR

A record 764,495 international students were enrolled in US colleges last year. China sent the most students — 194,029 — and the number of students from Saudi Arabia jumped 50%, to 34,139.

Filling Daytime Hours: Choosing (and Attending) Classes

*I*t will happen to you every semester when the new class schedule comes out: You get a little adrenaline surge. Even if some of your new courses might be boring or hard, there's always a chance that others will be amazing. You might even find out what you want to do with your life! But there are also the questions. What requirements should you do first? What if you're interested in everything and it won't all fit in your schedule? And how do you sniff out those life-changing professors among the cranky, the mediocre, and the just-ok? Read on for answers!

TAKE CLASSES THAT YOU ACTUALLY LIKE, that you're actually interested in. Everyone I know is taking all these intense classes in subjects that they're not interested in, and they're miserable. But I'm having a great time.

—LUCY LINDSEY
HARVARD UNIVERSITY, FRESHMAN

MAKE YOUR OWN PATH AND FIND YOUR OWN TEACHERS.

—EBELE ONYEMA
GEORGETOWN
UNIVERSITY, SENIOR

HEADLINES
Best Advice and Top Tips

- Avoid early-morning classes if you don't want to sleep through lectures.
- Experiment—take a class or two outside your desired major.
- If you think the first class of the semester is boring, drop the course—it won't improve.
- Talk to students who already took the class you're interested in to see if the professor is any good.
- Don't choose your major too soon - and don't be afraid to change it once you do.

I WOULD RECOMMEND that during your first year, you take a class that is outside what you think you want to do. You'll meet other people, and freshman year is a really good time to meet a lot of people. Take the P.E. classes; it's something active. If you're in a very academic school, go out and have something active in your life. It's a good release. I did martial arts—Tae Kwon Do. That was really fun and you meet a lot of different people there. And kick some ass.

—JASPER
UNIVERSITY OF CALIFORNIA AT BERKELEY, JUNIOR

• • • • • • • •

DON'T AVOID AN INTRIGUING COURSE just because it is notoriously difficult. It's much easier to study something interesting that is challenging than it is to study something dry that is simple. You'll surprise yourself when you end up doing better in the difficult class that inspires you!

—STEPHANIE DREIFUSS
DUKE UNIVERSITY, SENIOR

GO FOR THE GOOD TEACHERS and the bad times instead of the good times and bad teachers. I took calculus the first semester at 8 a.m. and that time just sucked. But I had a good teacher and I got an A. Second semester, I took a class at 1 p.m. and it was a hard teacher, and I got a C.

—*AMY SCEVIOUR*
GEORGIA INSTITUTE OF TECHNOLOGY, SOPHOMORE

• • • • • • •

" Never sign up for a 7 a.m. class. Yes, you did it in high school, but Mom was always there to keep waking you up, and if by some miracle you do make it to an early class, you will sleep through the lecture when you get there. "

—*J.T.*
UNIVERSITY OF FLORIDA, GRADUATE

• • • • • • •

FALL IN LOVE with someone in your class right away; student, T.A., professor, whomever. You'll be hard-pressed to skip class. If there is no one in your class to love, then pick someone to hate and show up every day to make his or her life a living hell.

—*S.P.*
UNIVERSITY OF GEORGIA, GRADUATE

ALL THE GOOD STUFF YOU DO ACADEMICALLY, you do in your junior and senior years. So, try to do all the crap in your freshman and sophomore years. Get it out of the way so you can enjoy your last two years.

—ANONYMOUS
JOHNS HOPKINS UNIVERSITY, JUNIOR

. . . .

Take the most interesting and easiest classes you can find, have a good time, and try not to flunk out.

—JUAN GONZALEZ
CLEMSON UNIVERSITY
GRADUATE

I WENT TO A JEWISH PRIVATE HIGH SCHOOL and we were in classes from morning until night. We still had a lot of work, but not like college. In college, we have classes a couple of hours a day and the same amount of work. Freshman year, I felt like I was falling off the cliff with all the work. But I got used to it.

—CHANA WEINER
BARNARD COLLEGE, SOPHOMORE

. . . .

LEARN A LANGUAGE. If you've taken a language in high school, take more of the same and become fluent. If not, learn a new language, but think about one you might actually use. Even if you aren't thinking about a term abroad, pick a language and go for it.

—ANONYMOUS
UNION COLLEGE

DEAD TIRED

Among the effects of sleep deprivation: irritability, vision impairment, stuttering speech, momentary loss of reasoning, confusion, hallucinations, nausea, and (very rarely) death.

DON'T BELIEVE PEOPLE when they tell you a professor is really good. They're probably wrong. I've taken about three classes because someone told me the professor was so cool and so good, and those are the three classes I hated the most. Then I hated the people that recommended the classes to me. Find the classes that interest you, and you'll be fine.

—*EBELE ONYEMA*
GEORGETOWN UNIVERSITY, SENIOR

• • • • • • • •

JUST BECAUSE SOME PEOPLE don't go to class and still get A's doesn't mean you can skip class and still get A's. You can try it, but I wouldn't recommend it.

—*J.D.*
EMORY UNIVERSITY, SENIOR

• • • • • • • •

I HAVE LEARNED THAT picking classes that end early in the afternoon is the best. I know that if I begin my day at 2 p.m., I will sleep to 11 a.m. and get nothing done. I like to have my classes begin at 10 a.m. and end around 1 or 2 p.m. This way, I don't have to wake up too early, but I'm still getting my day going at a decent time.

—*ANNIE THOMAS*
UNIVERSITY OF MICHIGAN, SENIOR

• • • • • • • •

ALWAYS RESEARCH THE CLASSES that you want to take (and that will satisfy major/graduation require-ments) a few weeks before registration opens up. Keep in mind that thousands of other students are researching classes. Chances are that you will be competing for a seat in a class with the students that have been doing the same thorough research. Research the professor of the class that you want to take and pick the best time. Most importantly, begin registering for classes as soon as your regis-tration time opens up – a few minutes can cost you a seat in the class that you really want to take.

—*ALEKSANDR AKULOV*
HUNTER COLLEGE, SOPHOMORE

Ask people what the best class they've ever taken is.

—*SUMMER J.*
UNIVERSITY OF VIRGINIA, SENIOR

THE CHILI PEPPER AND YOU

Everyone looks at ratemyprofessors.com before signing up for classes. But can you trust those anonymous scorecards? Do they tell you everything you need to know? Do you really care whether your professor got the chili pepper (the sign of personal attractiveness)? How can you get the most benefit out of the site?

Ratemyprofessors.com uses five measures:

1. Easiness
2. Helpfulness
3. Clarity
4. Hotness
5. Overall Quality

These categories will probably help you if you're looking for a fun elective or an easy 'gut' course. But if you're looking for a strong course in your major, you may need to ask yourself a few extra questions before you follow the advice on this site:

- Does the reviewer use foul language? This usually indicates a student is disgruntled over a grade, which means that he or she is not exactly objective.

- Is the reviewer's spelling and/or grammar on the pathetic side? Be suspicious if the low ratings are in the Easiness and Clarity categories; the issue was probably the student, not the professor.

- Are there enough reviews posted for you to make an informed decision? If there are just one or two, you probably want to find out more before you decide whether to register.

Frances Northcutt

DON'T OVERLOAD; don't take too many classes. I took too many classes. I was staying up to five and six o'clock in the morning, missing classes that morning. That's not fun.

> —ALBERT SO
> GEORGIA INSTITUTE OF TECHNOLOGY, SOPHOMORE

• • • • • • • •

USE THAT FIRST YEAR as your sandbox year. It's really important. It's OK to screw off. It's OK to go out and experiment.

> —W.J.F.
> GEORGETOWN UNIVERSITY, JUNIOR

• • • • • • • •

IF YOU PLAN TO WORK for Goldman Sachs in four years, your entire future seems to rest on whether you secure a seat in Accounting 101. But this is a misguided approach. You should use your first few semesters to take the courses most dissimilar to your goals. If you plan to major in business, take a course in French New Wave Cinema or British Lit. If you think you're a chemist, take physics. If you want to speak Hebrew, take Arabic.

> —DOUG
> WAKE FOREST UNIVERSITY, GRADUATE

• • • • • • • •

MOST PEOPLE JUST 'DO' SCHOOL—you don't see a lot of students doing research, playing sports, doing extracurricular activities—and one can sense the monotony. I suggest you take the perspective that grades don't count and take classes with professors who are passionate about what they're teaching. Learn, don't just take classes that you think will yield a higher grade.

> —YALDA A.
> UNIVERSITY OF CALIFORNIA AT BERKELEY, GRADUATE

Share your school supplies with fellow classmates. Believe me, there's going to be a time when you forget something in the future, so volunteer your extras.

> —J.S.
> UNIVERSITY OF GEORGIA, GRADUATE

Consider

When studying Far East religions, don't confuse a llama with the Dalai Lama, the spiritual leader of Tibet.

—*Lynn Lamousin*
Louisiana State
University
Graduate

IF YOU KNOW SOME PEOPLE who are already at your college, talk to them and see which professors are good and which ones suck.

—*Andrew Ouzts*
Georgia Institute of Technology, Sophomore

· · · · · · · ·

ACADEMICALLY, TRY TO GET TO KNOW PROFESSORS. He's not some guy in the Emerald City hiding behind the curtain. Your professor is just a person.

—*Phil*
University of Virginia, Senior

· · · · · · · ·

GO TO EVERY CLASS; that's half the battle. If you do, you'll pass. I went to the majority of classes freshman year, but I would've done so much better if I had gone to all of them.

—*Kristin Thomas*
James Madison University, Junior

· · · · · · · ·

EVERYBODY'S SMART IN COLLEGE. At least give yourself a semester before you dive into the hard classes. I was in the top 10 percent of my high school class and I felt real good about myself. But it took me the first year of college to realize I had to work real hard to make good grades.

—*Jonathan Cohen*
Emory University, Senior

· · · · · · · ·

STAY LATE AFTER CLASS and ask questions. It's good to be known by your professors; later on you'll need recommendations from them. It's important that you did more than just get a good grade, that your professor remembers you.

—*Jawan Ayer-Cole, M.D.*
Florida A&M University, Graduate

SLAVE OF APHRODITE

At the beginning of my freshman year, I was hit by Cupid's arrow. It was a direct hit—for the entire semester I was in love with my Introduction to Classical Studies professor.

Professor, whom I referred to reverently as "the 13th Olympian Goddess," taught an auditorium full of undergraduates about the follies, jealousies, battles, and—most prominently—the sex lives of Greek gods and mortals alike. I had always loved Greek mythology, but this class brought excitement and legitimacy to my obsessive hobby. I had read Catullus in my Latin class in high school, so I thought I was fully prepared for the unique and bizarre proclivities covered in my professor's 101 class, but those depraved Greeks and Romans surprised me time and time again! I think I was most surprised that this racy curriculum was discussed and taught in public! Can she talk about what seems clear to be the origins of NAMBLA at the podium?

Not all of Classical Studies was NC-17; I figure that a taste now and then kept the coeds awake and returning each week. But I loved all of it: the philosophy, the art, the architecture, the myths and poetry. Sappho, Euripides, Ovid, and Herodotus. I was hooked, to the class and to the deity who posed as our teacher. Vivid memories of hiding behind kiosks and trees while watching her every move attest to my naiveté and somewhat unhealthy fixation.

Once the semester ended, I pored over the class listings, hoping to fill my schedule with more classics and more chances to listen and catch glimpses of my professor. Alas, she was only teaching graduate classes, so my first encounter with the 13th Olympian Goddess turned out to be my last. However, I remained smitten with the subject and decided to join the Classics Department.

—PHIL CARMEL
UNIVERSITY COLLEGE–SALFORD (ENGLAND), GRADUATE

TAKE A WIDE VARIETY OF CLASSES. You may find that you are interested in a subject you hadn't previously considered. Plus, freshman year is the best time to experiment with that sort of thing. And before you decide to take a certain class, make sure you know something about the professor teaching it. Ask around, search the Web; anything. A good or bad professor can genuinely make or break a class.

—*DANIELLE FRIEDMAN*
DUKE UNIVERSITY, SENIOR

"Figure out the social scene of your school before you make any schedules. It's no fun going to class hungover on Friday mornings!"

—*ERIN*
SUFFOLK UNIVERSITY, GRADUATE

I'M USUALLY THE TYPE OF PERSON who does all his work, but now, I actually have to think. The workload isn't harder, but it's different. I take a lot more notes now. I'm in a study skills class and they suggest a system for taking notes—dividing the page into three sections, writing notes in one part, cues for main ideas in another, and summaries in the other. I don't like that system, but it helps to try different things.

—*DUSTIN CAMAC*
UNIVERSITY OF DELAWARE, FRESHMAN

GET TO KNOW YOUR TEACHERS, because when it comes down to getting a better final grade you might need a little help. And if your professors know you, they might be willing to help you.

—MATT BURLESON
UNIVERSITY OF TENNESSEE AT MARTIN, GRADUATE

• • • • • • • • •

I TOOK COURSES THAT WERE HARDER, not what normal freshmen took. I ended up not doing as well as I should have. There's no harm taking a class you've taken already in high school. Because freshman year is about getting used to your environment, and if you're studying all the time, it's harder to do that.

—NATASHA PIRZADA
GEORGETOWN UNIVERSITY, SOPHOMORE

• • • • • • • • •

BE WARY OF CLASS TITLES like "Frodo's Epic Nightmare," "American Humor," and "Introduction to Comparative Politics." They might sound interesting, but the professors could be dry and boring.

—JACKIE
STATE UNIVERSITY OF NEW YORK AT BINGHAMTON, GRADUATE

FOUR PHRASES THAT TAME BUREAUCRACY

1. "I'm so sorry to bother you ..."

2. "I read all the information on your website and I just have one more small question ..."

3. "Hello, how are you today?" (So obvious, yet so rarely used!)

4. "My RA said you were a good person to talk to about ..."

TIME MANAGEMENT 101

Managing your time is a lot like managing your money. Once you spend it, it's gone, so you have to make it all count. With 24 hours a day multiplied by seven days a week, your weekly Time Budget is 168 hours per week.

Step #1: Figure out how you use your time each week:

Estimate the amount of time per week you spend on each activity:

_____ Class time (# of hours in class each week)

_____ Studying (Most colleges suggest three hours for every hour you're in class.)

_____ Job/Work

_____ Commuting/transportation time

_____ Athletics/physical fitness (team sports, working out, etc.)

_____ Co-curricular activities (clubs, student government, community activities, etc.)

_____ "Family" responsibilities (cleaning, cooking, shopping, communication, time with relatives)

_____ Socializing with friends and other hobby time

_____ Sleeping

_____ Eating

_____ Personal hygiene (bathing, hair, make-up, etc.).

Step #2: Assess your use of time:

a) Add together the totals for the above   SUBTOTAL = _____
   lines for your week:

b) Now subtract your subtotal from   TOTAL = _____
   168 hours per week:

- If the number in your TOTAL line is negative, you have committed more time than there is in a week. YOU ARE IN TROUBLE. Time to cut back in certain areas.
- If you have time left over, ask yourself what choices can be made. Do you have time for more sleep? Volunteering? Friends? Relaxation?
- If your time used equals 168, great! This is a good start. Now take a look at any hours you may be spending in some areas that you want to start using in other ways. This is how you manage your time to be most effective.

Step #3: Determine a goal and action plan for better time management/use:

What would you most like to do to better manage your time? You should also consider buying (and USING) a planner, which can help you keep track of time, projects, assignments and be more efficient. Some tips: Color-code your calendar/planner by the activities listed above, and once you make a schedule, do your best to stick with it.

Step #4: Repeat, when necessary:

You'll want to take a look at this again at the start of each term, if you get a job, or if you notice any changes in your physical or emotional well-being.

Scott C. Silverman

AND THE MORAL OF THE STORY IS . . .

There was one class I had when I gave a big speech to the whole class, while hung over. That was a bad idea. I had an economics professor who picked out a few people to give speeches; to teach his class, basically. The night before, I got pretty drunk. The speech was on Milton Friedman's theory on something or other. I was so hung over when I tried to give the speech, I couldn't talk; I just mumbled. The professor asked me questions: "Do you mean this means that?" I said, "Yeah, yeah, that. Yes, of course." And so we got through the whole thing, and afterwards he pulled me aside and said, "Wow, I've been teaching this class for 20 years, and that is the worst description I've ever heard." And yet, I passed the class. I talked to the professor. I realized I screwed up, and I made up for it. So the moral is, if you screw up, talk your way through it. Don't let it lie. People understand.

—*Anonymous*
University of Texas, Graduate

Before signing up for any class, find out who is teaching it, and go talk to them. At the beginning of the year, most professors are just sitting around waiting for students to drop in. You can learn way more about a class, and the professor teaching it, by spending 10 minutes with the professor, one-on-one. You'll get a sense of what will be required and how much of a hard-ass the teacher is going to be.

—*Don Wazzeneger*
Youngstown State University, Senior

IF THE FIRST CLASS of the semester is boring, drop it! If a professor can't make the first twenty minutes of the first class exciting, it is going to be a long semester. Go into add/drop week with a list of possible classes to take. Go to seven or eight classes in a week, or more. Then choose the best of those. It makes for a hectic week, but it will make the semester so much better.

—*SUMMER J.*
UNIVERSITY OF VIRGINIA, SENIOR

WHEN LOOKING FOR AN EASY ELECTIVE, ask a few athletes. As a former student-athlete who usually had taxing courses for my major, I was pretty good at finding less taxing electives, GPA boosters, blow-off classes, etc. This allowed me to keep my sanity. Also, ask around to find out if your chosen elective is as interesting as it sounds. I almost signed up for "Costumes Through the Ages." It sounded like it might be a good elective to take. After asking around, I found out the class is boring and difficult.

—*HASSAN*
UNIVERSITY OF TULSA, GRADUATE

ONE OF THE MOST IMPORTANT THINGS in college is to have a good relationship with your academic advisor. Meet with him/her a couple times a semester to work out your four-year plan and choose your classes for the upcoming semester. They have a wealth of knowledge and will make your time a lot less stressful. They appreciate involved students and are always willing to help you get the best schedule possible.

—*ILAN GLUCK*
UNIVERSITY OF MARYLAND, JUNIOR

DON'T TAKE MORE THAN ONE CLASS that has a lot of reading. I picked some classes that had too much reading, so I am always reading. I average four hours a day, maybe longer. I go to class, take a break, go to dinner, and then go to the library. I'll be in the library until 1 a.m.

—*BAYLESS PARSLEY*
UNIVERSITY OF VIRGINIA, FRESHMAN

. . . .

" Take the opportunity to participate in class. Never again in your life will you be confronted with such an open forum for sharing ideas; this is the time to develop your skills to make a persuasive point. "

—*SCOTT WOELFEL*
UNIVERSITY OF MISSOURI, GRADUATE

. . . .

IT'S ESSENTIAL THAT YOU BUILD up a grade cushion in your first year. That way when you're a junior or a senior and things get tough, you don't have to worry as much about your GPA.

—*YAP*
NEW YORK UNIVERSITY, JUNIOR

YOU. WILL. TEACH. ME.

One thing I learned my freshman year is that teachers don't have to have their Master's degree to teach; they just need to have one in progress. That's good for them because the school usually pays for it, but bad for the students because it means the professor doesn't already know everything he's going to be teaching you and will often be distracted by his own studies.

It's important to make sure your teacher actually knows more than you. Be brutal. Ask a million questions. I can't tell you how frustrating it is to be paying over $300 a class and hear, "I'll have to look that one up," in response to a question you already know the answer to. Don't be afraid to be very, very mean to your teacher. Bad teachers waste your time and should not be there. You have to believe they have no feelings and drive them the hell out.

Don't let your teacher be a slacker and don't let him forget things. This should be dealt with according to the size of the college and the amount of students. For the love of sweet Jesus, my class was the only one my teacher taught, and he'd sometimes forget his notes!

By the way, the best teachers don't use notes.

—STEVEN COY
SAN DIEGO STATE UNIVERSITY, SOPHOMORE

CRACKING THE ACADEMIC CURRICULUM

Choose one course from Category 3A. Pick two courses from different academic departments in Category 2E. If both 2E courses are taken on campus, and not satisfied by Advanced Placement, students may apply them toward Requirement PD/C or PD/D, but not both. The same course may be used to satisfy 3A and PD/A, but if the course is worth fewer than three credits it must be repeated for PD/A. This applies only to students matriculating before Fall 2014. All other students should consult the 2013-2016 Bulletin. We apologize for the delay in printing the 2013-2016 Bulletin. It should be available within six months. In the meantime, questions may be directed to the Dean of Arts and Sciences. Although this position is currently vacant, the new Dean should be selected...in around six months.

Are they kidding???

Navigating the general education requirements of your college can be as mind-twistingly complicated as filing taxes for the average multinational corporation or filling out your driver's license application. But don't despair; help is here.

- Does your college offer an online degree audit system? Use it! But whatever you do, don't be fooled into thinking that requirements are just a series of boxes to fill in, or annoying tasks to "get out of the way" so that you can go on to the good stuff. Your Gen. Ed. courses might turn out to be the good stuff you've been waiting for all these years.

- All those confusing letters, numbers, and symbols actually represent something: the range of skills and knowledge that the faculty of your college think every student ought to have. If you take half an hour to read up on the purpose and design of the general education curriculum, you'll start to see at least some method to all the madness. (Hint: Try the first few chapters of your college catalog and the Mission Statement online.)

- Still stumped? Go see your academic advisor or favorite faculty member. They will be happy to let you in on the secrets cleverly concealed behind the baffling charts and lists.

Frances Northcutt

GEOLOGY (AKA "ROCKS AND JOCKS") is much harder than the course description would lead you to believe.

—*LYNN LAMOUSIN*
LOUISIANA STATE UNIVERSITY, GRADUATE

· · · · · · · ·

I WISH I'D HAD A BETTER IDEA of the classes I wanted to take. When you get here it's a bit of a scramble; you have so many options. You have a course book that's 3,000 pages and you have to flip through it and find stuff.

—*TOBIAS*
HARVARD COLLEGE, FRESHMAN

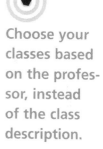

Choose your classes based on the professor, instead of the class description.

—*ROBIN JALEEL*
EMORY UNIVERSITY
GRADUATE

A MAJOR PAIN

It's getting harder to choose a major. Colleges and universities offered nearly 1,500 academic programs in 2010; 355 were added to the list over the previous 10 years, as colleges, to stay competitive and current, adopted new disciplines like homeland security and global studies, cyberforensics and agroecology.

ONE OF MY STRANGEST MEMORIES is attending a class taught by a dead man. One of the freshman-level psychology courses consisted of videotaped lectures from a professor who died in the 1960s. I don't remember his full name but his first name was Fred, so everyone called him—you guessed it—Dead Fred. I wish I had a picture of 500 students all staring at small monitors streaming a flickering, grainy, black-and-white, talking head three times a week. Maybe it was all just one big psychology experiment.

—SCOTT WOELFEL
UNIVERSITY OF MISSOURI, GRADUATE

. . . .

" Do not take an easy teacher who's boring. I'm in one of those classes this semester. I find it so much better if you like the teacher and it's a tough class than if you dislike the teacher and it's easy! "

—M.M.
BOSTON COLLEGE, JUNIOR

. . . .

ALWAYS TALK TO STUDENTS who took the classes in the past to find out whether the class or professor is hard or easy, good or bad, nice or mean.

—HASSAN
UNIVERSITY OF TULSA, GRADUATE

THE EARLY BIRD ... IS TIRED AND COLD?

TRY TO STAY AWAY FROM early-morning classes as much as possible. Even if you think you can do it, it'll start to take a toll on you halfway through the semester, when you are staying up late studying for midterms, and you have to get up at 8 a.m. after getting three hours of sleep.

—*MICHELLE Y. LEE*
EMORY UNIVERSITY, SENIOR

IF YOU HAVE AN 8 O'CLOCK followed by classes until the afternoon, make sure to eat breakfast. Even if you think you can power through a few hours of class without eating, you should still grab a quick granola bar or pop tart on your way to class. It definitely gives you enough energy to participate in labs and stay awake in lectures.

—*JONATHAN LIU*
UNIVERSITY OF TENNESSEE - KNOXVILLE, FRESHMAN

COMING FROM HIGH SCHOOL, starting class at 9 a.m. seems like a vacation. But only for the first couple of weeks. Waking up at 8 a.m. becomes legitimately painful after a while, especially if you go to school in the north.

—*ANNIE THOMAS*
UNIVERSITY OF MICHIGAN, SENIOR

ON THE DOUBLE 101

At the United States Coast Guard Academy, before you begin your studies, you have to survive Swab Summer, a seven-week "traditional military indoctrination . . . designed to help young civilian students transition into the Academy 'lifestyle.'" The training process includes general military skills, physical conditioning, seamanship, swimming, and—oh yes—academics. And forget about sleeping in after a tough day: morning formations are at that oh-so-friendly 6:20 hour.

LOOK THROUGH ALMOST EVERY SINGLE DEPARTMENT of classes and pick the ones that are really cool-sounding. Don't be afraid to take a class early in the morning... especially if it's only one day a week. You'll be okay. Probably.

—PETER STONE
TUFTS UNIVERSITY, SOPHOMORE

. . . .

DON'T TAKE CLASSES THAT ARE IMPORTANT for your major that first quarter. I entered school as a chemistry major, so I took a chemistry class right away and it totally kicked my butt. In high school I was so into science, and I had a great, hands-on science teacher, but lectures in college were nothing like that. It's fine to have a major in mind, but be open to the fact that it might change. You need time to adjust to college life, to being on your own, to having no one telling you what to do. If I could do it over again I'd only take GEs for a quarter or two.

—JESSICA DOSHNA
UCLA, GRADUATE

TALK TO YOUR COUNSELOR, especially if you're not certain what major to choose. A counselor can look at your interests and help you pick classes that apply to multiple majors, rather than to just one major. They also have a better understanding of when classes are offered; I had to wait a whole year for a required class once because I didn't know it was only offered in the fall, and I didn't sign up in time.

—COREY
SAN DIEGO STATE UNIVERSITY, JUNIOR

“ Take a variety of classses and make sure it's a variety not only in the type of topic but also in the type of work they ask you to do! ”

—CATIE
HARVARD COLLEGE, SENIOR

DON'T BE AFRAID TO STAND OUT. Speak up in your classes; free your mind in your application essays; go against the grain; say something outlandish that will make them remember you over the others in the bubble gum craze.

—HILLARY
BOWLING GREEN STATE UNIVERSITY, GRADUATE

ASK THE ADVISER

Can I fit all my classes into just three or four days a week?

I call that 'living the dream', and it's a dream most incoming fresh-men have! A four-day schedule can work out if the stars align and there's space in the classes you need. I don't recommend a three-day schedule, however, and here's why:

- If you get sick and miss a class day, you'll be behind in all or most of your classes. That's a lot to make up.

- A three-day schedule likely requires you to go from class to class to class with no time to catch your breath, talk to your friends, look over your notes – or eat lunch. Each day will seem like an endurance test that you can't wait to finish. Not fun, not sustainable.

- And finally, you need to take a good hard look at your personal habits. Will you have the discipline to wake up at a reasonable hour and study on your 'off' days?

When you're a junior or senior, you may very well choose to condense your class schedule so that you have days open for an internship. But for freshman year, give yourself a break and spread your classes over four or five days.

Frances Northcutt

LOOK UP REVIEWS ON PROFESSORS before you sign up for classes. I took a math class once that was really bad; the final was so hard that most of us failed it. Had I looked at his profile on ratemyprofessor.com, I would have known to avoid him. Don't go too far and avoid every professor, of course. Sometimes you won't be able to get around having a bad teacher.

> —*ANDREW*
> *UCLA, SENIOR*

ONE OF MY BIGGEST REGRETS about freshman year is that I let a lot of my friend-group peers pressure me into taking classes I wasn't interested in. That was a bummer because I didn't get to take the classes I should have taken, and also I didn't do as well, because I wasn't as interested, and that brought down my overall GPA. Make sure the classes you take are the ones you personally want to take. You'll make new friends in your classes so you don't have to sign up for classes with friends.

> —*CATIE*
> *HARVARD COLLEGE, SENIOR*

DON'T WAIT TOO LONG TO CHOOSE A MAJOR. I didn't declare until my third year, and I ended up needing to take four classes per quarter. It was intense, and not very fun when you're nearing the end of college and you want to have a good time with your friends.

> —*JESSICA DOSHNA*
> *UCLA, GRADUATE*

MAKE YOUR PROFESSORS think you care about their class. Get to know them one-on-one. Stay after, go to their office hours; even if you don't give a rat's ass about their class, make them think that you care.

—BRETT STRICKLAND
GEORGIA STATE UNIVERSITY, SOPHOMORE

• • • • • • • •

" Don't be afraid to change your major. My friend Chris thought he was going to be an engineer and now he's going to study philosophy. "

—PETER STONE
TUFTS UNIVERSITY, SOPHOMORE

• • • • • • • •

Consider

IN COLLEGE YOU HAVE TO STAY UP a lot later working, pretty much everyone does. So try to schedule your classes a little later. When I was a freshman, I ended up taking an 8:30 class, and I thought that wouldn't be so bad because in high school I had to get up at 6:30. But I ended up not making it to class a lot of days because I stayed up so late, a lot later than I would have in high school, and I found it really hard to wake up.

—MATTHEW GUTSHALL
ST. JOSEPH'S, JUNIOR

ASK THE ADVISER

If one of my classes isn't going well, can I drop it?

You'll probably need to see your real-life adviser to discuss the particulars of your situation, but here are some general principles to get you started.

Before classes begin, check on two things:

1. How many credits do you need in order to be considered a full-time student? (Financial aid, health insurance, and your eligibility to live in the dorm can all be linked to full-time student status.)

2. What is the last day to drop a class without receiving a 'drop' or 'withdrawal' notation on your record? One "W" is not terrible, but you don't want your transcript to be littered with them.

Once classes begin, if you want to drop a class and you're sure that dropping won't affect your full-time status or your transcript, ask yourself:

- 'Will dropping this class throw me off track for my major or pre-professional sequence?'

- 'Is dropping the class my only option? Can I switch sections, take the class pass/fail, or get help with difficult material?'

Your adviser can help you sort through all of this.

Frances Northcutt

CHOOSING A MAJOR

What's it going to be – Accounting, Art, Geology, History, Math, Nursing, Pre-Law, Psychology, Social Work, Spanish - or are you still undecided? If it's the latter, you just might be one of the smartest new students entering college this year.

Believe it or not, you simply don't yet know enough to make such a critical decision. Here's why: First, you may have the impression that your choice of academic major will dictate your career path as well. In reality, most people with college degrees will change careers 2-10 times in the 40 or so years they work, and often those careers are not in the major they chose when they started college.

Second, your decision might have been made due to pressures from others – for example, your family, your peers, and even yourself in the search for the "right" major for you. By giving yourself more time to decide, you might make a better choice.

Third, you are about to experience an academic and social environment in college that will provide you with many fields of knowledge, experiences, and opportunities that are completely new to you – and that may influence your decision.

So, how should you plan? Colleges often ask for your major when you apply and you might have to choose something. However, if the "Undecided" or "Exploratory" option is available – take it! It's ok to be undecided at this stage. But even if there's no such option initially, don't worry; you'll have the option to change your major later on if you want.

But how will you know what to choose? There's a very simple answer: major in what you enjoy studying. As you complete your courses during your freshman year and after, you will learn which subjects you like to think, read, listen to lectures, talk, do research, and write about. This should greatly influence your ultimate choice of a major.

"But what can I do with a major in _____?" you ask. Another good question, but it shouldn't dominate your choice of a major. Most Psychology majors do not become psychologists; most Math majors do not become mathematicians; most History majors do not become historians. Whatever your choice, be sure that you develop the skills that graduate schools and employers need, want, and expect when you graduate. These include: writing, speaking, using technology, and other more directly applied skills, as well as those that are more generic and that students often underestimate – including demonstrating leadership, responsibility, collaboration, a strong work ethic, and integrity. All of these can be developed in your college experiences both in and out of the classroom through student clubs and organizations, service learning, internships, volunteerism, work experiences, and more. Most importantly, these skills can be learned in any and all majors, if you choose your related options strategically and wisely.

Whatever you choose as your college major, be sure you make an informed choice, and you will become a better person, a better student, and a better employee as a result.

Thomas J. Grites, Ph.D.
Assistant Provost
The Richard Stockton College of New Jersey

DON'T BE AFRAID TO SAY what you need to in class. One time, a kid across the table from me and I got in a heated debate over the validity of fart jokes. I really care about that subject. They're a legitimate source of humor! And the teacher wasn't fazed, since it was a class called Theory of Comedy. Plus, she had just explained a very inappropriate (and highly unprintable) joke that Shakespeare made in "A Midsummer Night's Dream," so everything was fair game. That class was a blast. I got a pretty nice grade and am still friendly with many of my classmates.

—SHANNON KELLEY
KENYON COLLEGE, JUNIOR

Hitting the Books: Why, When & How to Study

A s if getting into college wasn't hard enough, now you have to get through it! Everyone told you that the readings would be denser, the papers longer, and the exams tougher, but you were hoping none of that would actually happen in your case. But here you are, and it's happening. Just remember, those college admissions officers let you in because they knew you would be able to do the work. This chapter might help, too.

FRESHMEN COME IN AND EXPECT TO GET AN A. But then you realize you were a big fish in a small pond in high school, and in college there's a bunch of other big fish and you've got to step it up a notch.

—K.K.
NORTHWESTERN UNIVERSITY, GRADUATE

SLEEP A LOT. AND ALWAYS GO TO CLASS.

—*SARAH*
GEORGIA INSTITUTE OF TECHNOLOGY GRADUATE

HEADLINES
Best Advice and Top Tips

- Find a place where you can study without interruption—most likely not your room.
- Don't skip classes—it makes the work that much harder.
- Self-discipline is the key to academic success.
- Don't wait until the last minute to get your work done—you'll only regret it.

DO HOMEWORK RIGHT AFTER CLASS. Study for a test the whole night before. Other students will understand why you look like hell.

> —RICHARD
> GEORGIA SOUTHERN UNIVERSITY, GRADUATE

Consider

IF YOU GET A B OR A C, DON'T WORRY. When you're going into the job world after graduating, there's no company that's going to say, "Well, you didn't do well in Western Civilization."

> —RHIANNON GULICK
> GEORGETOWN UNIVERSITY, SENIOR

ONE THING THAT IS DIFFERENT between college and high school is homework. College professors expect you to do the homework for your own benefit—which means for no credit. There is no homework given out to pad your grade. That's why it's important not to miss lectures.

> —JAMESE JAMES
> UNIVERSITY OF TULSA, GRADUATE

KNOW HOW TO ACCESS all the teachers' information. Most professors expect you to be able to download syllabi, assignments, labs, things to write up. Your grades are online. It's more difficult if you can't do these things. It's not impossible, but it's more difficult.

You need to study as much as you can during the day, between classes, rather than wait until the evening when it's more distracting, with TV and friends and social things.

—*LEAH PRICE*
GEORGETOWN UNIVERSITY, SOPHOMORE

. . . .

" Study individually 70% of the time, in groups 20% of the time, and seek the professor's or teaching assistant's help 10% of the time. Divide your time up like this and you're golden. "

—*SEAN CAMERON*
PRINCETON UNIVERSITY, SOPHOMORE

. . . .

DON'T MISS ANY CLASS, even if you think what the teacher is doing that day isn't significant. You never know what they could say that might affect the school year.

—*K.M.*
HOWARD UNIVERSITY, SOPHOMORE

THE MAP IS NOT THE JOURNEY and the notes are not the course. Take notes but don't try to be a stenographer. Use class notes to enhance your understanding of the course; for example, flagging areas for follow-up in text or with the instructor.

—SCOTT WOELFEL
UNIVERSITY OF MISSOURI, GRADUATE

• • • • • • • •

THE HARDEST PART IS KEEPING A SCHEDULE; having to do your work and putting that ahead of fun, because you can do whatever you want in college. But that will catch up to you. I went out the night before my Calculus 1 final; I ended up almost failing it.

—THEODORE SCHIMENTI
COLUMBIA UNIVERSITY, FRESHMAN

• • • • • • • •

DON'T READ IN YOUR BED; you'll fall asleep. I would read in my bed and I would, obviously, fall asleep. When you're in your bed, that's what you do. And then you start to associate reading with sleeping, so anytime you try to read anywhere, you fall asleep. So, don't read in your bed.

—BETHANY
JAMES MADISON UNIVERSITY, SENIOR

8 A.M. VS. 2 A.M.

A morning person is apt to get better grades than a late riser. In other words, late-nght studying does not pay off as much as one might think.

THE PROBLEM I HAD WAS THE PRIORITIZATION. You have a lot more free time in college than in high school. But you think you have more free time than you actually have. And by November of freshman year, you're behind. I don't know anyone who wasn't behind. You tend to forget to study when you first get here. You have parties, freedom from parents—you almost forget that you're in school. Freshman year, people would go to 60 to 70 percent of classes, at best, because they would stay up late and then miss morning classes. You almost forget how important education is. You worked for 12 years to get here, but just because you're here, the work doesn't stop.

—*ZAK AMCHISLAVSKY*
GEORGETOWN UNIVERSITY, SENIOR

• • • • • • • • •

ONE OF THE LESS POSITIVE MEMORIES from my freshman year occurred during final exams of first semester. I had stayed up until 4 a.m. studying material for my art history final, and was extremely confident that I would perform well and get the A that I had expected based on my 96 average going into it. I awoke the next morning to the horrifying realization that my alarm clock had not gone off and I had already missed the entire exam. I was so disappointed and angry at myself. The zero score averaged into my grade brought it down to a B-, which brought my GPA down almost half a point. To avoid this disappointment in the future, I make sure to set a backup alarm, and sometimes even a backup-backup alarm, on important test days.

—*MAXWELL HOCKSTAD*
STATE UNIVERSITY OF NEW YORK AT ALBANY, SOPHOMORE

The workload in college is like shoveling snow. If you do a little bit every day, you'll get by. If you wait until everything piles up, it becomes an impossible task.

—*NICHOLAS BONAWITZ*
UNIVERSITY OF ROCHESTER GRADUATE

IF YOU'RE QUESTIONING whether or not to go to a party, you better not go to that party, you know what I'm saying? Kids in college don't have good judgment. That's how you learn responsibility, learning how to listen to yourself. Some kids are like, "You think I should go to that party? Because I've got a midterm." It's like, "Keep your ass inside and study. You just answered your question." Learning how to answer your own questions; that's a big part of college.

—*ANONYMOUS*
BROWN UNIVERSITY, SOPHOMORE

FIRST SEMESTER IS KEY; this is what you need to prepare for. From there it is downhill. Get ready to work really hard and then establish a foundation. From there you will be able to just maintain. To do well you have to work hard and the time to begin is freshman year, first semester. So, enjoy your summer and come ready to work hard.

—*INSU CHANG*
CARNEGIE MELLON UNIVERSITY, JUNIOR

FLIRT WITH THE PROFESSORS. It comes in handy when you need to be late on your term paper because you partied all weekend.

—*ANONYMOUS*
UNIVERSITY OF GEORGIA, GRADUATE

THE SELF-DISCIPLINE is the toughest thing. You have to set up time to study.

—*Z.S.*
GEORGE WASHINGTON UNIVERSITY FRESHMAN

FRESHMAN YEAR IS A CRITICAL TIME to motivate yourself academically. Talk to your academic counselor. If you mess up in your first year, you get in a psychological track and will continue to spiral down. Then your self-esteem goes down and everything else breaks down. Then you drop out.

—*M.N.M.*
COLLEGE OF SAN MATEO, SENIOR

- - - - - - - - -

GET A LAPTOP LOCK. I've heard stories where people get up from their computer for a minute—to go to the bathroom or get a drink—and a minute later their computer is stolen.

—*DIANA SHU*
UNIVERSITY OF CALIFORNIA AT BERKELEY, SOPHOMORE

AFTER THE HONEYMOON

The first month of freshman year is often a happy blur of parties, new friends, and leisurely lessons. Often heard on the grassy quad or amongst the votive candles of the campus coffee shop:

"I can't believe classes are so easy."
"I learned all this stuff in AP Bio."
"4.0, no problem."

But beware—the honeymoon doesn't last forever. About a month into the semester, the *review* will be over. Your professors will start covering *new* material, fast.

Be ready!

5 TIPS TO IMPROVE READING SKILLS IN COLLEGE

Many new college students for whom English is a second language find that one of the greatest challenges to success in college is being able to keep up with – and fully understand – assigned readings. Here are five tips that may help you conquer college reading, whether English is your second – or first – language.

Study Tip 1: Using Index Cards to Study Vocabulary

One of the most challenging aspects of succeeding in college is to learn the new vocabulary and jargon typical of a subject. There are many ways to build vocabulary, but using index cards is a well-tested method. As you come across an unfamiliar word while doing a reading assignment, write it on the blank side of the index card. On the lined side, write the definition and a sample sentence. You can use a good online dictionary, such as the Oxford dictionary site, to do this exercise.

Study Tip 2: Focusing Your Attention

Does your mind ever wander while you are reading? There are many potential distractions that can interrupt our concentration and disturb our reading process. Your cell phone might ring or someone might start talking to you. You may be reading an adventure story set in India, but a voice in your head might be asking you where you want to eat lunch today. Do everything possible to keep your mind focused and "in the moment" when you are reading. Try to read an online newspaper or magazine article from beginning to end without any interruptions. Set up a plan to make this work! Hide away from others, turn off your cell phone and any other electronic devices you might have. If you can successfully do the reading without interruption, you will see how much easier it is to follow the ideas in the text.

Study Tip 3: Re-reading

It is one thing to say that you've completed a reading and another thing to say you understood what you have read. Just because your eyes have passed over a text does not guarantee that you have comprehended all of the ideas within it. Re-reading a section of a textbook, a story or an article can be very helpful. You might set up different goals for the first and second reading. For example, you can first do a reading straight through without stopping; then go back and re-read, but this time highlight key terms and concepts as you make your way through the text. Re-reading is not "wasting time;" it's a second opportunity to connect with what you are reading.

Study Tip 4: Communicating with the Professor

Students usually do not take advantage of the opportunity to meet with the professor individually. Most professors keep office hours specifically for the purpose of answering questions students may have about the course or assignments. In the meeting with the professor, students can ask clarification questions about a particular reading in the course and can ask for help with a difficult reading selection. Your professor may offer some insight, some helpful references or even a memorable anecdote about the topic of a class reading that can guide you toward a better understanding of the reading assignment.

Study Tip 5: Make Reading a Daily Habit

Strong readers frequently have their heads stuck in a book or magazine (whether paper-based or e-reader). Certainly, you will be assigned plenty of class readings from your professors. However, there is nothing like reading for pleasure. Find the time to read something enjoyable under a tree, on the bus or in your bed. Just as you need to nourish your body, you need some food for thought every day. As they say, a house without books is like a room without a view.

David Rothman and Jilani Warsi
Queensborough Community College

AVOID PUTTING STUDYING OFF until the last minute. After a lecture, I would always go back and go through my notes and rewrite them. If the professor says something more than once, that is a strong clue that it is important. In high school, I could get away with cramming the night before; that changes in college.

—*SARAH TIPPY*
WESTERN ILLINOIS UNIVERSITY, SENIOR

. . . .

GO TO OFFICE HOURS. Professors will tell you what to expect, and what you need to improve. I've gone to office hours and actually had T.A.'s change my grade because they read the paper again and realized that they graded it too harshly. I had it happen twice. I showed them that I did know the material, even if it didn't come out in the paper.

—*EVELIN OCAMPO*
UNIVERSITY OF CALIFORNIA AT SANTA BARBARA, JUNIOR

. . . .

WAKE UP EARLY AND STUDY. Even if you're not a morning person, make yourself one. It's the quietest time in the dorm and you'll be so productive.

—*SEAN CAMERON*
PRINCETON UNIVERSITY, SOPHOMORE

. . . .

GET INVOLVED WITH PEOPLE who are taking classes with you. When you have friends who are doing the same thing with the same goals, it's easy to work together, and you can build off each other, rather than trying to do everything by yourself.

—*COURTNEY WOLFE*
GEORGIA STATE UNIVERSITY, JUNIOR

I STUDY ABOUT three or four hours every night. For tests, you really can't cram it in, but I do about six hours before tests.

> —R.J.
> UNIVERSITY OF DELAWARE, SOPHOMORE

• • • • • • • •

I'M AN OVERACHIEVER, so I spent too much time studying my freshman year. My main advice is to make sure you balance studying with having fun. When you have fun, it's a lot easier to sit down and study.

> —KIRSTEN GIBBS
> GEORGIA INSTITUTE OF TECHNOLOGY, JUNIOR

If you don't have a laptop, you're probably screwed.

> —J.V.
> THE COLLEGE OF WILLIAM & MARY GRADUATE

WHAT TIME IS IT?

I PULLED AN ALL-NIGHTER LAST NIGHT. I get an adrenaline rush from the fact that it's the last second, and I can stay up late without a problem. But I don't recommend doing it, if you can avoid it.

> —M.M.
> NEW YORK UNIVERSITY, SENIOR

• • • • • • • •

MOUNTAIN DEW AND CAFFEINE pills help you get through all-nighters.

> —ANONYMOUS
> UNIVERSITY OF RHODE ISLAND, SOPHOMORE

• • • • • • • •

I ONCE STAYED UP THREE NIGHTS back-to-back. It was fairly intense. I drank coffee, but it was mostly adrenaline; you do what you've got to do. Also, I used to eat chocolate-covered espresso beans. They taste good and it gives you a little boost.

> —B.
> MASSACHUSETTS INSTITUTE OF TECHNOLOGY, GRADUATE

GETTING THE COLLEGE RHYTHYM

Many things will be different for you during your first year of college. One of the main differences, of course, is what is expected of you academically. Your college professors are not your high school teachers, and most likely will demand more of you, especially in your work outside the classroom. In college you'll have to master a subject in one 14- to 16-week semester, instead of the nine months you may have had in high school. To do this, you'll want to make some updates to your study skills. Learning to learn better is a process, and if you made it to college, you can do this, too; believe in yourself. Here are a few tips to help you succeed:

- **Study with others.** College has its own rhythm, just like taking on a new dance or learning to play a new video game. Instead of spending hours of your valuable time trying to learn everything on your own, find other students who seem to know the right steps or have reached the next level in the game. Join study groups for your courses; you'll learn from other students who are 'getting it' and at the same time *you* can teach other students what you know.

- **Spread out the studying.** The amount of information you are expected to learn can't be crammed into one night of studying for the dreaded Friday exam. Study an hour or two per class each day. Listen to the lectures, read the book, review your notes and participate in your study group, and you'll be surprised at how much you are able to retain.

- **Use college resources.** Don't be too proud to get a tutor for your classes, go to any supplemental instruction courses, visit the writing center or math center for help, and by all means, talk with your professors. Also, get to know the people who work in your campus library; they will be great assets in helping you find the information you need for any research projects.

Don't wait until midterms; it's better to use the resources early than to wait until *after* you receive a bad grade. Many people want to see you do well, but it's up to you to reach out to these resources. Remember, your campus resources are provided to help you succeed—wasting them will only make your first year more difficult.

- **Use technology.** There are wonderful programs for your computer and your mobile phone that can help you study better. There is an excellent flash card program (flashcardmachine.com) that allows to you study your notes wherever you are, without having to lug a stack of note cards around. Search for programs that you can use to quiz yourself, such as quizlet.com or studyblue.com. You also can find programs that help you take notes, including Google Docs and Evernote. Many of the resources are free.

By the end of your first semester you'll have a good idea about the best way for you to study. You will get to know the people with whom you study best, and you will have found the best places for you to study. It may not be your dorm room, the library or the computer room – but you'll find what works for you.

You'll learn the college rhythm; it just takes a little time, a lot of hard work, and, most important, some self-confidence.

Edwin B. Mayes, M.Ed.
Director, First Year Experience & Family Programs
Case Western Reserve University

An hour of class is worth more than five hours of poring over notes.

—DAN
MIAMI UNIVERSITY
FRESHMAN

NO MATTER HOW SICK YOU MIGHT BE during finals week, do not take any cough medicine. And read the labels on any cold medication you take for any reference that the medicine will make you drowsy. I was sick as a dog my first finals week, but I made the mistake of taking medication that made me so tired I couldn't stay up to cram. And no amount of caffeine can overcome the depressants in that medication. Just put up with the runny nose and drink coffee.

—ANONYMOUS
YOUNGSTOWN STATE UNIVERSITY, SENIOR

• • • • • • • •

YOU CAN'T PROCRASTINATE as much as you do in high school. You get behind, and you get behind, and you get behind, and then you get further and further behind, and you don't know what to do about it. I had a 4.0 in high school, when I could have slept through every class, and now I'm struggling. I have to pick up my study habits.

—KEVIN BUSHEY
GEORGIA STATE UNIVERSITY, FRESHMAN

• • • • • • • •

DON'T MISS EVEN ONE DAY of homework. If you fall behind, it's so much harder to catch up.

—NATASHA PIRZADA
GEORGETOWN UNIVERSITY, SOPHOMORE

• • • • • • • •

THIS IS SOMETHING MY DAD TOLD ME: You should look at college like a nine-to-five job. You wake up and you do all your work nine to five so that you're not stuck doing your work at 3 a.m., like I always am. Then you're tired and you end up sleeping through your first class, like I always do. So, get your work done early and then you have time to socialize.

—JENNA
BOSTON COLLEGE, FRESHMAN

GO OUT TO PARTY ON THURSDAYS, Fridays and Saturdays, but stay at home on the other days. I don't have classes on Friday; you should try to schedule that. And I don't study on Sundays; that's for watching football. During the week, I go to class and then study about two hours a night.

—FRED
UNIVERSITY OF RHODE ISLAND, JUNIOR

· · · · · · · ·

SOME OF MY MOST PRODUCTIVE STUDY SESSIONS were studying in groups. Find a classroom that's empty in the evening, write notes and questions on the chalkboard, quiz each other, and have fun with it.

—K. HARMA
WESTERN WASHINGTON UNIVERSITY, GRADUATE

· · · · · · · ·

I GO TO SCHOOL IN A BIG CITY, and there's always the temptation to go out and do something. You can't escape it. You have to realize, when night-time comes, you're going to want to go out. So you have to do your work in the day; otherwise, your work won't get done.

—CATHY
COLUMBIA UNIVERSITY, SENIOR

· · · · · · · ·

IN ENGLISH LITERATURE, don't watch the movie instead of reading the book. I didn't read all of *A Clockwork Orange* and I had an exam on it, so I watched the movie. I didn't know how obvious it would be that I substituted the book with the film. Never rely on the movie rendition or, for that matter, what you find online! Your professor makes you read the book for a reason.

—VERONICA
QUEENS UNIVERSITY, GRADUATE

Be careful when buying used books. The person who had the highlighter before you may have been an idiot.

—J.T.
UNIVERSITY OF FLORIDA, GRADUATE

TECHNOLOGY AND STUDYING

You need a computer, but not just any computer. You need a reliable computer. I've seen my friends' machines crash too many times right when they really needed them for a big assignment or presentation. I have a Mac and it's never broken down on me, and I hear the same thing from other Mac people on campus. Having a machine that won't break down when you need it is going to make studying way easier.

 —Barry Langer
  Oglethorpe University, Junior

While some people prefer to take notes on their computers, most of them also decide to surf the net while in class. Not only does it distract from your lectures, but it also distracts your peers. Plus, teachers know – I've seen plenty of people get busted. Just be careful and realize that at the end of the hour or so, you can search as much as you want.

 —Maya Newman
  Columbia University and The Jewish Theological Seminary, Graduate

In one of my classes, all my homework was online. You couldn't forget homework, it was due at midnight. It kind of sucked because I would get lazy about it, and copy/paste the question into Google. While I got good grades on the homework, I wasn't learning and was screwed for exams.

 —Tina
  Marist College, Senior

Most professors have everything online, so you have to use the computer or your phone to get your assignments. Some professors let you use your phones in class to research something, or to use it as a calculator.

 —Michael
  Rutgers University, Junior

DROPBOX (HTTP://GETDROPBOX.COM) IS the best way I know to share files with others so that everybody has the latest version of documents. It's great for projects, keeping files synced across multiple computers, and it backs up data online. Google Docs (http://docs.google.com) is another good way to collaborate with people on assignments.

> —REYNER
> OLIN COLLEGE, FRESHMAN

• • • • • • • •

COMPUTERS ARE A MIXED BLESSING. My computer is both the ultimate tool and the ultimate time-waster. I can spend hours on Facebook, Twitter, and other fun sites, which is pretty distracting. However, Bowdoin has a site called Blackboard which contains a lot of the information we need for class. This is extremely helpful.

> —LIZZIE
> BOWDOIN COLLEGE, FRESHMAN

• • • • • • • •

IT MIGHT SEEM THAT A LAPTOP is the best gadget to help with getting work done; however, the best way to study is with a notepad, a pen, and a quiet library. A laptop will offer distractions that anybody would be absorbed into. From my experience, a quiet library motivates and offers the opportunity to work and study the actual material that I need to learn.

> —ALEKSANDR AKULOV
> HUNTER COLLEGE, SOPHOMORE

• • • • • • • •

MY COLLEGE USES BLACKBOARD and it's actually pretty good. It organizes your classes and keeps you updated about your grades in detail. But if a project is due at midnight through Blackboard, DO NOT wait until the last five or even 10 minutes to send it, because everyone in your class is sending it at that time, and the site will crash!

> —CATLEYA
> UNIVERSITY OF MIAMI, JUNIOR

STUDYING WITH MUSIC WORKS for some people. It does not work for me. I wish I could focus on my work as well as I can focus on the songs on my iPod. For me, it definitely interferes with what I am trying to study or get done.

—*ANNIE THOMAS*
UNIVERSITY OF MICHIGAN, SENIOR

· · · · · · · ·

IN HIGH SCHOOL, I NEVER REALLY DID ANY WORK during the day. Here, it's essential to do some work during the day because I find myself easily distracted at night. There's so much freedom and you have so much time in your day, it's tough to balance it all.

—*MOLLY DERINGER*
BROWN UNIVERSITY, FRESHMAN

Watching the sun come up while studying is not a good thing.

—*JAMESE JAMES*
UNIVERSITY OF TULSA, GRADUATE

REALITY BITES (BUT YOU STILL NEED TO BE HONEST WITH YOURSELF)

Don't kid yourself thinking that you are going to work on a project or do any studying at all on weekends; it ain't gonna happen. I used to think like this: OK, test Tuesday. Today is Thursday. That means I have five days to prepare. But it never worked out like that. What really happened is that Friday was Friday (party day) and on the weekend the party continued. Monday was for recovery. You have to factor reality into your planning.

—*KEN KEEL*
UNIVERSITY OF VIRGINIA, SENIOR

" Set aside a time every day when you study. No matter what else you do that day, when that time comes, you sit down and study. It can be 45 minutes to an hour. If you do it every day, you'll do better in school. "

—JAKE MALAWAY
UNIVERSITY OF ILLINOIS, GRADUATE

THE POWER OF THE FRONT ROW

I took Introduction to Business and panicked when I got 7 out of 10 on the first quiz. One of my friends said to go to the T.A.'s office hours, because it was a huge class and the professor didn't know who you were. My friend also suggested I sit in the front row of the class. I then went to the T.A.'s office hours and she said, "Sarah, don't worry about it. I am happy that you are showing dedication by coming to my hours." A few minutes later, the professor walked in and said to my T.A., "How are your students in the section?" She said, "They're fine, and by the way this is Sarah Fass; she was concerned about her quizzes." My professor said, "Oh, I know who she is. She sits in the front of my class. And by the way, don't worry about the quiz, just keep sitting in the front row."

—SARAH FASS
AMERICAN UNIVERSITY, FRESHMAN

TIPS FOR ACADEMIC SUCCESS

You are probably used to getting good – maybe even excellent – grades in high school. Well, we have news for you...college is harder than high school! To get (more or less) the same grades in college, you'll have to work harder, despite dealing with enhanced opportunities and distractions, and taking care of yourself, perhaps for the first time. How do you get a leg up? Try any combination of these:

- **Sit in the "inverse T" of the class:** If you sit in the front two rows of class, or directly down the center (see, it makes an upside-down "T" from your professor's point-of-view), you'll be in his or her line of sight. So you'll be forced to be more attentive in class and caught up on the material, and your professor is more likely to get to know you and take an interest in you. When you have a question, she or he is more likely to see your hand go up. Of course, this also means that if you skip class, someone's going to notice.

- **Don't skip class:** You are paying far too much money for every hour of class. Skipping even one lecture is like flushing wads of money down the drain.

- **Go to office hours:** Your teaching assistants and professors are required to hold a certain number of office hours every week. Many times, these go by without anyone stopping in to visit or ask questions. When you go to office hours, your instructors will appreciate your interest and the fact that you're taking full advantage of your education. Try to go with a great question in mind - even if it's one you think you understand but you want to comprehend more fully. My advice: email a question, then go to office hours (your professor may begin to associate your name and face), then keep going to office hours, and ask meaningful questions in class. You may end up taking another class or getting a letter of recommendation from this person, or even pursuing research opportunities with them.

- **If your college offers supplemental services, check them out:** There is probably a department called the Learning Center, Study Skills Center or Academic Resource Center. In addition to study skills workshops (note-taking, time management, exam review tips), they may offer 1:1 tutoring for various classes. Or an upper division student who has excelled in that class may hold regular review sessions or help you work through homework.

- **Don't cheat:** You may not realize it, but there are many – many! – different forms of cheating beyond simple plagiarism and copying someone's answers on a test. For many assignments, your professor may not allow you to collaborate with others. You can even plagiarize *yourself* if you use any portion of work you had submitted for another paper, without citing yourself as a source! Don't violate any of these forms of cheating. You'll get caught, plain and simple.

- **Stress Less:** Stress can either empower you (meaning you over-come it), or devour (overwhelm) you. You can tap into resources from your Wellness Center or Counseling/Health Centers. Make a stress ball (balloon full of flour), work out regularly, go out with your friends once in a while, see a movie, schedule some 'down time' where you are not studying. Find some ways to de-stress or unwind, or you may find yourself getting sick frequently, or more irritable, or something else that you don't want to experience.

- **Find what works for you, and do it:** You might like to study in quiet spaces (i.e. the library) or in active spaces (i.e. a coffee-house). There are pros and cons to both. Libraries rarely let you bring food in, so if snacks during study time are important to you, or you have to be somewhat social with friends while studying, the coffee shop is the way to go. If you can't stand distractions, find a study carrel in the library. You may or may not be able to study in your room; your TV or wireless Internet may be too distract-ing. When you go home to visit family, you have to carve out study time in between family expectations for socializing.

- **Study before you party:** Suffice it to say, doing things in the reverse order will NOT be productive. Plus, where are your priorities? Look, we get it, college involves lots of opportunities to have fun, but you have a job right now: your education, and you may very well have some actual paying jobs as well. This may be the most important 'job' you ever have, as it will pave the way for most, if not all, of your future opportunities. Do not squander this chance. Above all else, be successful in your coursework. There's nothing worse than repeating a class that you didn't enjoy the first time but need to graduate...except, of course, for not graduating at all.

Scott C. Silverman

DON'T PARTY TOO MUCH and then cram. I did, which resulted in my very low GPA my freshman year. As a result, I had to work very hard to make up for it.

—*JESSICA TAYLOR*
STATE UNIVERSITY OF NEW YORK AT GENESEO, GRADUATE

• • • • • • • •

BY 9 P.M. ON THE NIGHT BEFORE I had two papers due the same day (for the first time ever), I hadn't started either of them. I was freaking out, I was not prepared. I was sure I wasn't going to finish everything in time. I called my mom close to tears on my way to the library, saying "I don't know what to do, how did I let myself get to this place?" And she said, "Emily, I know what you're saying, but it's time to put on your big-girl panties and get to work." Basically, freaking out wasn't going to help. I say that to people now, "put on your big-girl panties" .... even though I'm not really sure what that saying means!

—*EMILY*
HARVARD COLLEGE, SENIOR

I PULLED MY FIRST ALL-NIGHTER LAST WEEK. I did two nights in a row. I was up from 5 a.m. on Tuesday morning to 3 p.m. on Thursday afternoon. It was tough. I went to class to turn in my second paper on Thursday; I got there, sat down, and hit the desk. I fell asleep and someone woke me up at the end of class and I turned in my paper. Diet Coke with lemon pulled me through.

—*WHITNEY*
YALE UNIVERSITY, FRESHMAN

• • • • • • • •

TURN OFF YOUR CELL PHONE IN CLASS! One student forgot to turn his phone off in one of my classes, and the professor made this particular student hold a normal phone conversation in front of the entire class. At the end of the conversation, the student had to say "I love you" really loudly, so that everyone could hear. Professors frown upon cell phones in class.

—*LINDSEY WILLIAMSON*
VANDERBILT UNIVERSITY, GRADUATE

THREE WAYS TO BE A BETTER STUDENT – FAST

1. Sit in the front of every class. Now you'll stay awake.

2. Buy a different notebook or set up a separate binder section for each class—and use it! Now you'll keep up with the material.

3. Reread (or read for the first time, as the case may be!) all your class syllabi. Now the semester holds no unpleasant surprises.

It's good to go to class every day, at least to make an impression that you care.

—*Luke Moughon*
Georgia
Institute of
Technology
Sophomore

College is not high school; it requires you to think in very different ways than one is used to. Find one place on campus where you can study without being interrupted, and designate a portion of your time for that purpose. When reading, read for content, and know what you are reading (it makes skimming that much more effective). If you must cram, going to bed earlier and waking up at 6 a.m. to force a few more hours in is more effective, because at least you are awake for the test. But then again, that's just me.

—*Amy*
Princeton University, Freshman

• • • • • • • •

Buckle down early. Do your work early. The temptation gets greater the later in the year it gets.

—*Laura Gzyzewski*
DeSales University, Junior

• • • • • • • •

The key to surviving and having free time is to know what the teacher wants you to know and just study that. Skip everything else if it's not necessary to get a good grade in the course.

—*Anonymous*
United States Military Academy at West Point, Junior

• • • • • • • •

Get some friends who can edit a paper. They'll come in handy. And for every hour you study, do 15 minutes of fun stuff. It helps keep a balance.

—*Conor McNeil*
Emory University, Sophomore

IN COLLEGE, YOU HAVE these one- and two-hour chunks in the day with nothing to do. A lot of people spend that time taking a nap or watching TV or checking email or putzing around. It's a good habit to keep a homework assignment on hand, so when you have a spare moment you can pull it out and start reading it. It helps you keep up with it all.

—*CATE*
BROWN UNIVERSITY, JUNIOR

"Don't wait to write extremely long papers until the night before they're due. Writing under pressure is one thing; writing under extreme, debilitating pressure is something else entirely. "

—*DANIELLE FRIEDMAN*
DUKE UNIVERSITY, SENIOR

I STUDY AT NIGHT WHEN IT'S QUIETER; 10 p.m. to 4 a.m. Then I sleep all day. My roommate studies then, too. It's hard to find people you get along with who have the same patterns of sleep.

—*WALTER*
UNIVERSITY OF MARYLAND–COLLEGE PARK, SOPHOMORE

NEVER, EVER GO TO THE LIBRARY ON SATURDAY, unless it's during finals. Take a break one day a week and have fun.

—*STEVE DAVIS*
FLORIDA STATE UNIVERSITY, GRADUATE

THERE'S LESS DAY-TO-DAY WORK than you have in high school, so you think that you don't have that much and you continue not doing that much. Then it hits you. It all piles up. That's not good.

—*LUCY LINDSEY*
HARVARD UNIVERSITY, FRESHMAN

. . . .

" Get old tests from previous semesters; old tests and notebooks. There's a code name for this at most schools; find this out the first week of school. "

—*SEBASTIAN*
GEORGIA INSTITUTE OF TECHNOLOGY, GRADUATE

. . . .

Reward yourself for tasks completed by participating in an extracurricular activity or hobby.

—*DAVID*
ANDERSON
UNIVERSITY, SENIOR

DON'T GET TOO DOWN ON YOURSELF if your grades are not as good as they were in high school. You have to get used to each professor and how they grade. I was pretty much an A/B student in high school, but my first semester in college was B/C. Some of my friends went through the same thing and really got down about it and started partying more. I went the other way and started working harder. It really paid off.

—*JENNY PRISUTA*
YOUNGSTOWN STATE UNIVERSITY, SENIOR

DATE A GOOD STUDENT. Being around people who study and care a good deal about their grades is going to rub off. If the people you hang out with are less liable to ditch a study session to hang out, chances are you'll crack down and study – if for no other reason than a lack of available buddies to procrastinate with. This holds doubly true for dating.

> —*AMANDA*
> *UNIVERSITY OF COLORADO AT COLORADO SPRINGS, SOPHOMORE*

FACEBOOK VS. HITTING THE BOOKS

FACEBOOK IS YOUR WORST ENEMY during midterms or finals season. During my first semester freshman year, I approached an RA who is a computer science major and asked him for directions to block Facebook from my Internet browser. My plan was to unblock myself after midterms. However, knowing I could unblock myself anytime didn't help much. Over the past four years, I've trained myself to not be distracted by Facebook during studying, but it's still tempting to go on Facebook, comment on other people's statuses, look through photos, etc.

> —*MICHELLE Y. LEE*
> *EMORY UNIVERSITY, SENIOR*

EVERYBODY KNOWS THE FEELING of checking the Facebook News Feed for the umpteenth time the night before a big paper is due. That kind of study break is helpful – in moderation.

> —*REYNER*
> *OLIN COLLEGE, FRESHMAN*

FACEBOOK AND EMAILING ARE TOOLS that are specifically made to encourage procrastination in students.

> —*AMANDA*
> *UNIVERSITY OF COLORADO AT COLORADO SPRINGS, SOPHOMORE*

MAKING A STRONG FIRST IMPRESSION ON PAPER

When you think of first impressions, you probably think of your physical appearance, your clothing, your speech, and your manners. While all these things are important in a general sense, they probably won't influence your teachers or affect your grades as much as the first written assignment you hand in for a particular course. To make a strong first impression on paper, consider the following bits of advice:

1. **Make sure your assignment is typed and handed in on time.** You're in college now. That means handwritten papers are no longer acceptable. Even if you don't have a computer or a word processor at home, as a college student, you probably have a computer account on campus and numerous computer labs available to you. Take advantage of them, and give yourself plenty of time to complete the assignment on schedule. A first assignment that is typed and on time may lead your professors to think you are organized and prepared.

2. **Write to the correct length.** If your professor asks you to write two full pages, don't write one or three. Believe it or not, teachers have a specific purpose in mind when they indicate the length of an assignment. They may want you to be precise and direct in a short assignment, or they may want you to provide examples and background information in a longer paper. Writing to the requested length may lead your instructors to conclude that you can follow directions and are willing to do so.

3. **Use a strong thesis early in your paper.** Your thesis is your main idea, and your thesis belongs, generally, at the end of your first paragraph. Your thesis also lets your reader know where the essay is headed and how it's going to get there. Here's an example of a strong thesis: "The Hudson River should be dredged for four main reasons." A strong thesis in the proper location will let your instructors know you are serious about what you have to say.

4. **Use transitions to move your readers from one idea to the next.** If you're writing about the four reasons for dredging the Hudson, you should use words like "first, second, third, and fourth" to separate your reasons. Yes, a new paragraph will indicate that you're moving on to a new idea, but without a transition, the reader might not know if the new idea is still part of the previous reason or a new reason altogether. Transitions make your writing more clear and make you appear ordered and logical.

5. **Have a strong conclusion.** Just as your thesis introduces your main idea, your conclusion reminds the readers of that idea and allows them to remember your idea and think about it. You may want to conclude with a summary, a challenge, or a call to action. A strong summary shows that you are secure and confident.

6. **Use the spellchecker and the grammar checker on your computer, and proofread carefully.** In the days before computers, teachers may have been a bit more lenient. They might have forgiven a spelling error, for example, if it looked more like a typing error. Today, however, you can't let anything slide by. Your professors expect you to use the tools available to you. Your professors also expect you to catch the errors that the computers miss. A paper that is free of spelling errors and typos will show you to be a competent and careful writer.

First impressions – either positive or negative – are hard to overcome. This semester, take your time with that first writing assignment and make a great first impression on your instructors.

Copyright 2012 © by Jim LaBate

Jim LaBate
Writing Specialist in The Writing and Research Center
Hudson Valley Community College (Troy, New York)

I'VE LEARNED TO LISTEN TO THE PROFESSOR and what he's saying— not just scribble down everything that he says—and then try to summarize his thoughts in my notes. Not word-for-word, but the main points.

—JOSH
PRINCETON UNIVERSITY, SENIOR

• • • • • • • •

YOU HAVE TO KEEP WEIRD HOURS. Sometimes at 3 a.m. you're doing your work. But it's just what you have to do.

—T.O.
HOWARD UNIVERSITY, SOPHOMORE

• • • • • • • •

Don't try to study on a Friday night. Don't even try.

—NOURA BAKKOUR
GEORGETOWN
UNIVERSITY, SENIOR

DON'T STUDY IN YOUR ROOM; you won't ever get to it. Your phone and neighbors will be too enticing. I would suggest a quiet cube at the library, if you really need to get something done.

—J.S.
UNIVERSITY OF GEORGIA, GRADUATE

• • • • • • • •

YOU MIGHT ONLY HAVE CLASS AN HOUR OR TWO a day. The rest of the day, you have to figure out how to be as productive as possible, so you can go to meetings/clubs—and have some fun!—at night. The trick to this, for me, is multiple study spots. I found that I love the first floor of the library, the third floor of the student center, and one of the cafés on campus. After I spend a few hours in one place, I relocate to the other. It gives my mind—and body—a bit of stretch when I'm transferring places and the new location gives me a fresh, less-stressed perspective when I sit back down to get to work.

—EMMA
HAMILTON COLLEGE, JUNIOR

IT'S NOT SO MUCH TECHNOLOGY that interferes with studying as it is the notion of procrastinating. You will find the most ridiculous excuses to put off studying. But that's really what college is all about – learning to do the best job in the smallest amount of time because you were an idiot. Every year, you will convince yourself that you won't allow yourself to fall behind. And every subsequent year, you will learn that you are more full of it than the year before.

> —J.V.
> THE COLLEGE OF WILLIAM & MARY, GRADUATE

HAVE YOUR SCHOOL'S WRITING CENTER help you edit first drafts of your papers. I learned this later, but if I had started freshman year I would have had a much smoother experience, believe me.

> —MAYA NEWMAN
> COLUMBIA UNIVERSITY AND THE JEWISH THEOLOGICAL SEMINARY, GRADUATE

MY iPHONE AND ME

The iPhone is my right-hand man. Without it, I wouldn't be half as effective as I am now. I have this thing called MobileMe that works with it, and every time I add a calendar event on my computer, it pops up instantly on my phone. Same for email and contacts, and it lets me GPS my iPhone if I lose it. All the apps (and Internet access everywhere) make it singly the most useful tool in my arsenal, especially if I need to type up an email to a professor when I'm on the road.

It can be a distraction, though. Don't buy too many games or you'll find yourself wondering where the last hour and a half went – and the answer will be, "Flinging tiny cartoon islanders into a volcano."

> —BARRY LANGER
> OGLETHORPE UNIVERSITY, JUNIOR

THE LIBRARY: YOUR PARTNER IN ACADEMIC SUCCESS

Now that you are a freshman, it's time to begin getting to know your library. The college and university library is very different from your high school or local public library. Known as an academic library, they are teaching libraries, and genuinely so. Most academic librarians are faculty members with masters or doctoral degrees. Their purpose is simple and yet very important – to provide you, the student, with the research and information tools needed for your chosen profession so that by the time you graduate, your library skills will be developed enough to strongly support the research and information tasks in your profession. Academic librarians won't do your work for you or just give you the answers to questions, but they will teach you *how* to find the answers and to become an expert library user.

Remember this – the process of research is not difficult, but it is detailed. It is important, therefore, to adhere to the steps involved in the research process:

1. First, understand the topic about which you will be writing. Writing a research paper is not an opportunity to tell the reader what the topic is about. It is an opportunity to defend, refute, challenge, analyze, or suggest a new position on an opinion or topic. If you're not sure you really understand your topic, your library will have resources that can help you learn about and focus on topics. Select and develop a topic that is neither too broad nor too narrow.
2. Second, identify databases and other library resources which will provide you with the evidence to support your thesis statement. Remember to take an interdisciplinary approach, because no topic exists without being influenced by other topics.
3. Third, develop a search strategy, which includes discovering what words will be effective when you search. Open a new Word document and keep a list of the search terms you've discovered to be effective, since the searching process may extend over several

days or weeks, and it is unlikely you'll remember all the words you used. As you find articles and other materials, be sure to collect the citation information with each work. And, for articles and other sources that are available in PDF form, save them in a folder on your desktop.

4. Finally, critically evaluate the sources to ensure authenticity and objectivity. Make sure that they are scholarly and are published in a peer-reviewed journal, rather than a for-profit publication. Your paper is only as strong as the evidence you find.

Many library services and resources are provided to assist you in many ways. Check with your library to see which of the services are available, and how you can access them. Your library may have laptops and tablets you can take to class or home overnight, group study rooms where you can work undisturbed with your team, course reserves for items held specifically for your class, open study areas for collaborative learning or individual study, extended hours during final exams, and the option of scheduling a one-to-one consultation with a librarian.

Research is an important part of professional careers. Businesses conduct demographic research to ensure profitability. Doctors research new procedures to improve patient outcomes. Engineers discover new techniques to provide safety and design innovation. Regardless of your career choice, research is part of the job. And being an expert researcher is just another tool that you will need to "acquire" to be competitive in the job market, successful with what you do, and satisfied knowing that you are in control of your career. Your academic librarians are ready and delighted to help you learn to navigate the complex research landscape. But the responsibility of asking for help belongs to you – if you don't ask, you'll never find out. So, interrupt a librarian and ask for help. That's why we are librarians.

Prof. Douglas Hasty
First Year Experience Librarian
Florida International University

182

A LITTLE <u>TOO</u> CREATIVE . . .

At the University of Central Florida, a recent case of cheating had nothing to do with the Internet, cellphones or anything tech-related. A heavily tattooed student was found with notes written on his arm. He had blended them into his body art.

The same university prohibits gum chewing during exams, because it might "disguise a student's speaking into a hands-free cellphone to an accomplice outside."

COLLEGE IS NOT HIGH SCHOOL. You are responsible for doing your homework and making sure you are ready for the next class. Invest the time and go to class.

—*MICHAEL*
RUTGERS UNIVERSITY, JUNIOR

. . . .

IF PROFESSORS GIVE OUT EMAIL ADDRESSES, use them! Don't send anything raunchy, even if you are in love with your English professor. Use it to communicate about class work. Email them if you happen to have skipped class and want to know what you have missed. This is a sure way to win points with them. By humanizing them, you make them a friend. I have done this a few times and they seem to like it when you are involved in school, even when you are not.

—*EDIE SHERMAN*
KINGSBOROUGH COMMUNITY COLLEGE, SENIOR

STUDYING IS ALL ABOUT KNOWING YOURSELF. You don't want to end up in the library on the night before the final exam, crying. But you also don't want to be a shut-in book worm. Something as simple as using a notebook to take notes instead of a computer will help. Studying in small bits will be easier, and you are more likely to remember what you wrote rather than what you typed. Show up to your class 5 minutes early, flip through your notes from the class before. Small things like that will leave you over-prepared, so that you wont be cramming last minute and you will have weekends free during the year!

—*MICHAEL CUMMO*
BOSTON UNIVERSITY, SENIOR

• • • • • • • • •

IT WAS STRANGE – freshman fall I had the fewest hours of class of any semester so far. In high school, I was used to getting up early in the morning and staying at school all day, sometimes coming home late, depending on athletics or rehearsals, so it was so strange to find myself with five free hours in the afternoon. Which of course is the time you should be getting your work done, but I was excited about getting tea, and going biking on the river! After the first few weeks, once I started getting bigger assignments, I realized that if I wanted to get any sleep, I had to work during the day. Theatre rehearsals would often go until midnight; sometimes until 2 in the morning!

—*HALEY*
HARVARD UNIVERSITY, SENIOR

HAVING A COMPUTER IN CLASS is a plus and a minus. Typing is much faster than writing, but I know I'll always be tempted to check my email. Sometimes when I'm in an important lecture I'll turn the Internet off completely.

Using a computer isn't great for every class; in a small class or a seminar, computers can be disruptive, and in general if the lecture feels slow enough to allow me to just write, I'll always choose that. Don't just use your computer out of habit, think about whether it's right for your work methods or your particular class.

—EMILY
HARVARD COLLEGE, SENIOR

• • • • • • • •

THE FIRST WEEK HERE, I stayed in my room and studied too much. My second week, I realized I'd missed out on social life, so I stayed up really late socializing in the dorms and did my work only on the weekend. Neither of these methods worked very well. Then I started making a schedule for myself.

—CAROL
HUNTER COLLEGE, FRESHMAN

Extracurriculars: Making the Most of Your Free Time

So many clubs, so little time! Most college graduates will tell you they wish they'd done more extracurriculars during their four years. Those years will go by in a flash, so if you see a group you want to join, don't wait till next semester. Think big, think broad, think quirky: There's Dumbledore's Army for Harry Potter fanatics, a fencing team, singing groups, community service clubs—one of these groups is just waiting to give you the best experience and best friends of your college years. Sign up for whatever looks good. If, later on, you find yourself with too many things to do, you can always cut back.

TAKE FUN CLASSES. I took yoga and aerobics. I also joined the salsa-dancing club. These things break up the monotony of the usual classes.

—EMILY TUCK
CALIFORNIA STATE UNIVERSITY, GRADUATE

FREE TIME: USE IT. DON'T WASTE A DROP.

—ARIEL MELENDEZ
PRINCETON UNIVERSITY
FRESHMAN

HEADLINES
Best Advice and Top Tips

- Clubs are a great way to network with other people.
- Extracurriculars are also a good way to try out something new.
- Organizations in your area of academic interest may even offer scholarships.
- It's your free time, so make sure you're having fun.
- Physical exercise is a great way to relieve stress.
- Spend your free time on things that don't involve school.

BECAUSE COLLEGES OFFER SUCH A breadth of extracurriculars, it's important to learn about them before you decide which ones to devote yourself to. A lot of schools have activity fairs that allow you to sign up for any activity that interests you. After this, you will start receiving emails from the groups about meetings, events, and initiatives. With this information, you can decide if it is something you are passionate about or something you could eliminate from your résumé. And it's okay to back out!

—STEPHANIE DREIFUSS
DUKE UNIVERSITY, SENIOR

• • • • • • • •

BECAUSE I'M JEWISH I joined Hillel House. I love the activities that they do, such as visiting soup kitchens and organizing meetings where they bring in a speaker. I am going to join them on their trip to New Orleans for Habitat for Humanities.

—CAROL
HUNTER COLLEGE, FRESHMAN

CHECK THINGS OUT, PARTYWISE, when you first get to college, because after a while it gets too crowded with work. You get too busy, so it's important to have fun at first.

> —PATRICK
> UNIVERSITY OF RHODE ISLAND, FRESHMAN

I TOOK A DIFFERENT APPROACH to extracurricular activities and decided to intern instead. I started interning freshman year. But I found it better to spend my time with a few activities that are very important to me, rather than spread myself thin trying to build my résumé.

> —GERALDINE SARAH COWPER
> CUNY/MACAULAY HONORS COLLEGE, SENIOR

ASK THE ADVISER

I hear people talking about extracurricular activities, and other people talking about co-curriculars. What's the difference?

Guess what — there is no difference! A few years ago, we student-affairs advisors started using the term "co-curricular activities" instead of "extracurricular activities" in order to underscore the importance of the learning you do *outside* the classroom.

Although your classes are of vital importance, editing your college newspaper or running a tutoring program for local school children may be just as important in developing your intellect and professional skills.

Frances Northcutt

TO SLEEP OR NOT TO SLEEP

A DAILY NAP IS A GOOD IDEA. Come back from class and take a nap and you wake up and feel like it's a whole new day. An hour-long nap, or even a 15-minute power nap, is good.

> —*WHITNEY*
> *YALE UNIVERSITY, FRESHMAN*

· · · · · · · · ·

DON'T BE A WUSS YOUR FRESHMAN YEAR or you will have few friends. If you are the kind of kid who goes to bed at 10 o'clock, you will be in trouble. Learn to stretch yourself. Push yourself to be a late-night party person or you will have no social life. Everyone walks around here deprived of sleep, but misery loves company. We have weekends to catch up.

> —*TEJ SHAH*
> *CARNEGIE MELLON UNIVERSITY, SOPHOMORE*

· · · · · · · · ·

SO MANY PEOPLE ARE SLEEP-DEPRIVED that they become zombies. Once I woke up and went to class in the afternoon thinking it was morning; this is not unusual. People are always confused about dates and times. Learn how to survive without sleep and you will thrive in college.

> —*LINDSEY SHULTZ*
> *CARNEGIE MELLON UNIVERSITY, SENIOR*

· · · · · · · · ·

HOW DO YOU SURVIVE FRESHMAN YEAR? Nap. Get up for class. Go to class. Then nap. That's how you survive.

> —*MIKEY LEE*
> *STANFORD UNIVERSITY, JUNIOR*

I'M GAY. My college has a queer student union; their meetings take place every week, with typically 30 in attendance. Another organization, Queer Allied and Activism, discusses LGBT issues, and we try to implement actions to try and improve our community. This is definitely the more political organization, whereas the first is geared more towards social mixing, where hooking up is quite common. Some others prefer the "hooking up" scene.

—ANONYMOUS
UNIVERSITY OF VIRGINIA, JUNIOR

MY FRESHMAN YEAR at George Washington was a lonely experience. I didn't really know anyone on my first floor. But the more I talked to other freshmen, the more I realized there was opportunity to network with other people. I got involved with a bible group on campus; it was an amazing time of sharing the bible, meeting people who cared, and singing songs. It was a beautiful experience.

—MICHAEL CHOE
GEORGE WASHINGTON UNIVERSITY, GRADUATE

EXTRACURRICULARS ARE IMPORTANT for your college résumé, but they also help you meet lots of people with similar interests to yours and can really ease the process of making friends. I'm involved in a lot of organizations on campus (student government, Jewish Student Union, theatre, debate society, school paper, to name a few), and it helps me meet new people on a regular basis. Being involved in a fraternity or sorority is really good for this too.

—BARRY LANGER
OGLETHORPE UNIVERSITY, JUNIOR

USE THE GYM AS MUCH AS POSSIBLE, because when you get out, it's not free anymore. It's in your tuition, so you're paying for it.

—SANI G.
UNIVERSITY OF CALIFORNIA AT IRVINE, JUNIOR

FINDING A STUDENT ORGANIZATION TO JOIN...

Depending on how big your college is, you may find many types of organizations: political action, religion, culture, academic/professional, social, athletic, and more. Some groups tie directly into your studies, others provide great community service opportunities, and all of them will help you have fun and build skills. Here's how to find one that's right for you.

1. First, check with your student activities office – online or in person. They probably have an up-to-date list of all of the officially recognized student organizations on campus.
2. Anytime your campus holds a student organization fair or expo, be sure to check it out. These events will give you exposure to a large number of student organizations all in one place at the same time.
3. You can search on Facebook or other online sources to find groups organized around some of your interests.
4. Find a few that you like, go to some meetings and events, and then decide if you want to stick with those groups.
5. If you can't find a student organization that meets your needs or interests you enough, you can get a few friends together and create your own. You can usually get funding from the Associated Students to cover some of the organization's activities.
6. Take your time. Resist the temptation to join 15 organizations your first term. Start with two – *maybe* three. Eventually you can join others or assume leadership responsibilities, once you know you're ready.

Scott C. Silverman

CLUB SPORTS ARE FUN, non-threatening ways to get your exercise in, as well as a way to meet a variety of people. Most people who join club sports are a grab bag of personalities.

—STEPHANIE LEIGH DOCKERY
WILLIAMS COLLEGE, GRADUATE

...AND LEAVING IT

Good news: You signed up for an extracurricular. Bad news: You might not like it. How can you tell for sure? Here are three hints.

You don't want to hang out with the other people who also take part in the extracurricular. At least part of committing to an extracurricular is making new friends along the way, people you really connect with because you share some of the same passions. If you find yourself thinking you have nothing in common with the people around you – or worse, you don't like them – it could mean the activity might not be the best option.

It interferes with your studies. Extracurriculars are supposed to complement your studies in college, not compete with them. If you find yourself stuck at extracurricular activities to the point that your grades suffer, it's time to take a step back.

You'd rather sleep in than tend to your extracurricular. We know – sleep is precious. And wanting to catch a few extra z's is normal. But if you find yourself sleeping through an activity that's supposed to be fun and rewarding, then maybe it's not all that fun and rewarding. Find an activity that makes you *want* to get out of bed.

Frances Northcutt

CHANGING THE WORLD

I HAVE ALWAYS TRIED TO LIVE by the quote by Gandhi, "Be the change you wish to see in the world." At this point in my life I am still unsure about what to do or what my main purpose is. In fact, I am now doing my ninth internship since beginning college and still have no idea. All I can do at this moment is live in a polite, friendly manner and be compassionate towards my peers in life. I really do think it is the little things that count.

—*GERALDINE SARAH COWPER*
   CUNY/MACAULAY HONORS COLLEGE, SENIOR

I WANT TO CHANGE THE WORLD by learning self-defense techniques, and teaching other students and people what the art of self-defense is all about. It's a great way of increasing one's energy and knowing how to act in certain situations.

—*MICHAEL CHOE*
   GEORGE WASHINGTON UNIVERSITY, GRADUATE

AT SCHOOL, I JOINED AN ORGANIZATION called p3. P3 stood for Paraprofessionals Promoting Peer*fection. We welcomed all the new freshmen in and were the first faces they saw at orientation. Along the way we pretty much gave them a heads-up on what to expect, and at the end we served as their mentors throughout the year if they chose to have one. You didn't get any compensation for being a p3; just the gratification and rewarding feeling when one of your mentees tells you that they don't think they could've made it through their freshman year without you.

—*BRITTANY*
   ALBANY STATE UNIVERSITY, GRADUATE

COMMUNITY SERVICE organizations such as the Red Cross and Project Giveback not only help the community but they make you feel good about yourself, knowing that you made a difference is someone else's life. If you have free time, and you need something to do, helping others is the perfect way.

—*HAYLEY MASON*
   HOWARD UNIVERSITY, SOPHOMORE

WE HAVE A VOLUNTEER PROGRAM at the university called Madison House. They arrange all different kinds of activities to get involved in the community; helping out in classrooms, teaching English as a second language, and volunteering for hospital duties, among others. It's really heartening to see the school make an impact in the community and to know that the students truly care enough to wait in line just to volunteer.

—*Jo*
UNIVERSITY OF VIRGINIA, SENIOR

COLLEGE IS DEFINITELY a time to become an activist. There are many terrible things in this world that could and should be changed, but we can only do so much, so it's important to find a cause that is meaningful to you. For me, this cause is climate change.

—*DREW HILL*
COLBY COLLEGE, JUNIOR

THE BEST CLUBS AND ORGANIZATIONS to join on campus (outside of Greek life) are those that involve volunteering. It is a way to help others and to get to know your community at the same time. Sometimes it's easy to forget that your college/university does not exist in its own bubble. There are people, places and spaces that exist outside your classroom and dorm walls. Go out and explore. It will make you a more in-tune person in the end.

—*A.F.K.*
DUKE UNIVERSITY, GRADUATE

I DON'T WANT TO CHANGE THE WORLD; I just want to make individual lives better.

—*TIFFANY*
STANFORD UNIVERSITY, SENIOR

I WAS IN A SEMI-PROFESSIONAL *a cappella* group that travelled around the country and the world singing for thousands of people every year. I met my closest friends, became a confident public speaker, and gained invaluable leadership and time management skills. It was incredible, but it was a huge time commitment and did not give me much time to devote to other extracurricular activities.

—MAYA NEWMAN
COLUMBIA UNIVERSITY AND THE JEWISH THEOLOGICAL SEMINARY, GRADUATE

• • • • • • • •

YOU SHOULD DO LOTS OF EXTRACURRICULARS because when you're really busy, you don't waste time. If I had more free time I would probably just waste it playing Super Smash Bros.

—PETER STONE
TUFTS UNIVERSITY, SOPHOMORE

SOME EXTRAORDINARY EXTRA-CURRICULAR ACTIVITIES

- The Williams College Anti-gravity Society. Juggling is more than a hobby; it's a way of life.

- Kutztown University Medieval Renaissance Club. Gives you that opportunity to be a knight in shining armor and joust on a horse that you've always wanted! Pillaging not included.

- Students for an Orwellian Society (national society, founded at Columbia University). Attracts student from all over the nation who want to live in a 1984 (the George Orwell classic) inspired totalitarian society.

- University of Minnesota's Campus People Watcher's Club. Calling all creeps and stalkers – if we give ourselves an official name and slogan, it's socially acceptable!

I FOUND MY FRIENDS through a huge variety of different activities, including the rugby team, the residential college council, an *a cappella* group, Outdoor Action Leaders, not to mention people that lived right by me. My best friends come from activities; otherwise I would have never met them.

—*DENALI*
PRINCETON UNIVERSITY, JUNIOR

· · · · · · · ·

EXTRACURRICULARS ARE WHAT COLLEGE IS ABOUT; creating your own niche. If you're an academic, start a publication. If you're an actor, launch a theater. I started a debate team that competed against the Ivy League schools. Now I'm creating a theatre program located at Lincoln Center, with master teachers from Yale, Julliard, and NYU. At this great space, students and professional New York creatives will be working to produce plays together.

—*RON Y. KAGAN*
CUNY/MACAULAY HONORS COLLEGE, SENIOR

· · · · · · · ·

I'M IN A DANCE company on campus. It's student-run; we choreograph all of our own pieces, we set the lighting and the music. We rehearsed last night from 11 p.m. to 1 a.m. It's a lot of work, and I'm sleep-deprived because of it, but I love it.

—*COLLEEN*
PRINCETON UNIVERSITY, JUNIOR

· · · · · · · ·

THERE IS A HOWLING AT THE MOON CLUB at Mt. Holyoke; when it is a full moon, you can hear them all over campus.

—*RUTHANN*
MOUNT HOLYOKE COLLEGE, GRADUATE

My freshman year I tried archery and karate for the first time. I wasn't good at either of them, but it was fun being bad at something new.

—*AMY FORBES*
MISSISSIPPI STATE UNIVERSITY GRADUATE

ON DIVERSITY

ONE OF MY BEST FRIENDS here is from Nepal. Conversations with him have opened my horizons. I learned a lot about different cultures and how women are treated in Nepal. I was talking about visiting and he was like, "These are things you can expect." It's refreshing. Be prepared to ask questions when you don't understand things, and be open to new ideas and people.

> —*MEREDITH*
> *BROWN UNIVERSITY, SOPHOMORE*

. . . .

I AM CAUCASIAN and am definitely a minority at my school. I have embraced this and been able to immerse myself into a vast array of cultures and people. I know that most of my friends went to homogenous, "white" schools and have not been able to face racial or discrimination issues up front. Here at Hunter College, I'm able to interact with people from all over the world. This diversity has kept me open-minded and aware of the issues surrounding race. I am thankful that I have been able to attend West African dance classes or tasted Islamic food during the Dean's Hours.

> —*GERALDINE SARAH COWPER*
> *CUNY/MACAULAY HONORS COLLEGE, SENIOR*

BE A PART OF SOMETHING that you sincerely enjoy because it's your free time. Upon my arrival on campus, I decided to dedicate my time and efforts to Duke Africa. It served as a space where I could celebrate my Nigerian culture, learn about other African cultures, and become informed about issues and causes affecting Africa socially, economically and politically.

> —*D.A.*
> *DUKE UNIVERSITY, SENIOR*

I'M IN THE YALE ALLEY CATS. I spend a lot of time singing and hanging out with everyone in the group. We travel around the world. It has given me a solid group of friends. It's one thing to rely on roommates. But you have friends that you share so much in common with—be it singing, traveling, or performing. That common ground brings people together.

—DAN AMERMAN
YALE UNIVERSITY, SOPHOMORE

MY SOPHOMORE YEAR, I joined the mountaineering club. Their weekend excursions and the boulder time at the rock wall helped me to counterbalance the burden of intense classes and blow off some steam. I met a lot of cool people in this club and strengthened my relationships with previous friends.

—DREW HILL
COLBY COLLEGE, JUNIOR

THE COMPLETE STUDENT-ATHLETE

The college existence provided endless opportunities for me to display my athletic talent:

- Track and Field = Running to class, hurdling benches, hedgerows, and midget freshmen on the way.
- Football/Rugby = Getting into a pool-cue swinging, bottle-throwing, table upending bar brawl over a $5 billiards game.
- Swimming = Jumping naked into frigid Lake Mendota (Wisconsin) during the middle of November and frantically trying to reach the shore before hypothermia claimed my life.
- Beer-pong.

—JOHN
UNIVERSITY OF WISCONSIN AT MADISON, GRADUATE

BALANCING BOOKS AND SPORTS

IF YOU ARE INVOLVED in an extracurricular activity, you need to learn time management. Since I was a student-athlete in college, I found out first-hand what time management was. I had to keep up my grades and coursework in addition to practicing three hours a day, plus having games or meets to compete in. It was hard, but it was worth it in the long run. I can't tell you how good it looks on my résumé that I competed in an NCAA sport while keeping up my grades.

—*JAMESE JAMES*
UNIVERSITY OF TULSA, GRADUATE

IT'S TOUGH TO BALANCE doing a sport and being at school. You practice three hours a day, and you go to school all day. When you get home you're tired, and you have to find time to study. A lot of times you don't want to, but you have to learn how to do it. It took me all of first year to learn how. I mean, we're normal students in some ways, but in other ways we're not, because we're always doing something. We don't have the free time a lot of people do when they get out of class. When we get out of class, we have to go here and go there; we're traveling, we're on the road, we're in hotels. It's tough to make the grade when you play sports.

—*RUSTY BENNETT*
GEORGIA STATE UNIVERSITY, SOPHOMORE

CLUB SOCCER ROCKED! We road-tripped all over the place. You get to know people pretty quickly when you have to spend hours with them in a car.

—*LINDSEY WILLIAMSON*
VANDERBILT UNIVERSITY, GRADUATE

ONE THING THAT REALLY HELPED was that I played soccer my freshman year. The soccer team was more than just a team. It wasn't like it was from 4-6 p.m. on weekdays and then a game on Saturdays. It was a whole community. You saw people on campus; you yelled. We had a participation ceremony my freshman year, and I still remember the song we sang during the *a cappella* jam. We wore capes and magic wands and we were "super soccer firsties." It was more than just soccer; we were really part of the college community.

—*RUTHANN*
MOUNT HOLYOKE COLLEGE, GRADUATE

. . . .

FRESHMEN SHOULD JOIN CLUBS that fit their majors. This allows you to meet and get to know the people who will be taking the same type of courses as you, which is a good thing to know if you are ever sick and miss class or have a question about a course or professor. This also helps you form a bond with people you are likely to see years down the road, in your profession.

—*H.N.F.*
PENNSYLVANIA STATE UNIVERSITY, GRADUATE

Consider

. . . .

FIND A COMMUNITY to be involved with, whether that's getting involved with dorm life or getting involved in an extra-curricular right away. My freshman year I spent all of my time with the girls who lived with me and right above me and it was really great. And then when I joined my *a cappella* group I felt like they became the emotional support system that I had back when I was living at home with my family.

—*EMILY*
HARVARD COLLEGE, SENIOR

WHEN I WAS A FRESHMAN, I joined a Chinese club, because I was majoring in Chinese and it really helped me network. I still had that common network when I left Duke. I would advise freshmen to join an ethnic or religious club; I found that those were the clubs that kept people grounded.

—*SHEVON*
DUKE UNIVERSITY, GRADUATE

• • • • • • • • •

THERE'S AN ACTIVITY FAIR that takes place the first two weeks you're on campus. The gym is filled with tables for all the different groups—*a cappella* groups, dance groups, religious organizations, community-service organizations—and you put your name down on the lists of all the ones you might want to be involved with. The first two weeks of classes, you get emails from 20-25 organizations, but then you slowly whittle down to the ones you can see yourself actually dedicating your time to. It's difficult. Choose two or three organizations and just go with those. I try to be involved with something that keeps me active physically, along with something that keeps me involved with the community.

—*JOSH*
PRINCETON UNIVERSITY, SENIOR

• • • • • • • • •

ONE GREAT THING ABOUT JOINING everything freshman year—I still get random emails from, say, the Korean Society or the Indian Students Organization, inviting me to their open houses. So I can go and have all sorts of wonderful free dinners. I have a friend who managed to spend only $14 on food for a whole week!

—*DENALI*
PRINCETON UNIVERSITY, JUNIOR

VOLUNTEERING AND SERVICE LEARNING: WHAT'S THE DIFFERENCE?

Although quite different, both volunteering and service learning are important and valuable!

Volunteering	Service Learning
Volunteers give their time and energy to the community.	In a reciprocal arrangement, service learners help the community and receive the opportunity to hone their skills and deepen their learning.
Not connected with academic credit.	Often built into an academic course, and supervised by the professor.
Volunteers walk away with feelings of pride and virtue because they helped others.	Service learners also walk away with new knowledge.
Typically does not require extensive preparation.	The activity is bracketed by classroom learning of specific skills and/or background information.
Example: Students get together to clean up a local park.	Example: Based on what they've learned in class, environmental studies students design and implement energy-saving initiatives on and off campus.

Frances Northcutt

MAKING YOUR MARK: COMMUNITY INVOLVEMENT

In my work with students, one of my favorite things is to sit down with a student one-on-one and ask them how they want to make a difference – on our campus, in our community and in the world. Maybe they want to see a new major created on campus, or more shade trees in the courtyard. Or perhaps they want to establish a community volunteerism program where students go into the city to help feed the hungry or encourage children to go to college, or increase children's literacy in developing countries. Maybe *your* vision for the world includes something equally inspiring.

All of these changes are possible, and any of us can make them happen. We just have to take the first steps. Whether the changes you want to see are major or minor, this worksheet will help you identify how to make them a reality. You can make your campus, community and the world a better place to be, one step at a time.

- What is the one change that I most want to see happen (i.e. on campus, in the city, etc.)? NOTE: Assume time and money are not an obstacle. Feel free to think big.
  "I want to plant more trees and flower beds on campus."

- Why do I feel this change is important?
  "Adding more trees and flower beds will beautify the campus even more, and provide extra shade."

- Who do I have to talk to and work with to accomplish this change?
  "I should meet with the Associated Students, Dean of Students and staff from the groundskeeping department."

- How do I keep time and money from being an obstacle for me?
  "I will research the current funding allocated to landscaping on campus, and look into any grants to fund landscaping projects or materials that could be donated."

- When/where do I get started?
  "I will ask 10 of my friends, neighbors and classmates to bring a friend to a meeting to discuss the issue, and will schedule that meeting for before this term is over."

- What do I do if people say no or I encounter other roadblocks?
  "When decision-makers mention that this change isn't possible due to X or Y, I will ask them to help identify alternative ways of getting this done."

Here are some of the things you may end up doing to effect change. *Note: Try to go through these steps in order. For example, if the decision-maker agrees to the change – i.e. planting more trees – during a face-to-face meeting, then won't you be glad you didn't schedule a protest?*

1. Build a coalition of allies and supporters for your cause.
2. Send an email inquiry to discuss your issue and schedule a meeting.
3. Meet with the decision-makers so that you can present your case … and do your best to research the constraints and circumstances that led to the status quo.
4. Be willing to accept a compromise solution, if the circumstances are reasonable.
5. When necessary, collect petitions and present them to the decision-makers. Your student body association can be critical here.
6. If still no reasonable responses are forthcoming, protests and rallies may be a wise next step.

As you tackle your cause, remember the words of famed anthropologist Margaret Mead: "Never doubt that a small group of thoughtful, committed citizens can change the world; indeed, it's the only thing that ever does."

Scott C. Silverman

STARTING YOUR OWN CLUB

Every September, at least five of my freshman advisees stop by my office to ask me how they would go about starting their own club. They're full to the brim with energy and enthusiasm—they want to be entrepreneurs, pioneers, leaders, captains, or presidents.

If you're interested in starting your own club, congratulations to you on your creativity and initiative. But before you get too attached to the idea, check your college's club list to see if someone already had that bright idea for a board-game club, ultimate Frisbee team, or *Glee* discussion group. Most of the time, someone has. And, consider some of the benefits of joining an *established* club:

- The hassle of getting the club approved and registered has already been take care of by somebody else.

- You'll become part of a group—a group of people with whom you have at least one thing in common.

- The club may already have a presence and reputation on campus; when you join, you'll be able to build on that social capital.

- You can work your way up to a leadership position, learning good stuff along the way, so that you'll be ready when the time comes.

But if the club you want doesn't exist, and there's no other club even remotely similar, and you're ready for the energy- and time-consuming task of promoting your idea, getting other people to buy in, and working with the administration to get things off the ground, *and* you think your college just has to have such a club … go for it!

Frances Northcutt

JOIN DIFFERENT CLUBS FROM THE ONES that your roommate or friends are in. It's good to branch out of your comfort zone and connect with a variety of people.

—E.S.
DUKE UNIVERSITY, GRADUATE

EVERYONE HAS TO FIND SOMETHING: it can be just watching a movie on a Tuesday night, hanging out in the hall with friends at 2 a.m., a weekly yoga class, or just reading a book for fun. But you need something outside of schoolwork and the party scene or else you just run out of steam before each semester ends.

—SAMANTHA STACH
DUKE UNIVERSITY, JUNIOR

Enjoy any good weather you get. Study outdoors, play some Wiffle ball, anything to keep you busy.

—ARIEL MELENDEZ
PRINCETON UNIVERSITY FRESHMAN

IT BEATS STUDYING

While you're cramming in the library, here's how some other freshmen around the country are spending their time:

- Race track—Washington State University
- Toy design department—Otis College (California)
- Professional golf courses—Purdue University (Indiana), Augusta State University (Georgia), Kent State University (Ohio)
- Massage therapy room—Baker College (Michigan)
- International gaming institute—University of Nevada-Las Vegas
- Cross-country ski trails—SUNY Oswego
- Dance studio—University of Tampa (Florida)
- Rodeo arena—Oklahoma Panhandle State University

RAH! RAH! SCHOOL SPIRIT AND TRADITIONS

Now that you're settled into college, show the pride you have in your school. The first one's easy…wear a T-shirt from your school's bookstore - and pick one up for your kid brother, too! More importantly, you definitely do *not* want to be the person at your school wearing some other school's stuff, even if it is laundry day. Burn that other school's shirt, or better yet, donate it to a needy charity near campus. Here are some other ways to show your colors:

- **Go to sporting events on campus:** If you like sports, this is an easy one. If you don't, at least try to have fun at some of these events.

- **Participate in all of your campus's traditions and ritual events:** Every university has unique traditions that build a sense of pride and community amongst students, staff and faculty. The rituals or ceremonies (i.e. Orientation, Convocation and Graduation) are critical milestones in your college experience and some of your favorite college stories, friendships and memories. If everyone on your campus rubs the belly of your mascot's statue before finals week for good luck, then go with a group of friends to do the same. If there's a "spontaneous" stress-relieving run midway through the term, make sure you've got your running shoes handy. These traditions link you to all of the alumni of your institution, and to future students as well.

- **Take pride in the achievements of your university, and of other students, staff and faculty:** Any award or recognition someone from your campus gets is great, and will boost the value of your degree.

- **Wear facepaint and temporary tattoos:** These are inexpensive and temporary ways to show off your spirit.

Scott C. Silverman

COOLER THAN FACEBOOK: FACE <u>PAINT</u>!

Channel your inner child. You may not have worn facepaint since your 5th grade Halloween party, but this is college, so it's ok! You'll definitely see facepaint at sporting events, and maybe also at some other campus events, or ceremonies. If you want to look like a first year, feel free to go without facepaint. But if you want to look like you know what you're doing, then go big or go home. Paint your face with any of the designs described here, or any of your own creations, then add a school jersey or T-shirt.

Facepaint isn't about artistry... If you paint your face, it's because you have immense school pride, you like sports and cheering on your team, or you do it for fun.

Here are a few starter designs:

- Classics: Paint the jersey number of one of the athletes - or a football or basketball - on your face. The simple stripe under each eye works too.
- 50-50. Divide your face down the nose with each color, or do a yin-yang, or top-and-bottom, etc.
- Mascot-themed facepaint.
- Movie characters. If your school color is green, go as The Hulk; if it's blue go as a Smurf (though admittedly that's less intimidating).

Be creative! Once you know the basic designs, get creative. Use your fingertips, Q-tips or cosmetic wedges - and paintbrushes for fine detail. The first time you wear facepaint, you may want to put a small amount on one cheek and wait for 20 minutes to see if it irritates your skin (unlikely!). When you wear facepaint, don't scratch your face...you will adjust to the feeling of a painted face.

Now that you're all decked out (and even if you're not!) show your face at a sporting event. Whether your team is in first place or last, going to the games will be a blast.

Scott C. Silverman

SPORTS—I PLAYED A LITTLE BIT OF EVERYTHING in college. I had never played water polo in my life and I played that in intramurals and it was great. I played flag football, softball, volleyball; all that stuff. Sports are a great release. I played competitive sports in high school but I wasn't good enough to play on the college level, so it was a good way for a frustrated athlete to get out there and keep alive and be active. Intramurals were a way to be competitive, but it wasn't so competitive that you had to deal with the pressures.

> —JOHN BENTLEY
> TRINITY UNIVERSITY, GRADUATE

• • • • • • • •

IT'S NEVER TOO EARLY TO GET INVOLVED. Don't think, "But I'm just a freshman." If you join as a freshman, you could have enough experience to be president of the club by junior or senior year. That will look great on your résumé. In my freshman year, I got involved with the campus radio station, the campus newspaper, and the campus magazine. Since I was a journalism major, I wanted to get as much experience in the field as possible. My junior year, I became the editor-in-chief of the campus magazine.

> —LAUREN TAYLOR
> UNIVERSITY OF GEORGIA, GRADUATE

• • • • • • • •

WHEN I WAS IN HIGH SCHOOL, I was involved in everything. College is at a high level so you have to narrow it down. My favorite things in high school were theater and singing, so I just concentrated on those two things when I came to college. Pick what you enjoy and put your all into it.

> —DAN AMERMAN
> YALE UNIVERSITY, SOPHOMORE

NEED OTHER IDEAS?

DO STUPID STUFF. One time our R.A. randomly said, "I'm going to the beach to go swimming, you want to go?" It was 2 a.m. in the fall and it was freezing cold. But we said, "OK." So we all went swimming in freezing water at 2 a.m. in the ocean—and I've never felt more alive. You'll never remember staying up and studying for a midterm. What you'll remember is staying up and doing something *instead* of studying.

—*MIKEY LEE*
STANFORD UNIVERSITY, JUNIOR

DO THINGS YOU NEVER THOUGHT you would do. Ride the mechanical bull in that redneck bar, drink too much, and participate in karaoke. Do all these things while you can. Before you know it these behaviors will be frowned upon, so you need to get it out of your system.

—*P.G.*
UNIVERSITY OF GEORGIA, GRADUATE

COLD WEATHER FUN: Take lunch trays and go sledding. Build giant snow sculptures; if you pour water over them, they won't melt until spring.

—*JACKIE*
STATE UNIVERSITY OF NEW YORK AT BINGHAMTON, GRADUATE

AT MY SCHOOL, one of the freshman traditions is to go in this fountain. By the end of my freshman year, I still hadn't gone in that fountain. One night, one of my guy friends and I decided to go. The fountain wasn't turned on, but we sat up at the top of this dry fountain for three or four hours. It was one of the best experiences. We talked about everything—our expectations for college and for life. I think we started to understand what life is really about.

—*KERRY*
GEORGETOWN UNIVERSITY, GRADUATE

TIPS FOR LGBT STUDENTS

All students face a transitional experience as they enter their collegiate careers. Many LGBT (Lesbian, Gay, Bisexual or Transgender) students may experience additional challenges as they develop their own identity and find new friends. Ultimately, it can be (and should be) a liberating experience.

Here are some tips for LGBT students to help in this transition:

- Get to know new people. Do not make the mistake of limiting yourself only to the LGBT community, but also meet new friends who identify with other sexual orientations. College is a chance to expand your group of friends and get to know many new people with different perspectives and values.

- Some students find it helpful to join a Gay Straight Alliance organization on campus. Research your campus alliance online and communicate with the president of the organization. Determine if you feel comfortable with it and if it is aligned with your own personal values and goals.

- Be prepared to address questions that may be asked of you from other students. How open or private you want to be with your sexuality is your decision alone. But if you decide to talk about it, take these opportunities as a way to show an accurate picture of the LGBT community. If you do experience discrimination or harassment, be prepared to approach your resident assistant or hall director, as they are valuable resources and can help you address the inappropriate behaviors you are facing.

- Know that your resident assistants, hall directors, professors, the counseling center, university staff, and friends are there to talk to you, and that they want you to succeed.

Justin Long
Assistant Director for Assignments & Student Relations
University of Southern Mississippi

THE GREATEST THING WAS TAKING MUSIC; the camaraderie in general is great. I'm in a quartet and I'm in the orchestra. The orchestra was great in that you can play lots of different pieces that are new and keep up stuff that you've been doing for a while. In the quartet you get to know people on a very individual level and get to know how they play. You get to hang out with them at different times, so it just makes it that much more special. That was a big highlight of my year.

—IAN MOK
HARVARD UNIVERSITY, SOPHOMORE

Never underestimate the power of a Tuesday night game of cards.

—AMY FORBES
MISSISSIPPI STATE UNIVERSITY GRADUATE

WHEN YOU HAVE FREE TIME, enjoy things that are nonschool-related and healthy: Join a really random club, be in a play, volunteer, run a marathon, become a film noir enthusiast. Your free time can really give you a chance to meet people of similar mind-set and interest, and can also expose you to interests and ideas you can't find in the lecture hall. Also, make sure you watch a little bit of TV now and then, to prevent college "bubble" syndrome.

—AMY
PRINCETON UNIVERSITY, FRESHMAN

" Try new things. I never acted in high school, but I tried out for a play and got one of the lead roles. It's a lot of fun. I'm going to do a lot more of that now. "

—CONOR MCNEIL
EMORY UNIVERSITY, SOPHOMORE

PLANET COLLEGE

IT IS A COLLEGE STUDENT'S RESPONSIBILITY to educate himself or herself on the climate change issue. Saving the environment and taking on global warming isn't for everyone, but if a student feels passionate about the cause it is a worthwhile pursuit, just like any interest.

—*PARISA BASTANI*
UNIVERSITY OF PENNSYLVANIA, SENIOR

• • • • • • • • •

I DO NOT THINK THAT EVERY STUDENT HAS AN OBLIGATION to become actively involved in an environmental organization. University provides every student with many opportunities to become civically engaged. I do think that every student has an obligation to act responsibly towards the environment, from thinking about how many pages they print to how often they turn off the lights before exiting a room. Simple steps like this can create an environmentally conscious person.

—*JOSH*
PRINCETON UNIVERSITY, SENIOR

• • • • • • • • •

I'M EXTREMELY CONCERNED with Americans' sense of sustainability. I fear that older generations have completely failed us by creating a society where a $10 gallon of gas will crush the economy. Living in Atlanta is a study on how not to plan a city with the future in mind. Americans need to reevaluate their desires to ensure that our society remains sustainable. Hopefully my college education will not only enable me to live a sustainable lifestyle, but also allow me to influence others to do the same.

—*ALEX*
EMORY UNIVERSITY, SOPHOMORE

• • • • • • • • •

MY SCHOOL IS VERY ENVIRONMENTALLY CONSCIOUS, with recycling bins everywhere and an emphasis on recycled goods. Take shorter showers, don't use styrofoam if at all possible, and be aware that your actions almost always affect the environment.

—*JACOB*
UNIVERSITY OF MARYLAND, SOPHOMORE

I WAS PART OF MY SCHOOL'S Sustainable Food Initiative, which was building an urban garden. During my second semester at school, I spent a lot of time hauling rocks out of dirt. Those less masochistically inclined will probably find that there are lots of easier ways to become involved in environmental issues on campus.

—MOLLY
BROWN UNIVERSITY, SOPHOMORE

BECAUSE OF A VARSITY SPORT AND A MUSIC GROUP, I personally have not had the time to commit to any environmental organizations. That being said, I have found I can still make a substantial difference just in my own dorm. A lot of kids on campus will leave windows cracked in the winter, leave lights on, and throw away recyclables. These things take very little effort to do but make a huge difference when hundreds of students are doing them together. You don't have to join an environmental group to avoid being wasteful.

—ANDREW ALCORTA
HARVARD UNIVERSITY, FRESHMAN

THERE ARE TONS OF WAYS TO LEND SUPPORT. One group here sponsored a meal where students were encouraged to bring their own bowls and utensils to cut down on wasted water needed to wash dishes. Even if you don't want to become a member of a group, I think it's important to listen to and cooperate with the environmental groups' programs. They are doing them to make the campus a better, cleaner place. It's so easy to take part in a program and give them the support they need. It's easy to try to change little things, like drink water out of the bubblers instead of bottled water, actually put your cans in the recycling, and turn out the lights in your room. Starting sustainable patterns of living at college will prepare you to continue them for the rest of your life. It's every student's responsibility to put in the effort.

—TOBIAS
HARVARD UNIVERSITY, FRESHMAN

ANIMAL HOUSE?
HAVING A PET IN COLLEGE

A lot of us have grown up having a pet at home. But before you bring a dog, cat, hamster, lizard, goldfish, or another animal to your house or your dorm room, here are some things to consider:

- **If you live at home:** Consult you family first. As a college student you will have many new responsibilities and due to your class schedule you might not be able to take care of your pet all by yourself. As long as everyone's ok with it – and there are no allergies! – then you should be good to go.

- **If you live in the Residence Halls:** Odds are, that your university does NOT allow pets in the Residence Halls. Some residence halls may allow a small fish tank, but remember – even a fish needs daily care and that takes time from your daily schedule. Of course service animals or pets as emotional support are generally ok, but written permission from staff may still be required.

  You should also ask your roommates to make sure they will be ok with you having a pet and that they don't have any allergies. You have to consider that your pet might be noisy and disturb others in the residence hall. You may want to have a back-up plan if something goes wrong and you can't keep your pet due to barking, damage to the room, etc.

- **If you live off-campus:** Always check with your landlord first. He may ask for an extra pet deposit or monthly pet rent to cover potential damage and clean-up-related expenses. Some or all of it may be returned – or this might simply be an extra fee that you won't get back. There also might be breed restrictions that you have to be aware of. And each state has its own laws regarding the number of pets in a household. Finally, you probably want to check with your roommates to make sure there won't be any conflicts.

- **General rules about caring for a pet:** So let's say you can bring an animal into your family/household. You still need to make sure that you have the time and ability to truly take care of your new family member. If you live in an apartment, your dog will most likely have to be walked several times a day. Exercise and having plenty of room to play and run is important for every pet. If you plan to live in a house, it would be great if there was a fenced backyard so that your pet can have access to the outdoors without you having to worry about your pet running on the street and potentially harming itself.

Having a pet is like having another family member in the household, and pets get sick just like humans do. It is important to take the responsibility to take care of your pet as well as you can, even when you have papers or projects due or if it is in the middle of your final exams. Among other things, you should get your pets spayed and neutered, get their yearly vaccinations, and get them checked by a veterinarian on a regular basis to prevent the possibility of major medical diseases. For more information about pet care, visit the following websites:

> www.peteducation.com
> www.hillspet.com/index.html
> www.healthypet.com
> www.ASPCA.org

Find a great local veterinarian near your home or school, and if you do decide to adopt a pet, get one from a real pet store or animal shelter.

Peyvand Mirzadeh Silverman, DVM

IT'S REALLY HARD TO FIND TIME to be alone in college. You're always surrounded by people: your roommates, your friends, your classmates. In high school you have your own room; in college I always shared a room. It's important to find time to be alone so that you can reflect on everything you're going through. Go on walks, and write in a journal. If you go through your routine every day, the days pass so fast; if you don't think back on your day, it doesn't seem as meaningful. You don't treasure the memories that you make if you don't record them in a journal. In the future you'll be able to look back and see how your freshman year was. Try to find yourself and think about your experiences.

—MEGHAN
UNIVERSITY OF NOTRE DAME, JUNIOR

• • • • • • • •

I WAS INVOLVED WITH THE CRISIS HOTLINE. The most common call we had by far was what we called the loneliness call. It would be a person on a huge campus who felt lonely—a person who doesn't know how to meet people, who's away from home the first time.

My college has more than 250 student organizations—fraternities and sororities, hang-gliding club, bungee-jumping club, weight-lifting club, all kinds of ethnic organizations, every religious group. There has to be a group out there that has your interest.

—MICHAEL A. FEKULA
UNIVERSITY OF MARYLAND, GRADUATE

It's very important to do something physical. That's how I release all my stress.

—B.M.
UNIVERSITY OF
MARYLAND, JUNIOR

IT'S VERY EASY TO OVER-COMMIT to a lot of extra-curriculars because they're all really wonderful and you want to try everything. I thought I wasn't over-committing since everything I was doing was arts related – dance and music and theater – but I had no idea what huge time commitments those three things would all be. Things take up much more time than they do in high school!

—*HALEY*
HARVARD UNIVERSITY, SENIOR

THE BEST CLUBS to join are the ones that incorporate your major. Many offer scholarships, field trips, invite guest speakers, and can give you a bit of background on what you need to do to succeed. They also provide community service, which is a great experience for anyone. Many of these clubs also connect you with professionals whom you can shadow and get internships with.

—*WHITNEY*
VALDOSTA STATE UNIVERSITY, JUNIOR

JOIN A GROUP! That's the way I made my best friends in college. I like to sing, a lot. And I knew that I wanted to join an *a cappella* group while I was in college. So I learned about the groups and the auditions and within two weeks of being on campus, I had a new *a capella* family!

—*ELIZABETH*
UNIVERSITY OF ILLINOIS AT URBANA-CHAMPAIGN, GRADUATE

GET INVOLVED WITH CLUBS, or sports teams… join a sorority if that's what you're into… Joining the soccer team really made me feel like a part of the college. You have a group of people you get to know quickly and you feel like a part of the campus, which is awesome.

—*TAYLOR WHITNEY PETTIS*
BLOOMSBURG UNIVERSITY, JUNIOR

• • • • • • • •

HAVE FUN DOING ANYTHING, and just smile and laugh at least once a day. You've got to find ways to have fun and relax every day, or else you'll go nuts. You can tell the kids that don't: they just suck at life and are no fun to be around.

—*ANONYMOUS*
UNITED STATES MILITARY ACADEMY AT WEST POINT, JUNIOR

Technology: Facebook, Twitter, and the Online College Experience

As the students in this chapter will tell you, social networking sites like Facebook are great—in moderation. They're powerful tools for fun and making positive connections, especially if they lead to real-world interaction and don't replace it entirely. (You'll know you've gone too far if you forget what to do when you meet that cute sophomore in the bookstore line, or if "dinner with friends" starts to mean carrying takeout food to your computer desk.) After all, a tool is only as good as its user. As Sir Roger L'Estrange said so poetically: "It is with our passions as it is with fire and water; they are good servants, but bad masters." Sure, this was three centuries before the Internet, but Sir Roger really knew his stuff. Read on for some 21st-century wisdom about socializing in the computer age.

MAKE YOUR FACEBOOK PASSWORD difficult to type when drunk. Drunk Facebooking is horrendous and usually leads to stuff you don't want to deal with when you're hung over the next day.

—J.V.
THE COLLEGE OF WILLIAM & MARY, GRADUATE

Use your privacy settings.

—MICHAEL
NORTHWESTERN
UNIVERSITY
SOPHOMORE

HEADLINES
Best Advice and Top Tips

- Facebook can be a great way to begin to meet people, but follow up soon with person-to-person encounters.
- Don't post information about yourself that could be viewed negatively, even though you have some control over who will see your photos and details.
- It's easy to misjudge people when all you have to go by are their Facebook profiles.

Try to have a variety of pictures rather than one where you look exactly the same in 300 different poses.

—RON Y. KAGAN
CUNY/MACAULAY
HONORS COLLEGE
SENIOR

COMPARED TO MY FRIENDS, I am not a Facebook addict. Some people are on it 24/7. I use it to keep in touch with old friends. I also notice that you get a lot of random Facebook invitations from random people. I don't recommend sending random invitations to people unless you're willing to get to know them.

—MORGAN
COLUMBIA UNIVERSITY, FRESHMAN

• • • • • • • •

ON TWITTER, I always try to remember the point of a hashtag: they can either be ironic or useful. Nothing in between. For example, you can label your tweet with a hashtagged name of a movie you just saw, frat you just went to, or sports team you're following. But don't hashtag too much (#girl #cute #hair #party), and please, please, please don't hashtag long sentences. No one has the time or energy to read all of that.

—SOPHIE STONE
FRANKLIN AND MARSHALL COLLEGE, JUNIOR

AVOID PUTTING UP ANY PICTURES that you would not want your grandmother to see. Freshmen should do their best to untag pictures that portray possibly incriminating activities, such as underage drinking. You never know who can look at your profile.

—*KAMALI BENT*
CORNELL UNIVERSITY, GRADUATE

" Putting your telephone number, your address, your relationship status, pics of yourself with cups in your hand (or 150 pictures of yourself, in general) is way too much information to put on Facebook. Your friends know where they can find you. "

—*DANIELLE*
DUKE UNIVERSITY, GRADUATE

FACEBOOK HAS BECOME a vital tool in college life. Most of the information about important events is listed through Facebook. Popular groups, career services, student clubs, student government, and now even the college administrators use Facebook to distribute information.

—*ALEKSANDR AKULOV*
HUNTER COLLEGE, SOPHOMORE

SOCIAL NETWORKING 101

Your digital identity is something you need to work hard to protect. I'm not talking about your passwords and logins...even though those are important, too. But what's really important is how you portray yourself. The image you post online – and I don't only mean your photo - will influence people's perceptions of you.

- Keep your contact information and profile (including pics) up to date. That's the basic reason online social networking is so popular, as a constantly up-to-date address book.
- Be smart about what personal or contact information you share, and with whom.
- Adjust your privacy settings so that you are confident about what content you're showing to various people. Create friends' lists, and you can more easily adapt privacy settings by category. It's also a useful way to distinguish between close friends, acquaintances, family, university staff and random people.
- Interact with staff and faculty online. You may find that you have common or similar interests or tastes in music and movies. Maybe you play Farmville on Facebook with family members. Maybe you write a note, and friends from multiple spheres of your life (college, back home, family and university staff) might read and reply to it.
- You might be worried that university staff monitor everything you post. They don't. No university has the time or money to monitor all of their students' online profiles. That being said, if content on your profile came to the attention of someone working in Student Conduct, they would be duty-bound to follow up on it.
- Think before you post. Would you feel comfortable if your grandparents or parents saw that particular picture, comment, or other content on a billboard, or the front page of the newspaper? If not, you may not want to post it.

- Remember that anything you ever post on Facebook, regardless of your settings, could eventually get out. A "friend" who can view that picture of you doing illegal things can save it, send it to friends, or print it out. And you no longer have control over it.
- Make sure you understand the Terms of Use and User Agreements. Did you know that anything you post on Facebook is co-owned by them, until it is removed from Facebook ... so if you have a great invention, don't write about it on Facebook!
- Keep your passwords secure, change them from time to time, and don't use the same password for your Facebook and other social media as you do for online banking and email. Social media sites are equally susceptible to hacking, if not more so... and you don't want a Twitter hacker to be able to tap your bank account dry.

Scott C. Silverman

TOP FIVE THINGS *NOT* TO SHOWCASE IN YOUR PROFILE

1. Drugs

2. Alcohol, even if you're 21

3. Destroying or "improving" university property

4. Anything naked, sexual, or both

5. Yourself with half your face in light and the other half in darkness—it's not illegal or against school rules, but you'll look just like the other 10 million people doing the same dumb thing.

TAG: YOU'RE IT

What is your favorite thing to do on Facebook? If you're like many people, it's probably looking at your friends' pictures. You can see what they're doing, what parties they attended, who they're dating, etc. And they can see exactly what you're doing, too.

This doesn't present a problem if all your pictures show you at your finest. But what happens when you're caught on camera doing something … well, *embarrassing* or even *illegal*? Your friends (and possibly your parents) will probably see it, and you'll be *embarrassed*.

Further, friends of friends will also see it – possibly hundreds of people you don't know. Even worse, the picture (depending on what you're doing in it) might in the future make its way to the computer screen of an HR person at a company where you are applying for a post-college job.

You know all this. We're not trying to be your parents. But we do have some advice if you wake up one morning, log on to Facebook, and see a version of yourself that you'd like to delete forever.

1. First of all, look at your privacy settings. There's a special section that allows you to pick who can see photos that have you tagged in them. If you're a private person, choose the option that says "Only me" – or customize your privacy options to allow only certain people to see tagged pictures of you. Depending on the latest Facebook features, this might give you more, or even complete, control over the picture in question.

2. Another option is to untag yourself from the picture, so that you are no longer identified – unless your friends happen upon the picture, retag you, or just tell everyone you're in it.

3. Politely ask the person who posted the picture to remove it from Facebook and the Internet. They might get miffed and say you're being uptight – or they might tell you that you shouldn't have done the embarrassing thing on camera if you didn't want others to see it. They might have a point. You can tell them that they're absolutely right on all counts, and to *pretty please* take down the picture. If they still don't, you might want to consider what kind of "friend" they are. If the picture is really embarrassing/damaging to your reputation, know you have the right to hound them until the matter is resolved.

Most of all (and here's where we sound like your parents again): Be as vigilant as possible about controlling what pictures you end up in. Before the camera flashes, ask yourself if your mom – or your future self who's applying for that job – would want to see you in this situation.

Granted, college is at least partly about doing slightly embarrassing things and letting loose every once in a while. But pictures are worth a thousand words – and when they make it on the Internet, they have a way of *not* disappearing.

Elizabeth Lovett
Angie Mock
Robert Rhu

THE IDEA THAT A RELATIONSHIP is "official" when it's listed on Facebook is totally ridiculous. It's led to a fight with my last girlfriend and a confrontation with the friends of a girl before that. It's totally ridiculous but its part of college life; it's unavoidable. My friend who is just starting college couldn't find his new roommate on Facebook and now is worried that the guy's a social recluse, just because he's not on a website.

—ANONYMOUS
WASHINGTON AND LEE UNIVERSITY, JUNIOR

• • • • • • • •

"It's good to avoid half-naked pictures and full body shots. Generally, a nice close-up of your beautiful face is best!"

—STEPHANIE LEIGH DOCKERY
WILLIAMS COLLEGE, GRADUATE

• • • • • • • •

SOMETIMES YOU MEET A PERSON, talk with him online, and become good friends; then you meet in person and you wished you'd kept it online. The awkwardness factor is pretty big when you meet people through sites like Facebook. I don't usually interact with people online unless they had some other real-world connection to me already.

—TERRY
DUKE UNIVERSITY, SOPHOMORE

FACEBOOK 101

Being able to "friend" people on Facebook and learn a little bit about them gave me more confidence to approach them in person and hang out. I'd encourage incoming freshmen to not be afraid to friend (but not stalk) other incoming freshmen, if they can find even one thing in common with them—for instance, the same residential college, or the same prospective major. The worst that can happen is that the friend request will be denied. In that case, they can always try again once they meet that person face-to-face.

—EMILIA
RICE UNIVERSITY, JUNIOR

I USE MY SMARTPHONE basically like a computer. I check my email every chance I get, and I can look at assignments, check grades and important school emails. That way, I can act fast.

—AMANDA
UNIVERSITY OF MIAMI, JUNIOR

* * * * * * * *

WHENEVER SOMEONE TAGS ME in a picture or posts something on my wall, I ask myself, "Is it okay for my mom to see this?" I know a lot of people do not really use that rationale for Facebook. But it is definitely going to wake people up when they are trying to apply for jobs. I know for a fact that employers do look on Facebook to find out what their potential employees are up to.

—G.I.
GEORGE WASHINGTON UNIVERSITY, SENIOR

* * * * * * * *

ON TWITTER YOU CAN FOLLOW your school's sports teams and newspapers as a way to stay connected to what's going on.

—TAYLOR WHITNEY PETTIS
BLOOMSBURG UNIVERSITY, JUNIOR

STATUS UPDATES

Facebook status updates can be funny, cute, sexy, and a great way to strike up a dialogue among your friends. They can also be annoying, offensive, boring, and a great way to drive your friends insane, one keystroke at a time. What's most important to remember is that every time your friends log in, your status update is right in front of them. It's in front of your best friend from home, the guy you met at a party last week, and your mom's best friend who (irritatingly) joined and friended you immediately. When brainstorming your next update, remember the following things:

Be a Fickle Self-Editor: Picture the scene: You and some friends from your dorm show up at a senior party. You're excited to be there, but also a teensy bit intimidated by all the upperclassmen who seem so hip and self-assured. One of the friends accompanying you walks right in and announces loudly, "I have the worst sinus infection ever." Can you imagine anything more mortifying (and gross)? Status updates deserve equal consideration and reservation. Gross status updates make you look gross. Boring status updates make you look boring. There are no exceptions. No one on earth cares that you are waiting in line at the bookstore, or that you just blew your nose, or what you had for breakfast. No one. If you can't think of anything more interesting to write, don't write anything at all.

Use It: Because everyone sees your status updates, they can be a fantastic way to get a message out, show the world a quirky, introspective side to you, or start up a conversation. For example, recently we saw one we loved that read, "Jenny zigged when she should have zagged." It was clever, intriguing and gave Jenny an air of mystery. Everyone who read it had to wonder what she meant, and many asked her.

Another great way to use a status update is to get a message out. Asking a question ("Anyone have a suggestion for a good beach read?") or making a recommendation ("Loved the new Batman movie. Get out and see it today!") can be a great way to show your friends what you're up to and start a dialogue.

Updating Under the Influence: Just as using your cell phone or emailing after partying are bad ideas, so is Facebooking. We all tend to think we're hilariously funny after a drink or two. But we're not as witty or clever as we think. When you wake up the next morning and all your 472 friends have seen your (witty) status update (and whatever else you've written on your friends' walls, etc.), your pride will be hurting as much as your head.

Update in Moderation: Like everything else in this world, the trick with status updates is moderation. Update your status too often and you look like you have nothing better to do. As a freshman in college, we know that you have *lots* of better things to do, from bonding with new friends, to cramming for a midterm, to getting a load of laundry done.

Elizabeth Lovett
Angie Mock
Robert Rhu

I WOULD TELL FRESHMEN to think about where they want to be ten years from now and try to evaluate what you put up on your Facebook profile based on that. If you are trying to go into law or politics, and you have a scandalous picture up, someone could copy it, paste it, and save it for later.

—*J.M.G.*
DUKE UNIVERSITY, GRADUATE

. . . .

" Facebook has become as much a part of the college experience as beer and books. Heck, people probably spend more time with Facebook than they do with the other two combined. "

—*ANONYMOUS*
WASHINGTON AND LEE UNIVERSITY, JUNIOR

. . . .

THE APP THAT LETS YOU ACCESS BLACKBOARD on your phone is pretty useful; your professor can post the readings as a PDF and you can access them on Blackboard. And you can email the other kids in your class if you need help with anything. It works pretty well.

—*NINA*
TEMPLE UNIVERSITY, JUNIOR

WHEN I FIRST GOT INTO COLLEGE and found out who my roommate was, I looked him up on Facebook. All of his pictures were sketchy; I didn't know what his deal was. He was always wearing some sort of flower crown and frolicking with girls. I thought, "This will make for an interesting year."
I definitely judged him, which probably wasn't the best thing to do, because he ended up being nothing like his Facebook pictures. He's now one of my best friends. I wouldn't judge anybody by their Facebook pictures, because a lot of people don't put enough thought into them to give a good first impression.

—DAN AMERMAN
YALE UNIVERSITY, SOPHOMORE

WITH HIGH SCHOOL FRIENDS, Facebook is useful because you can write on their walls from time to time. But soon, a silent understanding develops that you have new lives and new interests, and it's not personal if your high school crew doesn't call you all the time. When you all go home for Christmas or summer, it'll probably be like nothing ever changed, so focus on developing your new friendships in college.

—MICHELLE Y. LEE
EMORY UNIVERSITY, SENIOR

THE BEST PART OF FACEBOOK is how it allows you to stay in touch with friends from other schools. They can see what you're doing and vice versa. The one bad thing about Facebook is that you become more accountable for the one-night stand from the night before. You're going to hear about it the next day.

—ILAN GLUCK
UNIVERSITY OF MARYLAND, JUNIOR

IN THE SUMMER LEADING UP TO COLLEGE, I received what felt like hundreds of Facebook friend requests from students who were about to go to Penn State as well. But currently, I'm not friends with any of the people who friended me before I was at school. Though FB is a great way to talk with your roommate about what things to bring before move in day, I would not recommend looking for hundreds of friends before you set foot on campus.

—*ANDREW OSTROWSKY*
PENNSYLVANIA STATE UNIVERSITY, JUNIOR

A LOT OF MY COLLEGE FRIENDS DEACTIVATED their social networks during midterms and finals week because it was too distracting. For myself, I'll work on a paper, take a quiz, or read, and all the while I'll go back and forth between Facebook and Twitter. Download the app, "Self Control". It helps you block certain websites, in order to help you avoid getting distracted when doing schoolwork.

—*CHARLINDA HAUDLEY*
UNIVERSITY OF ARIZONA, SENIOR

I WAS EXTREMELY ACTIVE in social networking before college. Joining groups of incoming freshman was invaluable; I met my floor mates and roommates, and it made the initial meet and greet completely seamless. Once you know the university you are attending, there are tons of Facebook groups that coincide with your interests. It's a great way to get started in meeting people and joining clubs.

—*MICHAEL CUMMO*
BOSTON UNIVERSITY, SENIOR

USE STORAGE WEBSITES FOR YOUR FILES! There's nothing like the panic of your first midterms when your laptop dies, your friends are using all of theirs, and you can't get to any of the papers you may or may not have started. Not only that, but you have to find a way to figure out what the assignment was to begin with. Storage websites - Mediafire, Dropbox, etc. - help you access everything you've already done from any computer. Even the one you're using as a personal desktop/tissue holder in the public computer lab where everyone can see you panic. This way, you can relax. It's all there at your fingertips.

—*KATHARINE*
BRYN MAWR COLLEGE, GRADUATE

INSTAGRAM IS MY FAVORITE social site because it acknowledges its pretentiousness and tackiness and then embraces it. Everyone knows that an Insta'd photo makes your eyes gleam, your skin glow, and your imperfections fade away; basically, you could not be more fake. But who cares? Just use this sparingly, and don't link it to your Facebook or Twitter. Your friends/followers didn't sign up to follow your Insta... they don't want to see every sunset, selfie, or cat pic that you post.

—*SOPHIE STONE*
FRANKLIN AND MARSHALL COLLEGE, JUNIOR

IF YOU REALLY WANT TO BE TECH-SAVVY, invest in programs and technology platforms - i.e. if you want to be in finance, learn Bloomberg and FactSet - as opposed to spending time tweeting at your friends across the room.

—*D.D.*
SYRACUSE UNIVERSITY, GRADUATE

FRESHMEN GO CRAZY with their picture uploading on Facebook. But that's understandable! We all do it. Everyone is eager to show off all the fun they're having at their new school with all their new friends and their new going-out clothes. But one too many pictures of you tagged with a Natty Light in hand is not only a bad idea as far as the legality of things; it is also just tacky. Tuck your red cup out of the frame and stay away from people who want to take pictures of you chugging from handles. Instead you can save these pictures on your computer in a separate folder (I'd call my album "#sloppy") and then you can enjoy them privately with your friends.

—SOPHIE STONE
FRANKLIN AND MARSHALL COLLEGE, JUNIOR

• • • • • • • •

I DON'T HAVE A SMARTPHONE so I never really had a problem with that in class. But in the library with my computer, it's so hard to focus for a long time without checking Facebook. I ended up deleting Facebook for a while, and then there was nothing distracting me from working!

—MATTHEW GUTSHALL
ST. JOSEPH'S, JUNIOR

• • • • • • • •

I THINK FACEBOOK and the ability to stream TV on my laptop were the two biggest procrastination tools I had in college. They were the two things that most kept me from getting work done when I actually sat down to do it. I think I watched more TV freshman year than I ever had before; it was the first time I had a laptop so it was the first time I could watch episode, after episode, after episode... Be careful how much time you spend doing that!

—NINA STOLLER-LINDSEY
HARVARD COLLEGE, GRADUATE

WHAT TECHNOLOGY IS GOOD FOR

USE ANY TECH YOU CAN to keep pursuing the things you love. Take advantage of computers in art studios to do graphic design and have some peace and quiet from your fellow freshman on your hall. Use your smartphone, if you have one or have access to one, to jot down stanzas of poetry that will inevitably come to you when you're walking across the quad to get to the cafe. Bookmark every single biology article in the New York Times on the app you have and read them when you get a break from classes and clubs. Take any moment you can to ground yourself in what you're sure of.

Use tech to keep in touch with old friends that you love. If you have people from your high school life that make you happy and keep you calm and safe and loved, use Facebook to keep in touch. Or Twitter, or Tumblr, or the "heyTell" app on your smartphone to send stupid, 10-second voice messages to people who still know you best, even if you're in the process of making new lifelong friends at school.

> —KATHARINE
> BRYN MAWR COLLEGE, GRADUATE

BE CAREFUL WITH FACEBOOK STALKING. In college, there is always something to be doing: another party, another club meeting, another rehearsal. Facebook stalking can become a toxic habit which feeds jealousy and distracts you from your own needs and schedule. Seize the day and enjoy your life, but avoid feeling left out or like you're falling behind. Most likely, you are just fine and on the same page as everyone else. The grass is always greener, so minimize Facebook stalking.

> —SARAH
> VANDERBILT UNIVERSITY, GRADUATE

FACEBOOK: PRO AND CON

I UNDERSTAND THE APPEAL of flipping through glamour shots of friends and acquaintances, creeping on crushes and ex-boyfriends, and catching up on the latest from That Girl with the Constant Pregnancy Updates from high school. All I can say is that when you really stop to think about it, every minute spent on Facebook is a minute wasted. It is so easy to get sucked into the mindless pleasure of other people's (carefully edited) lives, but you only get so much time to spend in college, and trust me, you'll wish you could get it all back when it's over. Using that time to compare yourself to others - consciously or not, that's really what you're doing - is something you'll regret; spending time living in the real world is not. Facebook is a great way to tell people about the textbook you're selling, or to ask about which Philosophy teacher to take, or to advertise your charity flip cup tournament. But I'd really encourage you to ask yourself, every time you log on, what you're really gaining.

—CAITLIN
GEORGETOWN UNIVERSITY, GRADUATE

. . . .

USE FACEBOOK! I certainly did. For one, you can link with people in your classes really easily. If you're Facebook friends with people in your classes, then when you have questions and problems it is really easy to get in contact with them. However, as we all know, college lends itself very easily to "pictures with beer" and "beer bongs" and things like that. Just be careful. It's time to start thinking about privacy settings (if you haven't already!). I'm sure your mom has already told you this, but the summer internship or campus job you want to get will not want you if there are pictures of you getting super-drunk and high and whatnot every weekend. Once the necessary precautions are taken, I say, "Utilize social media." That's what it's there for! It certainly enhanced many aspects of my college experience.

—ELIZABETH
UNIVERSITY OF ILLINOIS AT URBANA-CHAMPAIGN, GRADUATE

LEARNING HOW TO DO LABELS AND SORTING in your inbox is one of the most important things because everything is so email-centric. You get so many more emails than you ever got in high school. Having a system to sort through all the craziness makes it easier to find the things you want. Definitely get a GMail account because it's easier to organize. I try to keep my inbox pretty empty so that I don't miss things. I filter out email lists for any clubs or organizations right into a folder and then I can read it when I have time. Like if I'm interested in the free food list, I can read that when I want, but then my inbox is just people emailing me directly, personally, like friends and professors.

—*CATIE*
HARVARD COLLEGE, SENIOR

· · · · · · · ·

A LOT OF SCHOOLS OFFER FACEBOOK GROUPS where you can see everyone in your grade and post on the wall. You can ask questions; a lot of people ask questions about different professors, and whether they should take certain classes. That's how I found my roommate, I could see different people who needed roommates and what they liked to do.

—*TAYLOR WHITNEY PETTIS*
BLOOMSBURG UNIVERSITY, JUNIOR

· · · · · · · ·

THERE WAS ONE PERSON WHO FRIENDED literally everyone in our class on Facebook before getting to school. Now I'm actually kind of friends with him and see him around a lot, and still every time I see him I think of him as the guy who friended everybody. I wouldn't recommend doing that because people will remember it forever.

—*HALEY*
HARVARD UNIVERSITY, SENIOR

Inevitably you're going to misplace a power adapter - in class, at home, or at the coffee shop – which will quickly render your nice new laptop completely useless. Keep a spare one at your residence, plugged in.

Consider

THERE'S AN APP FOR THAT: STAYING ON TRACK

With all the activities available on campus, you may find it challenging to balance your personal and academic life while in college. To help manage your workload, consider going beyond standard "to-do lists", Post-Its, or reminder alerts on your phone. Here are a few apps that can help you keep important tasks in focus:

- Pocket Schedule – You can enter your course schedules and requirements into this application, and you can color-code courses, which helps when multiple assignments are due within a couple of days of each other. You have the option to separate assignment descriptions and titles from other tasks.
- Evernote - If you remember images more readily than lists, this task master enables you to add images to your notes. Images may be saved on your phone or tablet, or taken while using the application. You also can record voice messages.
- Remember the Milk (RTM) - This app will send you text or instant message reminders. It's also accessible from a desktop computer, and can sync with other calendars and social media feeds.
- Awesome Note - Consider the value of looking at a month's worth of activities on a calendar. You can color code activity types, and place activities into "folders." The travel folder, which logs daily activities for travelers, may appeal if you study abroad.
- ClassTrack – This app helps you keep track of pending assignments and upcoming exams, as well as completed credits towards graduation, and your GPA. You also can store grades on individual assignments.

Tatum Soo Kim
Director of Academic Services
New York University-SCPS
Division of Programs in Business

WOULD YOU LIKE RICE WITH THAT?

Best remedy for a liquid spill on your computer? A bag of uncooked rice. Not instant rice; inexpensive, uncooked plain white rice. Should a spill occur, immediately cut power to the computer and remove the battery. If the battery can't be removed, shut the computer down. Put the device in a sealed container (typically a trash bag) with that uncooked bag of rice and wait 48 hours before trying to turn it on. The device may be okay after that. (Suggestion: you probably want to throw away the rice rather than using it for your next meal.)

I VIDEO CHAT with someone almost every day - either one of my friends, family, or my long-distance boyfriend. It makes the distance between you and your loved ones seem much shorter. Which, in turn, can almost make me homesick. Whenever I talk to my friends and family, it's always hard to say goodbye, to go back to my life in a new place. But I just have to remember I'll see them soon. I just have to remember all the great things I have with me in college and that semesters aren't very long. (Also, when you go home, you'll very quickly realize you miss college and want to go back.)

—EVA DINES
UNIVERSITY OF MIAMI, JUNIOR

• • • • • • • •

IT'S EASY TO GO ON FACEBOOK and start looking at pictures and writing on walls. I just make it a policy not to do it while involved with academic work.

—JOSH
PRINCETON UNIVERSITY, SENIOR

LOTS OF IPHONES have been getting stolen recently. You have to be careful about walking around by yourself talking on the phone. If you have electronics, don't be too showy with them, especially if you go to an urban school.

—*NINA*
TEMPLE UNIVERSITY, JUNIOR

• • • • • • • •

FOR SOME REASON, it is so much more socially acceptable to tweet 10 times a day than it is to regularly update your Facebook status... so I take advantage of this and tweet about just about anything. Funny thoughts that cross my mind, observations about my friends / my school / society as a whole - anything is fair game. But don't use it as a Facebook wall - tweets back and forth between friends just clog people's Twitter feeds. Also, stay away from the mundane; although the occasional picture of your lunch is fun - if it is extra expensive, arranged in some crazy way, or breathtakingly large, for example. No one really wants to track your meals with you.

—*SOPHIE STONE*
FRANKLIN AND MARSHALL COLLEGE, JUNIOR

Money for Your Life: Working & Finances

No matter what else you learn this year, you'll learn that nothing is free. Wait, sorry, that's not true – we're about to tell you how to score free food at extracurricular events. However, there's a reason college students have figured out where to find freebies – because school is expensive! In this chapter, you'll see how other students managed to keep their costs down and even get some money coming in. Read on to find out why working (especially on campus) isn't so bad. We also offer some advice on how to control the money you earn so you can afford to pay for a good meal now and again, and maybe even save a little cash.

TOSS EVERY CREDIT CARD OFFER. Don't entertain the thought of new shoes, or that surround sound system. You don't need it right now; that's what Christmas and birthdays are for!

—AMANDA
UNIVERSITY OF COLORADO AT COLORADO SPRINGS, SOPHOMORE

I HAVE A CHECKBOOK AND I RECORD WHAT I SPEND.

—JESSICA
BARNARD COLLEGE
JUNIOR

HEADLINES
Best Advice and Top Tips

- Beware of credit card offers. But if you decide to get one, make sure you pay off the balance each month.
- A part-time job on or near campus is a good way to earn spending money, and to meet new people.
- There are easy budgeting programs for your computer – or just keep track of your expenses on paper. Whatever works best for you.
- Use your meal plan to its fullest potential – otherwise, it's wasted money.

DON'T THINK THAT WHEN YOU GO to the ATM machine and do a "current balance" check, the figure it spits out is really your current balance. I thought it was. I amassed probably $500 in bounced check fees my first semester. No one ever taught me how to balance a checkbook. Get your parents to teach you that before you go, and then make sure you do it when you're at school.

—K.E.R.
FLORIDA STATE UNIVERSITY, GRADUATE

• • • • • • • •

I HAVE AN ON-CAMPUS JOB in the women's studies department and in the dance department. Also, they have a bartending agency here and you get paid $20 an hour. I took the course so I can do that when I want to. I don't think all colleges have a bartending course, but usually there's a babysitting agency. Working on campus doesn't pay as much, but it's so much easier. There's nothing to do; I get paid for doing my homework.

—LAUREN WEBSTER
BARNARD COLLEGE, JUNIOR

TAKE AS LITTLE FINANCIAL ASSISTANCE as possible; debts stink. Work hard and try to pay as much up front as you can. I worked in the summers and at night leading up to college, and that helped pay bills during my first year of school.

—MICHAEL ALBERT PAOLI
UNIVERSITY OF TORONTO, GRADUATE

I THINK IT'S GOOD TO WORK A FEW HOURS a week at least, and that can be your weekend spending money. I worked at a restaurant and I used my tips as my spending money. It's also a good way to meet people in your school's town, so you get away from college, so you can vent, so you can be well rounded.

—MEGHAN
UNIVERSITY OF NOTRE DAME, JUNIOR

I REFEREED FOR INTRAMURALS. I was lucky, because my parents helped me out quite a bit. But even if you do get help or are on scholarship, I would recommend getting a job at some point. I know some people who work at the library, and they just sit there and study while getting paid for it. On the other hand, I knew people who did research for work in college, and that was like adding another three- or six-hour class; that was tough.

—JOHN BENTLEY
TRINITY UNIVERSITY, GRADUATE

FRESHMAN FACTOID

How students cover the cost of college:

- Financial aid and scholarships (37%)

- Pay for it themselves (9%)

- Parents pay (13%)

- Some combination of the above (41%)

STARTING IN THE HOLE

The average college undergrad carries $3,173 in credit card debt, and the average senior will graduate with $4,100 in credit card debt.

ON FINDING A JOB . . .

1. **Find a sweet on-campus job:** Campus employers are generally flexible and will let you work around your class schedule. The pay is often better than minimum wage, you can take extra time off during Finals week, and when you work on campus you're more plugged in to what's going on around campus. Some jobs might allow you to make money while staffing one of the athletic games, or help plan a major campus event.

2. **Work for a professor:** You can help a professor read and grade assignments, papers and exams. Some of these jobs are for graduate students, but many departments hire undergraduates to help, too.

3. **Tutor local school children:** What school subjects are you good at? You can tutor some local kids, motivating and helping them to do well in school. This is meaningful work that puts money in your pocket.

4. **Use your campus Career Center:** Go to a workshop and visit their website. They probably have a really easy way to search for any kind of job, whether it's on-campus, in the surrounding community, or for a big-name corporation. They can also help you create/update your résumé and practice your interviewing skills.

You need a résumé! Visit your Career Center's website – or Google – to find tips on how to create a résumé. Prepare a draft, then meet with a staff person, your peer mentor, or someone else you respect and ask them to review it and make edits.

Generally, you will want to have contact info on the top, then Education, Work Experience, Community Involvement, Leadership Experience, Honors and Awards, then finally References.

No one has the perfect résumé – and you'll constantly be adding to and revising yours. But the sooner you have something, the better, so that you can pull it out whenever you apply for a job – and if you wait, you may have a hard time remembering every important activity that ought to be included.

... AND SOME OTHER WAYS TO MAKE (OR SAVE) MONEY

5. **Start a free internship:** You won't make any money right away ... but if you do a good job and the department or company you intern for finds the resources, they may offer to pay you later.

6. **Be a test subject: Seriously!** Your college's psychology department is probably running a program where they pay students $10 to answer some questions or participate in a study. Just make sure you read the fine print before you take part in any study.

7. **Sell stuff you don't need:** eBay is a great place to start. People can make big bucks buying things cheap, and then selling them for normal prices on eBay, but selling stuff you don't need can definitely bring in spending money. Classified ad websites like craigslist.com can also be useful.

8. **Go to campus events:** A lot of them offer free food for attendees. You can probably find a few free meals every week!

9. **Fill out online surveys:** Companies need feedback, and offer cash incentives to get it. A simple Google search can point you in the direction of websites that offer you cash in exchange for filling out surveys online.

10. **Search for more scholarships and apply, apply, apply:** A lot of scholarships are given out online with only a handful of candidates, so when you apply, you have pretty good odds.

11. **Take odd jobs:** Mow the lawn, babysit, housesit, etc. Maybe you're really good at fixing things (computers, anything around the house, etc.).

12. **Minimize how often you eat out or buy fancy coffee drinks:** At $5 each, fancy coffee drinks can drain any wallet. Fast-food and sit-down restaurants are great for socializing and going out. But if you eat out just to save time cooking, know this: You can probably feed yourself, at home, for $2-3 per meal.

Scott C. Silverman

IT'S BETTER NOT TO WORK your freshman year, or at least the first quarter, because you're still adjusting. I was overwhelmed by the homework. And if you work your first year you don't get to meet as many people. But later, working helps to keep you focused. You gain skills and it helps you learn to budget your time. It's good to work on campus because they're flexible, and they'll give you time off during finals.

—*ABBY HERNANDEZ*
UNIVERSITY OF CALIFORNIA AT SANTA BARBARA, JUNIOR

. . . .

I WORK AS A WAITRESS ON CAMPUS. I work 11:30 a.m.–2:30 p.m. so it fits well into my work/study plan. My nights are open, I'm paid in cash, and I get tips. I keep a car at school, which is an expense, so I enjoy working; it's empowering. My parents are generous, but again, I enjoy having my own income and have been able to save a lot, which is important to me as I plan for my future.

—*VANESSA VALENZUELA*
SONOMA STATE UNIVERSITY, SOPHOMORE

. . . .

DON'T GET A JOB YOUR FRESHMAN YEAR. You don't know how involved in organizations you'll be or how much time you'll have to dedicate to school. But definitely work during Christmas and summer vacations, and save the money you earn.

—*SHEILA CRAWFORD*
NORTH CAROLINA STATE UNIVERSITY, SOPHOMORE

. . . .

A CHEAP EAT CAN be found at Mexican restaurants that have large portions for a reasonable price.

—*KANU*
HUNTER COLLEGE, SOPHOMORE

GET THE FLOOD INSURANCE

In January of my freshman year I was woken up one cold morning at three o'clock by the fire alarm going off in the hall of my dorm. I ran outside as fast as I could in my pajama shorts and T-shirt. They turned off the fire alarm, but something in the sprinkler system had malfunctioned, setting off the sprinkler in our hall, so we had a good five inches of disgusting, rusty water on the floors of our rooms. I had stored all of my schoolbooks under my bed, and they were now completely submerged in water, along with a good deal of dirty clothes strewn about, my printer, and all the electronics. The school informed me that because I hadn't bought insurance through them, they wouldn't cover any of the damage.

So keep your room neat, because you never know when you'll have gallons of rusty water flooding your room. And if the school offers insurance for a reasonable price, it's worth getting.

—MOLLY DONAHUE
SYRACUSE UNIVERSITY, SOPHOMORE

IF I WERE WRITING A BOOK about the things they don't tell you when you enter college, the first chapter would cover the hidden costs of living away from home—travel and school supplies, for example. However, the most shocking expense is food: the midnight pizzas, the birthday dinners, the celebration dinners, and the random exoduses from campus when you just can't take it anymore, add up in a hurry.

—ADAM
ELON UNIVERSITY, SOPHOMORE

FEDERAL WORK-STUDY PROGRAMS

For financial reasons, some students have to secure employment during college to off set the high costs of college tuition, while others want to begin to build a résumé that demonstrates a strong work ethic to future employers. Regardless of the reason, various part-time job options exist and include Federal Work-Study programs.

Federal Work-Study (FWS) is a campus need-based program that is administered by the Financial Aid Office at each participating college. The amount of work study funds you are awarded depends on your financial need, the amount of other aid you receive, and/or the availability of funds at your college. FWS provides each participating school a specific amount of funds that can be administered each year from July 1 through June 30. Therefore, it is essential to apply for federal student aid early, by completing your Free Application for Federal Student Aid (FAFSA) form. It is best to complete your FAFSA as early as January 1st of each academic year.

Upon securing FWS, you will be paid by the hour; the rate of pay will equal at least the current federal minimum wage. Students are also required to carry a minimum course load, usually 12 credits or 36 units. FWS jobs are usually located on campus in various student support and services offices and departments. However, in some instances you may be assigned to work for a nonprofit organization or a public agency affiliated with your college. There is usually an office on campus that maintains a current list of FWS positions; check with the Financial Aid or Career Services Offices on your campus.

Lastly, there is an added perk for FWS positions. While the money you earn is considered taxable income, your earnings will not be used in determining your financial need when filing the FAFSA form the following year.

Pamela M. Golubski, Ph.D.
Director of Training and Implementation at Brightside Academy
and Associate Editor for the International Journal of
Adult Vocational Education and Technology

GET SOME FIRSTHAND OFFICE EXPERIENCE before you graduate. You learn how to interact with people, and you have your own money for the first time in your life. You can pay for tuition and rent; you can live on your own. That freedom can help you achieve more.

—*M.B.*
SAN JOSE STATE UNIVERSITY, GRADUATE

● ● ● ● ● ● ● ●

" Whatever is left after school expenses, invest it in either money-market accounts or CDs. Within four years you have a nice little bundle saved. "

—*NIROSHAN RAJARATNAM*
UNIVERSITY OF MARYLAND, GRADUATE

● ● ● ● ● ● ● ●

EVERY TIME YOU GO OUT, when all your friends are having that last drink, cut yourself off; don't have that last drink. Then, go home and put the money you saved in a piggy bank. You'll be surprised how quickly it adds up. And you can go out and buy a new outfit.

—*S.G.*
COLUMBIA UNIVERSITY, SENIOR

Consider

● ● ● ● ● ● ● ●

LOOK FOR STUDENT ADVANTAGE CARDS. Craigslist is great for furniture. Buy in bulk at large grocery stores to get the best value.

—*MANNY*
GEORGE WASHINGTON UNIVERSITY, SENIOR

MONEY MANAGEMENT 101

Complete the chart below, and see if you've still got a positive balance at the end. If you're in the negative, figure out which cash outflows can be cut back or eliminated.

CASH INFLOWS	Amount	Tips	Your Notes
Employment income			
Parental support		Thank your family for their ongoing financial support.	
Financial aid/ scholarships		Keep your grades up. Most Financial Aid packages and scholarships require a minimum GPA, and if your grades don't make the cut, neither does the check.	
Other sources:			
TOTAL INFLOWS			
CASH OUTFLOWS			
Fixed Expenses			
Tuition		Pay this on time. If you don't, your college may drop you from your classes, and you'll have to pick classes all over again.	
Rent or room/board costs			
Car payment		This, and a number of other expenses, may very well be paid for by your parents.	
Car insurance			
Health/dental insurance		Your college may also provide this for you.	
Cell phone bill		Watch your minutes and usage to minimize overages.	
Personal computer		Most colleges have computer labs you can use for free, with limited printing, and many have, or are getting, free wireless Internet access, in case you have a laptop.	

Laundry		Unless you live close enough to do laundry at home.	
Variable Expenses			
Books			
School supplies			
Eating out & entertainment			
Gas		Carpool, use public transportation when possible.	
Luxuries/spontaneous shopping			
Groceries			
Utilities		Whether it's built into your room/board or not, turn appliances/lights/water off when not in use to help the environment and reduce costs.	
Periodic Expenses			
Clothing		You can always ask family for gift cards to your favorite stores.	
Gifts (Holidays, birthdays)		You don't have to spend a lot to give something meaningful to friends and family. It is the thought that counts!	
Car repairs/maintenance			
Toiletries			
Doctor visits/medicine			
Other:			
TOTAL OUTFLOWS			
CASH BALANCE			

Tips:
1. Create a budget based off of this table, and as cash flows in and out, track it.
2. If you have a checking account, keep track of transactions using your ledger.
3. When you have a positive cash balance, put it into a savings account to earn interest.
4. Watch out for credit cards…the ability to buy things you otherwise couldn't afford is very tempting, but you'll suffer for it in the long run, until you're ready to handle it.
5. Many banks and college Financial Aid Offices offer workshops and suggestions on how to manage your money effectively.

Scott C. Silverman

BUYING BOOKS

You can buy books online but then you have to wait two days for the shipment. I bought mine like that, but then realized how long it would take them to get here, so I had to cancel the order. The problem with buying used books is that sometimes there will be pages missing. And don't get used books if there is a new edition out. I know people who did this; the page numbers don't match up and the problems don't match up. They're constantly coming to my dorm to ask me what's going on.

—MORGAN
COLUMBIA UNIVERSITY, FRESHMAN

It's a good experience to have a job.

—M.B.
SAN JOSE STATE UNIVERSITY GRADUATE

I SPENT WAY TOO MUCH MONEY my freshman year on ridiculous things. Did I need the giant flag which eventually became home to three-week-old Easy Mac? No. Did I need the knockoff Gamecube controllers that eventually broke? No. Just don't spend money that you don't have. I've had a job since the summer before my freshman year, and it really ensures that I manage time well and also have a steady stream of income.

—BARRY LANGER
OGLETHORPE UNIVERSITY, JUNIOR

• • • • • • • •

YOU NEED TO FIND A JOB that allows you to work around your schedule. Living at the shore, I was able to work during the summer and save up some cash. Don't skimp on your classes, they are just as important as your job.

—MICHAEL
RUTGERS UNIVERSITY, JUNIOR

KEEPING A WORK-SCHOOL BALANCE

If you get a part-time job during school, it requires effective time management. Here are a few tips to help you manage your hectic schedule:

- Determine a strict limit on the number of hours you can work each week, based on the time you need for reading, attending classes, homework, joining organizations, sports, and having fun. As a guide, you should not be working more than 15 hours a week.

- As soon as you begin a job, provide your supervisor with a copy of your class schedule as well as a list of other weekly commitments. Your employer should NEVER require you to be at work during a class. You should also let your supervisor know the maximum hours you can work each week.

- If an academic or personal emergency arises, notify your supervisor as soon as possible if you will be late or unable to work. Ask him/her for the preferred method of contact (email, telephone, text, etc.).

- Opt to turn your cell phone off during work hours, and inform your friends of your schedule. This will make you appear more professional and will ensure you're not interrupted or tempted to answer incoming e-mails and text messages or Facebook posts.

Pamela M. Golubski, Ph.D.
Director of Training and Implementation at Brightside Academy
and Associate Editor for the International Journal of
Adult Vocational Education and Technology

DON'T SIGN UP FOR CREDIT CARDS just for the possibility of discounted prices. I faced a near disaster with a credit card company, because I signed up for a card that would give me points and discounts at various stores. Little did I know that there was a minimum fee required to keep the card, and it would accrue fees every month. I didn't read the fine print. I eventually canceled the card.

—*MICHELLE Y. LEE*
EMORY UNIVERSITY, SENIOR

. . . .

" Avoid credit cards unless they belong to your parents. I spent over $1,000 my first semester, over half of it on booze. "

—*J.V.*
THE COLLEGE OF WILLIAM & MARY, GRADUATE

. . . .

MAKE SURE YOU KEEP YOUR FINANCES in order in terms of how much you're spending. I usually give myself a monthly allotment of money I can spend on miscellaneous items such as going out to eat, going to the movies, ordering in, and any other random expenses. If you can successfully map out a good spending plan, you will find it much easier to keep track of money.

—*ANDREW OSTROWSKY*
PENNSYLVANIA STATE UNIVERSITY, JUNIOR

OWNING A CREDIT CARD led to dreaded experiences for me. Before college, I had no account and no financial responsibility. Once I got my first credit card, I would spend money occasionally on food and clothes. I came to think that spending a small amount of money every time meant that my expenses would be kept at a minimum. I didn't take into account that the expenses could add up to uncomfortable amounts. Eventually, I had to control how much I would eat, what I would eat, where I would eat, how often I would shop for clothes, where I would shop for clothes, etc.

—RAJ MATHEW
MACAULAY HONORS COLLEGE AT CUNY HUNTER, JUNIOR

• • • • • • • •

THE REASON I USUALLY HAD LITTLE MONEY was that I ate dinners at restaurants all the time. It is so easy to just stop at Jimmy John's between classes, but that money really adds up. Get things to make lunch with. Wait until you get home to eat lunch. Bring a snack. Make a sandwich. All of these will save you more money than you even realize!

That being said, since I tended to make the financially irresponsible decision to eat lunch in restaurants and found myself with little money, I got a job! There are hundreds of campus jobs that are lucrative and that work around student schedules. With those, you (usually) don't need a car either! You don't have to work 40 hours a week, just work enough to not overwhelm yourself and to make up for the money you're spending!

—ELIZABETH
UNIVERSITY OF ILLINOIS AT URBANA-CHAMPAIGN, GRADUATE

Use meal points! You already paid for them, and so there is no use saving them like money.

—HANNAH
UNIVERSITY OF
CALIFORNIA AT
BERKELEY
FRESHMAN

THE BENEFITS OF WORKING ON CAMPUS

After years of supervising college student employees and working alongside them, I'm convinced that if you want (or need) to work as a freshman, you should work on campus rather than off. Here's why:

A good place to acquire basic job skills.
The campus worksite is often a safe place to pick up the "common sense" you'll need when you go out for your first real job. Example: some students need to be told to call their employers if they are going to be late to work or won't be in due to illness. Many campus jobs are not high-stakes – no one is likely to die, the business won't tank, etc. – and campus job supervisors know that students are developing, so they tend to have more patience than the local fast-food shift manager.

Decent wages and perks.
On my campus, the hourly wage is often above the state's minimum wage. Additional perks:

1. Campus employers try to accommodate students' fractured days – working in between classes, for example, and their cyclical needs – a day off to finish a big paper or study for an exam.
2. A relaxed dress code (or none at all). This saves you money, too, since you don't have to go out and buy a special 'work' wardrobe.
3. No cost for transportation to and from the job site.
4. Some campus offices allow you to study while on the clock, if you've finished all your work tasks, the phone doesn't need answering, and no customer needs assistance. Just be sure not to post on Facebook about how bored you are at work when your supervisor is one of your FB friends.

Insight into your future.
Sometimes the campus job reveals the answer to what major and career path would be a good fit. Two years ago, my office hired a freshman biology major. She started out as a receptionist, which was

an appropriate first job for her personality and her class standing, and then she applied and was hired as a fiscal clerk. She likes this work so much that she has switched her major to accounting.

Sometimes a student lands a job that is at the throbbing center of the university: research. While the tasks may be routine, these jobs can build skills that complement or expand your interests and awareness. You may find yourself working for – if not quite "alongside" – a world-famous scientist, and be part of a project that alters understanding of the cosmos. In any case, you get to experience research methods and to contribute to the advancement of knowledge.

A 'home base'.
Campus jobs can offer a kind of home base and community. Most everything else changes each quarter, semester, or year: living arrangements, roommates, instructors and classes, your interests, majors, significant others, etc. But I've known students who stuck with the same work environment from matriculation to graduation and actually credited the job for keeping them in school: it was a place where they were known, measurably productive, where they clearly mattered and were missed when they weren't there.

Some worksites resemble kinship groups. They have developed customs and traditions – end-of-semester luncheons to honor those graduating, celebration of birthdays, regular food sharing, decorating for the holidays, and inside jokes. Students get to know faculty outside the classroom – no grades! – and are often the keepers of specialized knowledge: how to prepare travel requests, process reimbursements, provide instruction on using Excel or PowerPoint, and so on. Who wouldn't enjoy a reversal of roles - especially as a freshman?!

Christine Kirk-Kuwaye, Ph.D.
Coordinator, Student Development
University of Hawaii at Manoa
Publisher of collegewisdom.com

THERE ARE TONS OF CHEAP OPPORTUNITIES for students, you just have to search for them. For instance, students should take advantage of that free condom service they have around the dorms.

—BEN MILLER
UNIVERSITY OF NORTH CAROLINA AT CHAPEL HILL, SENIOR

· · · · · · · ·

MONEY GOES FAST AS A FRESHMAN. Dining hall meals only go so far. Let's be real, most of your spare money goes to alcohol. And it's a worthy expense, but money goes quickly. My advice to students who don't have jobs right away is to be smart about what you buy. Alcohol is a good use of college money, McDonald's is not.

—MICHAEL CUMMO
BOSTON UNIVERSITY, SENIOR

· · · · · · · ·

GETTING A JOB IN A HOTEL is a great idea, especially if you go to school in a city with a good-sized tourism industry. Jobs at larger hotel chains like Marriott or Hyatt offer decent pay and don't require a lot of hours per week. If you work in a bar, restaurant, or banquet within the hotel you get hourly pay plus a share of the tips - and things are quite expensive inside hotels, which means higher gratuity. It's more versatile than you think, too. You might start off as a server, but if you're a business major you can try to transfer to the business side, or if you're a marketing major you can try to move to that department. There's a lot of room for growth and they like to hire from within. It's an untapped resource.

—COREY
SAN DIEGO STATE UNIVERSITY, JUNIOR

IF YOU NEED TO WORK, GET AN ON-CAMPUS JOB.
On-campus employers understand your situation
better and are used to working around student
schedules. Take advantage of the job boards
around school, and the job fairs, too. I went to a
job fair and it was the best thing I ever did. It was
so easy to get hired; I did my interview right there
and got a job at the student union.

—JESSICA DOSHNA
UCLA, GRADUATE

• • • • • • • •

COLLEGE IS NOT CHEAP. If you need to apply for
financial aid, just do it. Make college affordable
for yourself. Even if you end up having loans to
repay when you come out, it is definitely worth it.
Invest in your future.

—MICHAEL
RUTGERS UNIVERSITY, JUNIOR

• • • • • • • •

THERE ARE A LOT OF GOOD BUDGETING programs
for your computer; that's what helped me. You
have to stay on top of it. Come up with a system
for tracking your bank account or you will get
screwed. Those charges will add up.

—RUTH FEINBLUM
BRYN MAWR COLLEGE, JUNIOR

• • • • • • • •

GET A CHECK CARD instead of a credit card. But
be careful with it. And don't use the on-campus
bank—it's always the worst bank.

—ANONYMOUS
JOHNS HOPKINS UNIVERSITY, JUNIOR

The more college money parents provide, the lower their children's college grades, according to a recent national study. Students who get a blank check from their parents may not take their education as seriously as others.

USING THE CAREER CENTER
(YES, EVEN THOUGH YOU'RE JUST A FRESHMAN!)

You might think that the career center – sometimes called a career development center, or career planning and placement center – is a place to visit when you're a senior looking for a full-time job. Actually, freshman year is a great time to use some of the services offered by your career center. Here are some ways they can help you now:

1. Your career center can help you develop your résumé. They probably have résumé templates on their website, as well as helpful tips on making your résumé stand out. Once you've created a résumé, visit your career center to get it reviewed. (If that's too intimidating, send it to your mom, ask your roommates to review it, or find an English major who has some extra time.) Either way, make sure that your résumé is free of errors so that you make the best first impression on an employer.

2. Your career center will have resources to help you find a work-study position or a part-time job on campus, and can give you tips on applying. Many career centers offer an online job posting service (sort of like Craigslist), where employers can post jobs and internship opportunities for students. Be sure to sign up to access this important resource.

3. Most career centers offer online videos or workshops, with tutorials to assist you with résumé writing, interviewing for summer jobs and internships, and getting involved in your campus community. Peruse the career center website and see if any of the videos appeal to you!

Remember that freshman year is a process of self-exploration and assessment: discovering what you're actually interested in and good at. Career exploration means trying anything-- a new club, an internship, or volunteering-- to find out what appeals to you and how you can best use your skills and talents in your life, not just your career. And if you end up hating what you signed up for – change it, but first ask yourself what was so bad about it. Was it the tasks, duties, people, environment, or something else? And if it's awesome, why did you love it so much? It's not so much what you decide to sign up for; it's what you learn from the experience that will help you get to the next step.

Lee Desser
Student Services Advisor
University of California at Berkeley

GET A JOB. Even if your parents are supporting you. All my jobs during college, from barista to research intern, helped develop my people skills, build my résumé, introduce me to great contacts, and pad my wallet. Even though it's not a ton of money, a part-time job in college goes a long way in reducing stress. It's also important to remember to strike a balance between following your personal budget and feeling like you can treat yourself occasionally. Many of your friends at college will have more financial flexibility than you; don't feel pressure to keep up if they're spending money on dinners, shows, and trips that you don't feel financially comfortable partaking in.

—*CAITLIN*
  GEORGETOWN UNIVERSITY, GRADUATE

IF YOUR SCHOOL HAS A CAREER SERVICES department, utilize that as soon as possible. They'll be able to help you get a job in your field early on. You really need career services. A lot of firms end up recruiting on campus, and through career services you can find a job easily.

—*MATTHEW GUTSHALL*
ST. JOSEPH'S, JUNIOR

. . . .

I LITERALLY JUST TRY NOT TO SPEND any money at all unless I absolutely need something. I've skipped out on a lot of little "luxuries". Write a list and don't buy anything that is not on it!

—*AMANDA*
UNIVERSITY OF MIAMI, JUNIOR

. . . .

BUDGETING IN COLLEGE IS EXTREMELY HARD, and budgeting while living and working in a metropolitan area is even harder. We don't have meal plans at Hunter so when you are living in the residence hall, or even if you commute from home, you have to either learn how to cook, get meals from home, eat out and/or order in a lot, or find some other way to "make it work." It is definitely not the best for the wallet or the waistline to eat out every night. You'll learn to grocery shop and also get really comfortable with eating leftovers and stretching large portions over multiple meals.

—*REBECCA*
HUNTER COLLEGE, SENIOR

. . . .

INTERNSHIPS ARE A GREAT WAY to know what type of career path you want to go on. Start looking for one of those immediately.

—*MICHAEL*
RUTGERS UNIVERSITY, JUNIOR

Food for Thought: Pop-Tarts, Beer & Other Essential Nutrients

s it humanly possible to eat pizza every day for a whole semester? Is the "Freshman 15" a myth-or an unhappy reality? Will your 10 a.m. history professor mind if you bring your breakfast to class? Does the maraschino cherry on top of your sundae count as one of those five fruit and vegetable servings you vaguely remember hearing about? Yes, freshman year means you must face many food-related quandaries. For possibly the first time in your life, you have total freedom to eat when, where, and what you want. Let our friendly guides steer you around the Pop Rocks.

THE FIRST INCLINATION when you get to college is to eat anything you want. Mom isn't there making sure you eat your vegetables. But three months and 15 pounds later you find out why a mom is a good thing when it comes to food.

—D.R.
UNIVERSITY OF NORTH CAROLINA, GRADUATE

THE MICRO-WAVE IS DEFI-NITELY YOUR BEST FRIEND.

—*REBECCA
HUNTER COLLEGE
SENIOR*

HEADLINES
Best Advice and Top Tips

- Food is an adventure at school. Treat it that way and you'll seldom be disappointed.
- If you eat the pizza, you will gain the weight. The Freshman 15 is real.
- Cheap college food: Mac 'n' cheese, ramen noodles, yogurt, fruit, trail mix.
- Try to eat healthy at least half the time. Your mother is worried about this.
- Take advantage of your meal plan. Otherwise, it's wasted money.

GET A GEORGE FOREMAN GRILL, or even just a toaster oven. You'd be surprised at how much you can make with those, from bagel pizzas to steak.

—JESSIE
VILLA JULIE COLLEGE, JUNIOR

. . . .

I HAVE WEIRD EATING HABITS. I eat rice cakes and dried pineapple. I don't know why. Also, chocolate helps.

—ANONYMOUS
YALE UNIVERSITY, SOPHOMORE

. . . .

If you drink the beer, you're gonna gain the weight.

—BRIAN ROSEN
PRINCETON
UNIVERSITY
GRADUATE

THIS IS THE FOOD HERE: They have all the basic food, and then they have these huge vats of sauce. And they just slosh the sauce over the food and it becomes disgusting.

—LUCY LINDSEY
HARVARD UNIVERSITY, FRESHMAN

TAKE EVERY FREE MEAL you can get. Generally, the dining hall is not bad. But when you eat it seven days a week, it gets pretty old, no matter how good the food is. Every time someone wants to take you out, take them up on it. If nothing else, it's a good way to make friends or meet people.

—*JONATHAN COHEN*
EMORY UNIVERSITY, SENIOR

BUY LOTS OF TUPPERWARE CONTAINERS to take to the cafeteria and sneak food out, so you don't have to buy it. You're paying for a meal plan anyway.

—*MEG*
UNIVERSITY OF NORTH CAROLINA, GRADUATE

I RECOMMEND THAT ONE ACQUIRE a taste for hummus. Hummus can really be put onto anything, it comes in all sorts of flavors, it's healthy, and it's relatively cheap if bought in bulk. Seriously, try and think of something that hummus wouldn't be good on; you can't!

—*STEVEN COY*
SAN DIEGO STATE UNIVERSITY, SOPHOMORE

I MAY SOUND LIKE AN ANNOYING PARENT when I say this, but please, for the love of God, do not spend all of your money on alcohol. There are so many ways to still be able to enjoy yourself (and drink) for less. Have your friends pitch in when you buy it (legally) at the store. Share it! Buy just one drink if you're at a club or pub because that stuff's expensive. Steal it from home. I don't care. It can just turn into a huge money-eater.

—*SHANNON KELLEY*
KENYON COLLEGE, JUNIOR

DON'T BUY THE FULL MEAL TICKET, unless you're sure you can eat breakfast every day. I made it to breakfast once the whole year. When I got up, I didn't have time to go downstairs and eat; I had to go to class.

—JAKE MALAWAY
UNIVERSITY OF ILLINOIS, GRADUATE

. . . .

BE CAREFUL WHAT YOU COOK in your toaster. My friend bought some frozen hot dogs—like, six of them—and then one day she was hungry so she tried to cook them in the toaster in her dorm room, and smoke came out of it and she set off the fire alarm. So she had to go to peer review, which was funny because most of the cases they get in peer review are people using excessive bandwidth from downloading too much, and then they get this interesting case. For punishment they said she had to make a few posters saying, "Be safe—don't put hot dogs in toasters."

—J.R. MCKINNEY
UNIVERSITY OF CALIFORNIA AT BERKELEY, SOPHOMORE

. . . .

MOST IMPORTANT PIECE OF ADVICE I ever received about college food: If you find a hair in your food in the dining hall, just assume it's yours and move on.

—MATT LACKNER
PRINCETON UNIVERSITY, GRADUATE

. . . .

DON'T BE FOOLED by the Freshman 15. Real men go for the Freshman 30; at least that's how I cope with it.

—ADAM
ELON UNIVERSITY, SOPHOMORE

The Freshman 15 happens to everyone, and don't believe anyone who tells you otherwise.

—AMY
PRINCETON UNIVERSITY FRESHMAN

DON'T ASSUME YOU WON'T GAIN WEIGHT just because as a teen in high school you ate a lot. In my first year of college, I didn't understand the concept of self-control with food. The all-you-can-eat buffet seemed like a good idea at the time, especially where the cookies and brownies were concerned. I used to stash as many as I could carry under a folded napkin and was so proud of myself for being able to sneak out with it—as if it were an accomplishment! I didn't realize that all I accomplished was a good 15 pounds. I was convinced that I couldn't fit into my clothes anymore because the dry air in the dorm room shrunk them all.

> —*VERONICA*
> *QUEENS UNIVERSITY, GRADUATE*

• • • • • • • •

GET YOUR OWN MINI-FRIDGE and buy your own food. Buy Easy Mac—it's microwaveable macaroni and cheese—so you don't need a stove.

> —*SIERRA*
> *CAL POLY SAN LUIS OBISPO, JUNIOR*

• • • • • • • •

DON'T EAT THE EGGS IN THE DINING COMMONS— they're fake. Anything you can eat from a bowl, like cereal and salad, is good. Don't eat a lot of fast food just because it's there and it's cheap. Jamba Juice is the way to go: it won't make you fat, it's kind of healthy, and it doesn't smell bad so you can take it to class and no one will yell at you. You get these people who go to class with a burger and onion rings and sit there for an hour in class and it's gross.

> —*KYM*
> *SAN JOSE STATE UNIVERSITY, SOPHOMORE*

BEST THINGS TO COOK UP IN A DORM KITCHEN

Brownies (from a mix)

Instant noodle-and-sauce packages

Pasta and sauce in a jar

Precooked chicken meat

Store-bought cookie dough

COOKING FOR 1 OR 2 ON A BUDGET

When you're sick of dorm food and can't get home for some of mom's, it may be time to cook something for yourself. You want something tasty that doesn't cost a lot. Believe it or not, it is entirely possible ... even though it may take some practice. Here are some tips to get started:

Budget Cooking

Saving money by cooking for yourself is easy. You can easily supplement your on-campus meal plan with meals you make yourself.

- Use store and manufacturer's coupons, and bring ads from other stores if your store matches prices.
- Buy fruits and vegetables when they're in season, and local produce (particularly at farmer's markets).
- Shop around a bit, to find the best price for the items you want.
- Buy only what you need, and only the quantities you can consume before the expiration date.
- The store-brand is often just as good, and using some canned food in a meal isn't a bad thing.

Pros and Cons of Leftovers

Cooking for one or two people is a challenge. Most recipes serve 4 or 8 or more. If you can reduce the recipe, great, but here's what you can do if you can't:

- To save cooking time during the week, you can choose to make meals in larger batches, and freeze single-serving portions.
- Buy frozen foods in bulk, thaw as needed. You can freeze almost anything too.
- You can stretch any meal a little further by adding tortillas, potatoes, pasta, rice and vegetables of any sort (or salad!) as a side.

- After you finish dinner, if the leftovers aren't enough to make an entirely separate meal, weave them into another. Chicken can go into a salad, rice, meat and corn can be added into a casserole, or chili and rice, etc.

Random Food Tips

- Eggs are a great source of protein. So are combining beans and corn tortillas.
- Chicken and turkey legs and thighs are good deals. After you consume the meat, you can freeze the bones and boil them later to make stock (broth).
- Sandwiches are really cheap to make, which may be why you probably ate a lot of them when you were in grade school. You don't have to eat PB&J or Turkey/Cheese sandwiches every day, but you can spice up your meal with different types of jelly, different breads or different spreads.
- Add other things to Mac 'n' cheese for something quick but full of flavor. Try hot dogs, hamburgers, chili, diced tomatoes and chili peppers, tuna, chicken strips, sour cream, multiple types of cheese, etc. I wouldn't recommend trying all of those in the same meal, but see how a little creativity can spice up any dish.
- Keep canned soups and frozen food/packaged meals on hand for quick and nutritious meals.

Team up with some friends: You can each make a separate dish and split it up, for added variety.

Here are a couple of useful websites to give you some more professional inspiration:

> http://www.kraftrecipes.com/home.aspx
> http://www.foodnetwork.com/quick-and-easy/index.html

Scott C. Silverman

AFTER I COULD NO LONGER AFFORD a meal plan, my friend and I would scour the campus paper and fliers for events with free food. Then, we would fill in our own "Free Food Calendar" with all the times and places of those events. We would end up at academic speeches, random barbecues, or various group meetings, none of which we belonged to or knew anything about. But they put out free food at these events. We wound up eating for free at least three to four times every week. You can't beat that!

—*CHAVON MITCHELL*
XAVIER UNIVERSITY, GRADUATE

● ● ● ● ● ● ● ●

" You're going to gain weight and you're going to take it off the next summer. Don't worry about it. Buy some fat pants. Everybody I know gained a lot of weight. "

—*HANNAH*
EMORY UNIVERSITY, JUNIOR

● ● ● ● ● ● ● ●

I HAVE A LOT OF SNACKS IN MY ROOM—macaroni and cheese and peanut butter and jelly. You might want to bring that kind of stuff, in case you can't make it to the cafeteria or don't want to go, for whatever reason.

—*ANONYMOUS*
UNIVERSITY OF MARYLAND
FRESHMAN

TOP THREE ZERO-EFFORT HEALTHY SNACKS

1. **BANANAS:** Requiring no preparation and no utensils, these wonders of nature are also easy to carry in a backpack.

2. **NATURAL YOGURT:** Try to avoid the brands full of artificial sweeteners and other chemicals, and you're all set. Spoon is recommended but not absolutely mandatory.

3. **FROZEN ORANGE JUICE:** No, not the concentrate that comes in a can. Instead, buy the smallest cartons you can get at the campus store, wedge them in the freezer section of your mini fridge, and pry them out the next day for frosty deliciousness.

DON'T THINK THAT YOU WON'T GAIN that Freshman 15 by ordering pizza while watching late-night TV (in my case, David Letterman), eating Burger King, and drinking every night.

> —*K.E.R.*
> *FLORIDA STATE UNIVERSITY*
> *GRADUATE*

THE HOT-DOG vendor will become your new best friend.

> —*J.G.*
> *FLORIDA STATE UNIVERSITY, GRADUATE*

COLLEGES WITH THE BEST CAMPUS FOOD

1. Bowdoin College, Brunswick, ME
2. Virginia Tech, Blacksburg, VA
3. University of Massachusetts Amherst, Amherst, MA
4. James Madison University, Harrisonburg, VA
5. Washington University in St. Louis, St. Louis, MO

HOW TO DECIDE IF YOU WANT THE MEAL PLAN: If you like to eat lots of food and you're not picky about quality, then eat at school. But if you care about things like taste, plan on buying your meals elsewhere. I bought the meal plan and was happy with it. You could eat tons of food cheap. Was it good? No. But as long as I was full, I didn't care.

—*DON WAZZENEGER*
YOUNGSTOWN STATE UNIVERSITY, SENIOR

• • • • • • • • •

PEOPLE NEVER EAT BEFORE PARTIES because they think there's going to be food at the party. Not in college! Eat a lot. Pizza is always a fun option.

—*CATLEYA*

• • • • • • • • •

FIND A FEW THINGS in the dining hall that you like. Often times the dorms are far from the city, so you don't have the option of going out to eat. My friends and I ate at the dorm dining hall pretty much all the time. I found the meat especially disappointing; I missed the steaks we made back at home. I ate a lot of chicken that year, and cereal.

—*ANDREW*
UCLA, SENIOR

I HATED COLLEGE FOOD! College food is a hard adjustment on the body. I stopped going to the cafeteria and started bringing food that I could make in my room. Microwavable meals are great and cheap.

—*DAVID*
KEAN UNIVERSITY, JUNIOR

• • • • • • • •

LIVING IN MIAMI, I've learned a lot about Cuban food. I'd say a necessity in any college student's home is a rice cooker. I like to fry up two over-easy eggs and break them on top of some garlic rice. Apparently it's a traditional Cuban comfort food. It's also nice to keep slice-and-bake cookie dough in the fridge. Easy to make, and they make your house smell so yummy. Your friends will think you're quite the baker when they come over.

—*EVA DINES*
UNIVERSITY OF MIAMI, JUNIOR

FRESHMAN 15: FACT OR FICTION?

A 2011 study determined that the so-called "freshman 15" – the weight gain phenomenon said to go along with starting college – is little more than a myth. The study showed that while new college students do tend to gain between 2.5-3.5 pounds on average, the weight gain has little to do with college and much more to do with natural body change as students enter adulthood. In fact, even 18-19 year olds who didn't attend college were shown to gain weight at an almost identical rate.

QUALITY CONTROL

I often see first-year students get really excited about the "all you can eat" dining options. I would encourage students to pick a few options that look tasty and manage the portions of those options. You don't need to try every dining option to get your money's worth. You can eat a few great items and avoid gaining weight during your first year of college. Quality over Quantity!

Jen Miller
Director, The Well
University of California, Riverside

RAMEN. I KNOW IT'S WILDLY UNHEALTHY, but I lived on it freshman year. It's fast and it's filling. What more do you need? I had two big staples when I decided to make my own meals. First: I would always get large bags of frozen chicken breasts and keep them in my freezer. I'd thaw them, throw them in the oven with BBQ sauce, and then I'd steam or microwave a frozen vegetable. When I wanted to be really balanced, I'd add some rice, but I had to really plan ahead for that. My other big staple was stir fry, which exclusively happened within three days of grocery shopping. I'd get some vegetables and then I'd cut up chicken and throw the vegetables together with some teriyaki sauce, creating a stir-fried miracle!

—*ELIZABETH*
UNIVERSITY OF ILLINOIS AT URBANA-CHAMPAIGN, GRADUATE

• • • • • • • •

YOU SHOULD ALWAYS have chips in the dorm room when you're up at four in the morning writing a paper.

—*DAN AMERMAN*
YALE UNIVERSITY, SOPHOMORE

13

Ready to Wear: Fashion & (at Some Point) Laundry

*I*gnore what the fashion magazines tell you to wear this season; those people don't know anything about your lifestyle. You don't have a laundry service, dry cleaner, tailor, personal dresser, makeup artist, stylist, and airbrush technician greeting you in the morning with a cup of herbal tea. Instead, you have a pile of semiclean clothes and 10 minutes to get dressed and get to class. This chapter will give you some handy tips for looking (and smelling!) good, despite all that. And why not read it in the laundry room? Could be a conversation starter.

AS LONG AS YOUR WARDROBE doesn't consist of only leather pants and tiger print shirts, fashion isn't a big deal.

—Jo
UNIVERSITY OF VIRGINIA, SENIOR

IT'S FUN TO TRY OUT DIFFERENT SMELLING LAUNDRY DETERGENTS.

—ANNIE THOMAS
UNIVERSITY OF MICHIGAN, SENIOR

HEADLINES
Best Advice and Top Tips

- College is casual these days. T-shirts are standard.
- Don't be the one who waits too long to do laundry or take a shower.
- Freshmen are known for wearing school-themed apparel. We're just letting you know.
- There's a "best" time to do laundry in your dorm. Figure it out.

You can wear your pajamas around campus; you won't be the only one.

—AMY FORBES
MISSISSIPPI STATE
UNIVERSITY
GRADUATE

BIG FASHION FAUX PAS—the lanyard with the ID in it. We have what is called a "one-card." It gets you into the dorms and some other buildings. The sure sign of a first-year is the lanyard with the one-card, especially the "Wellesley College" lanyard in your class color. Some first-years don't catch on and the poor dears wander around with them all year.

—SARAH
WELLESLEY COLLEGE, SOPHOMORE

HISTORY CORNER

Oberlin College has long been known for its progressive ideals, and admitted women students as well as men back when higher-education opportunities for women were rare. But all was not equal, even at Oberlin. In the 19th century, female students were responsible for the male students' laundry.

Consider

IF YOU LIVE IN A DORM AND YOUR BATHROOM is down the hall, get good shower shoes. If you go barefoot, by mid-October they'll be studying the stuff on your feet in biology class.

—*J.T.*
UNIVERSITY OF FLORIDA, GRADUATE

* * * * * * * *

“ No one will really notice if you wear the same two or three (or one) pair of jeans or khakis—it's the shirt that people notice. So get plenty of shirts and one or two pairs of jeans and you can cut laundry efforts in half. ”

—*DAN*
MIAMI UNIVERSITY, FRESHMAN

* * * * * * * *

DON'T TURN COLLEGE into an uncomfortable place to be. There is no sense in wearing high heels to school!

—*ERICA LANGE-HENNESEY*
TEXAS STATE UNIVERSITY, SENIOR

* * * * * * * *

USE MOM'S LAUNDRY detergent and fabric softener to make your dorm room smell a little bit more like home!

—*LAURA WOLTER*
UNIVERSITY OF TEXAS AT AUSTIN, GRADUATE

Just get lots of underwear and only do laundry when you run out.

—MEREDITH
BROWN UNIVERSITY
SOPHOMORE

LAUNDRY IS EXPENSIVE, and you have to be careful because people will steal your stuff. I had a problem with that. I had to take my homework down there and do it while doing laundry.

—B.M.
UNIVERSITY OF MARYLAND, JUNIOR

• • • • • • • •

RESIST CONFORMITY. We have too many Gap kids and Abercrombie look-alikes running around campus.

—KHALIL SULLIVAN
PRINCETON UNIVERSITY, JUNIOR

• • • • • • • •

IF YOU WANT TO BE COOL, don't wear anything with your school name or colors on it. It's called Freshman Fashion Wear for a reason.

—J.G.
FLORIDA STATE UNIVERSITY, GRADUATE

• • • • • • • •

IF YOU FIND YOURSELF IN THE LAUNDRY ROOM and don't know how to wash your own clothes, do not push the "help" button. This button is for security purposes only; for example, if you are attacked. No little helper will come and help you wash your clothes. Instead, you will sound the alarm and call the police.

—ANONYMOUS
UNIVERSITY OF PENNSYLVANIA, SENIOR

• • • • • • • •

DO NOT BRING CLOTHES that require ironing or dry cleaning or special handling. And do not loan your favorite shirt to a party-happy friend if you want it back in the same condition. If you are female, leave your handbag at home. No one brings a purse to a party, and during the day your backpack is your bag.

—J.
UNIVERSITY OF GEORGIA, GRADUATE

SPECIAL HYGIENE SECTION

Thanks to all those imperfectly socialized freshmen who made this page possible—and necessary.

IF POSSIBLE, TRY TO FIND THE SHOWER IN YOUR DORM with the best pressure and the most considerate bathroom users and ask politely to share it with them. A nice hot shower under a showerhead with good pressure is a great way to unwind. Be considerate of other bathroom users! Don't leave a mess for your janitors; they are there to maintain a standard of hygiene, not to clean up your messes.
> —ARIEL MELENDEZ
> PRINCETON UNIVERSITY, FRESHMAN

• • • • • • • •

EVEN IF IT DOESN'T BOTHER YOU to walk around for a few days without a shower— please, oh God, before you forgo the morning cleaning, please think of the person sitting next to you in class.
> —ADAM
> ELON UNIVERSITY, SOPHOMORE

• • • • • • • •

SHOWERING EVERY DAY IS A MUST. There are college students who think they can go more than a day without showering, but they are sorely mistaken. Trust me when I say that it can be painfully (and nauseatingly) obvious when someone has not bathed properly. As a courtesy to those around you, remember to take a shower.
> —JOSHUA BERKOV
> BROWN UNIVERSITY, JUNIOR

• • • • • • • •

JUST BECAUSE YOU CAN'T SMELL IT, doesn't mean it's not there. Shower at least once a day and especially after coming from the gym.
> —KHALIL SULLIVAN
> PRINCETON UNIVERSITY, JUNIOR

GUYS, BRING KHAKIS in the fall and then cut them off in the spring.

—STEVE DAVIS
FLORIDA STATE UNIVERSITY, GRADUATE

• • • • • • • •

66 During crunch time, you need only a few pieces of clothing: Sweatpants in school color of choice, comfy tank top or ratty T-shirt, and a hoodie. 99

—AMY
PRINCETON UNIVERSITY, FRESHMAN

• • • • • • • •

MY FRESHMAN-YEAR ROOMMATE and I were polar opposites. She was a city girl from D.C., really stylish, and she hated the way I dressed. When I got up in the morning to go to class, I would throw on my jeans, a sweatshirt, and my Birkenstocks, and for the first couple of weeks she would block the door so I couldn't leave. She would say, "Uh-uh, girl. You are not leaving the room like that." I would say that I was just going to class, and she would say, "Girl, you could be cute if you changed your style or did your hair. You could get yourself a boyfriend!" Finally, by Thanksgiving break, we came to an understanding: She would never wear Birkenstocks, and I would never wear tall, black, leather boots. But as I left for break, she told me, "Girl, do two things for yourself over break: Style your hair, and buy black shoes."

—SUMMER J.
UNIVERSITY OF VIRGINIA, SENIOR

LAUNDRY 101 (FOR GUYS)

Just about the last thing I ever feel like doing in college is my laundry. Either I don't have quarters, don't have soap, or just don't care that my clothes are more wrinkled and dank than Bea Arthur on a humid day. If this sounds like you, try sticking to the following strategies for avoiding the laundry room:

For shirts, pants and the like, divide your clothes into two categories. Category One is the stuff you wear every day. Keep these items as clean as possible and when you're done wearing them, fold them neatly, put them in your drawer, and pretend they're clean. A squirt of Febreze might help as well.

Category Two is your "going-out-to-parties clothes." This should be only one or two shirts and a pair of pants, which will stink of beer and smoke after a night out. Keep these in a trash bag on your closet floor. Wear them on Friday nights. No one will know the difference.

Tempting as it may be, you're not allowed to wear underwear twice. It's just wrong. You'll need to go to Wal-Mart and get 30 pairs of tightie-whities and 30 pairs of white tube socks. Wear each pair one day, and then once a month, throw all of them in the wash. It's all white, so you can do one load, and because it's just socks and underwear, you don't have to fold or sort anything. Just put them in another trash bag, next to your Friday night clothes. Keep two pairs of clean boxers on hand for dates.

—ADAM F.
GEORGE WASHINGTON UNIVERSITY, GRADUATE

STRANGE BUT TRUE UNDERWEAR TALES

I WAS ON THE WAY TO THE LAUNDRY ROOM and I dropped my underwear on the dorm stairs. I didn't realize until someone came up to me and said, "You dropped your underwear on the stairs." I was so embarrassed.

—CONSTANCE A. LINDSAY
DUKE UNIVERSITY, GRADUATE

I HAD THIS GIRL WHO DID MY LAUNDRY and I would notice that I was losing underwear. I rummaged through her stuff one day and found six pairs of my Fruit of the Looms! I haven't trusted anyone with my clothing since.

—RYAN BOWEN
UNIVERSITY OF GEORGIA, SENIOR

ONE TIME, THE WASHERS WERE BROKEN at the dorms. So I asked my new guy friend, who was six years older, if I could wash some clothes at his place. I finished washing and left but had forgotten a load at his place. His friends came over that night and saw my yellow thongs and pink granny panties. Needless to say we stopped hanging out.

—M.T.
GEORGIA STATE UNIVERSITY, SENIOR

I HAD GIRL'S UNDERWEAR in my laundry one time; she must have left it in the dryer. They had her name in them, so I went to her room to give them back. It was kind of awkward, at least for me.

—ALEX
EMORY UNIVERSITY, SOPHOMORE

KEEP TRACK OF THE TIME when you are doing your laundry. During my freshman year I was late to take my clothes out of the dryer and someone stole my Victoria's Secret underwear and left my granny panties. I was so mad!

—DANIELLE
DUKE UNIVERSITY, GRADUATE

SWEATS ARE ALL THE RAGE, especially if they have Greek letters on them or a logo of an organization that you are in. But don't wear the ones that simply have the school logo. I heard someone say that they were able to identify all of the freshmen because they wore our school's logo on everything.

—SUSAN MORGENBESSER
PENNSYLVANIA STATE UNIVERSITY, GRADUATE

• • • • • • • •

WARNING: DON'T WASH DOWN COMFORTERS. You'll flood the laundry room and ruin your blanket.

—ETHAN WASSERMAN
BOSTON UNIVERSITY, JUNIOR

• • • • • • • •

I HAVE NOT USED MY COMB YET. I have not worn any college shirts, either. A lot of the kids do that, but I haven't worn one, and my mom packed 15 of them.

—BAYLESS PARSLEY
UNIVERSITY OF VIRGINIA, FRESHMAN

• • • • • • • •

YOU KNOW IT'S TIME to do laundry when you run out of underwear. I know guys who said it was time to do laundry when you've worn your underwear inside out. That's pretty gross.

—NAT
UNIVERSITY OF RHODE ISLAND, SOPHOMORE

• • • • • • • •

THE TIME I GET UP determines what I wear to class. Sweats, sneakers, and slip-on shoes make it easy to hop out of bed and head to class. Unless I am going out with friends, I want to be comfortable when I am sitting at a desk.

—DAVID
KEAN UNIVERSITY, JUNIOR

I'VE BEEN DOING MY OWN LAUNDRY since I was 12, but in college, I got a really big laundry bag and saved it and took it home, an hour and a half away.

—MELISSA K. BYRNES
AMHERST COLLEGE, GRADUATE

. . . .

FOR LAUNDRY, I WAIT until I have no clothes left, and then I do two big loads all at once and I'm done with it in a couple of hours.

—ANONYMOUS
UNIVERSITY OF PENNSYLVANIA, SOPHOMORE

. . . .

COLLEGE IS A GREAT PLACE TO MEET all kinds of new people. But sometimes you can get into a rut—your daily routine becomes so regimented that you don't encounter as many new people as you did in the beginning. That's when it's time to try something new or go someplace different. In my case, this was the laundry room. I found that on the rare occasions I went to the laundry room, I would make friends with one or two of the people waiting for their clothes to dry.

—BRANDON WALKER
JAMES MADISON UNIVERSITY, SOPHOMORE

. . . .

I FIND MYSELF BUYING UNDERWEAR instead of actually doing laundry. My advice is to wait until after the holidays and get the holiday packs of boxers for $1.99 at the Gap. I do that a lot. I have a lot of boxers with holly on them. And you can get a lot of free T-shirts from clubs.

—MARTIN
GEORGETOWN UNIVERSITY, SOPHOMORE

IF YOU HAVE A LIMITED CLOTHES BUDGET, spend it on jeans. Jeans never go out of style. If you have some extra cash, buy socks and underwear. They seem to disappear between the dorm rooms and the Laundromat.

—DON WAZZENEGER
YOUNGSTOWN STATE UNIVERSITY, SENIOR

• • • • • • • •

IF AT ALL POSSIBLE, GO TO A SCHOOL in a state where your grandmother lives an hour away and just take your laundry there. You need to visit her every once in a while, anyway. So take your laundry there; she'll cook you dinner.

—ANONYMOUS
UNIVERSITY OF VIRGINIA, SOPHOMORE

• • • • • • • •

FIND SOMEONE WHO REALLY KNOWS how to do laundry. You get here and you realize that you don't understand how not to dye all your clothes pink.

—LUCY LINDSEY
HARVARD UNIVERSITY, FRESHMAN

• • • • • • • •

BEWARE OF WHAT YOU PUT in the communal washing machines. When I was a freshman, I decided to wash my orange rug. There was so much lint on it that it got on everyone else's clothes in that washing machine. Everybody knew it came from me.

—GLENDA L. RICHARDSON
DUKE UNIVERSITY, GRADUATE

• • • • • • • •

LEARN ABOUT YOUR CAMPUS before you decide to wear high heels! I've seen a girl fall down a hill in her stilettos—not a good look!

—JANELLE
UNIVERSITY OF GEORGIA, JUNIOR

READ THE LABELS! Whenever I did laundry, I made it a point to read the directions on the detergent boxes and the labels on the clothes. I also read the directions on the washing machines. I didn't want anything going wrong; clothes are too expensive!

> —JOSH
> MISSOURI STATE UNIVERSITY, GRADUATE

. . . .

NEVER, EVER MOVE SOMEONE'S LAUNDRY from the dryer. I did this once. When I came to pick up my clothes, I found a girl sitting in a chair she'd dragged into the laundry room, waiting for me to come back so she could give me a piece of her mind.

> —ALLISON GRECO
> MONTCLAIR STATE UNIVERSITY, GRADUATE

. . . .

HANG UP CLOTHES IF THEY'RE NOT REALLY, really dirty. It keeps them from getting wrinkled.

> —JOEL
> PRINCETON UNIVERSITY, GRADUATE

. . . .

MAKE FRIENDS WITH KIDS whose parents live close by and do laundry at their parents' house. I lugged laundry home on a two-hour train ride just so I didn't have to do it. It was a real pain. And do the essentials so that you don't run out of underwear and towels.

> —J.P.G.
> UNIVERSITY OF PENNSYLVANIA, SOPHOMORE

. . . .

BUY A LOT OF UNDERWEAR before you go. You can wear jeans until they walk. But you have to wash your underwear.

> —CHRISTINE
> UNIVERSITY OF RHODE ISLAND, SOPHOMORE

WHEN TO DO IT

DO YOUR LAUNDRY IN THE MIDDLE OF THE WEEK, not on the weekends.
> —*KELLI*
> *UNIVERSITY OF DELAWARE, SOPHOMORE*

DO LAUNDRY IN THE MIDDLE OF THE NIGHT or early in the morning—no one's there.
> —*CASEY*
> *GEORGETOWN UNIVERSITY, SENIOR*

DO NOT DO LAUNDRY ON FRIDAY, SATURDAY, OR SUNDAY. Wait until Monday, midday, when most people are at class. The maintenance staff has already fixed the machines from the weekend, and you don't have to worry about people taking your laundry out.
> —*H.D. BALLARD*
> *UNIVERSITY OF VIRGINIA, FRESHMAN*

I DO LAUNDRY A LOT, BETWEEN CLASSES in the morning or afternoon, during the week, and on the weekend. I do it whenever I can, to get it out of the way.
> —*JENNIFER A. SICKLICK*
> *GEORGE WASHINGTON UNIVERSITY, FRESHMAN*

DON'T DO LAUNDRY ON SUNDAY. Everyone does it that day.
> —*ANONYMOUS*
> *UNIVERSITY OF MARYLAND, SOPHOMORE*

I DO MY LAUNDRY SUNDAY MORNING. I set my alarm clock early. By the end of the week, all my clothes are dirty, and during the week I don't have time.
> —*AMY HOFFBERG*
> *UNIVERSITY OF DELAWARE, FRESHMAN*

I HEARD SOME HORROR STORIES about people's room-mates forgetting to wash their sheets. That will keep people out of your room.

> —MIKE PARKER
> GEORGETOWN UNIVERSITY, SOPHOMORE

● ● ● ● ● ● ● ●

I'M THE GIRL IN JEANS, a university T-shirt, and flip-flops. At the beginning of every fall semester I would see freshman girls walking around campus in high heels, and I would always smile and nod because I knew by the end of the day their feet would be in so much pain. The only advice I can give about fashion is to be comfortable in whatever you are wearing.

> —QUONIAS
> UNIVERSITY OF WEST GEORGIA, SENIOR

● ● ● ● ● ● ● ●

SOME FRESHMEN TRY TOO HARD. They try to be too radical, or too preppy. I mean, fashion is part of who you are. But don't try too hard.

> —THEODORE SCHIMENTI
> COLUMBIA UNIVERSITY, FRESHMAN

● ● ● ● ● ● ● ●

AFTER LIVING IN THE DORM for a week my friends and I decided that we needed to do laundry. Being the freshman that we were, we didn't want to leave the laundry room while our clothes were in the washer and dryer, so we stayed down there for the whole time. One of our friends brought down his iPod and speakers and we ended up having a dance party in the laundry room. It is one of my fondest college memories and we still talk about it today.

> —ANNIE THOMAS
> UNIVERSITY OF MICHIGAN, SENIOR

THE LAUNDRY ROOM is a pretty competitive spot. Stay with your clothes while they are in the washer and dryer. Bring homework with you, your phone, your laptop, whatever. Don't leave! If you do, there is a significant chance you will come back to find your underwear strewn all over the room because someone wanted your machine. This will probably happen as you enter the laundry room with a member of the opposite sex.

—*LAURA TRUBIANO*
HAMILTON COLLEGE, JUNIOR

Always dress a cut above the rest. College has a lot to do with image.

—*SEAN CAMERON*
PRINCETON
UNIVERSITY
SOPHOMORE

" Shower. Don't go to class in your sweaty gym clothes. I know your mom is not at college with you to dress you, but get cleaned up; it's distracting. "

—*MOLLY*
BROWN UNIVERSITY, SOPHOMORE

HOW TO MANIPULATE YOUR PARENTS into doing your laundry: When my mom was scheduled to visit, I'd throw practically all my clothes—clean or dirty—around the room. I knew that she wouldn't be able to take the sight of it. She'd take my stuff, clean it, fold it, and bring it back. That's a service you just can't beat!

—*JENNY PRISUTA*
YOUNGSTOWN STATE UNIVERSITY, SENIOR

IF YOU SEE A FREE LAUNDRY MACHINE, be on the ball and grab it. I have a little card I keep with me that says, "Dibs on these machines—Molly." If I see a free machine, I put the card on it, run upstairs and get my clothes.

—*MOLLY*
BROWN UNIVERSITY, SOPHOMORE

· · · · · · · ·

" Tip: Blue jeans don't get dirty for roughly seven days of consecutive use unless you spill something visible on them. "

—*BARRY LANGER*
OGLETHORPE UNIVERSITY, JUNIOR

· · · · · · · ·

I NEVER DID MY OWN LAUNDRY before college, so I had no idea what to do. I felt embarrassed because I thought that I should know how to do this and I was the only one at college who didn't. But that isn't true; most people don't do their laundry at home. My roommates were more than happy to help me. My roommate and I pooled our laundry into one big laundry bin. The first couple of times, he did it. Then I took over.

—*DAN AMERMAN*
YALE UNIVERSITY, SOPHOMORE

DON'T OVERSTUFF the incredibly small dorm washers. Your clothes won't get washed and you'll end up with detergent stains all over your white tank tops. Just pay the extra dollar and do another load.

—SAMANTHA STACH
DUKE UNIVERSITY, JUNIOR

- - - - - - - -

MY WORST LAUNDRY EXPERIENCE happened during my freshman year; someone stole all but four pairs of my jeans out of the laundry in my dorm. I was pissed off, but my parents gave me money for new clothes, so that was a plus.

—M.G
VALDOSTA STATE UNIVERSITY, SENIOR

- - - - - - - -

IF IT DOESN'T SMELL BAD or have stains on it, it's not dirty.

—HASSAN
UNIVERSITY OF TULSA, GRADUATE

3 TIPS FOR LAUNDRY, PART 1

1. Don't let laundry (especially damp/sweaty clothes) sit around for weeks on end. It smells and your roommates will be angry.
2. When using a dorm laundry room, you have to be patient because everyone tends to leave their clothes in the washers and dryers until it's convenient to get them out, even though it's extremely inconvenient for everyone else. (Flip side of this: Time your laundry and get it out immediately. It's just common courtesy.)
3. Don't bring anything to school that's "hand-wash only" or "dry-clean only." Unless you're a diehard fashionista and will go out of your way to find a dry-cleaner AND pay the extra money for it, you'll never get it washed and thus never wear it.

—LIZZIE
BOWDOIN COLLEGE, FRESHMAN

AT STANFORD, the majority of students ride bikes around campus. I attempted to wear a miniskirt and ride a bike. I immediately realized the awkwardness of it. I tried to push my skirt down and cover my underwear with my hand, but I don't think it really worked.

—*TIFFANY*
STANFORD UNIVERSITY, SENIOR

• • • • • • • • •

IT WAS AN EXCITING ACCOMPLISHMENT that I was able to take care of things like laundry by myself. I would wash my clothes at two in the morning. It was a relaxation thing. After I spent the whole night studying, I could just put my laundry in and watch it spin. I also realized I didn't have time to separate my clothes, so I just did everything in one cold batch.

—*ELIZABETH ROTH*
UNIVERSITY OF PENNSYLVANIA, SENIOR

HOW TO MAKE YOUR OWN DETERGENT

Just like you, we have access to the Internet. Which means we can come across a site that offers a way to make your own laundry detergent, should you run out of yours. Want to try it and see if it works? Don't try this at home! But since you're in your dorm ...

Homemade Detergent

Melt a grated bar of soap in a saucepan over medium heat. Stir in a cup of water. Pour mixture into two gallons of HOT water and mix well. Add 2 cups of baking soda (not baking powder).

Now see if it works: Do a load of laundry with a cup of it.

CONTRARY TO THE LAUNDRY INDUSTRY'S CLAIMS, all clothes can be washed and dried in one load. Over time, this will amount to a considerable saving, as well as create more time for partying.

—BRIAN TURNER
UNIVERSITY OF GEORGIA, GRADUATE

• • • • • • • •

GET BACK TO THE LAUNDRY ROOM on time! Time your cycles and don't be late. There were way too many times when people took my clean clothes out of the washing machine or dryer and put them on the dirty folding table.

—RENE
DUKE UNIVERSITY, GRADUATE

• • • • • • • •

DOING LAUNDRY CAN BE REALLY VICIOUS, especially Saturday and Sunday nights. That's when everybody wants to do their laundry, because they're going out. At 6 p.m. everyone wants to wash their clothes. You've got to do it in the morning, or on a weekday.

—MOLLY
BROWN UNIVERSITY, SOPHOMORE

Pajamas are okay for 8 a.m. class but not for 4 p.m. class.

—DANIELLE
DUKE UNIVERSITY
GRADUATE

3 TIPS FOR LAUNDRY, PART 2

If laundry isn't your cup of detergent (get it?) and you do not want to take on the task, I have three tips for you.

Tip #1: Be nice to Mom.
Tip #2: If Tip #1 fails, buy Mom jewelry.
Tip #3: If Tip #1 and #2 fail, find a very caring girlfriend.

—ALEKSANDR AKULOV
HUNTER COLLEGE, SOPHOMORE

NEVER WEAR ANYTHING FROM YOUR HIGH SCHOOL.
I mean, we all went to high school, but you don't
have to advertise it.

—*J.T.*
UNIVERSITY OF FLORIDA, GRADUATE

14

Friends:
Good, Better,
Best – or Former

Research shows that one in 10 babies is blessed at birth by a good fairy, and grows up with the ability to make and keep perfect friendships with no effort whatsoever. The rest of us, on the other hand, could use a few suggestions on how to find those new, lifelong friends in college while still holding on to the high school friendships that matter. Read on for down-to-earth wisdom on everything from casual connections to kindred spirits.

SURROUND YOURSELF WITH GOOD PEOPLE. It's more about quality than quantity when it comes to friends.

—JESSICA
BARNARD COLLEGE, JUNIOR

IT TAKES TIME TO MEET GOOD FRIENDS.

—ZAK AMCHISLAVSKY
GEORGETOWN
UNIVERSITY, SENIOR

HEADLINES
Best Advice and Top Tips

- Reuniting with your old friends can be strange when you realize you all have new lives.
- Be open to meeting new people, but remember it's the quality – not quantity – of people around you that matters.
- It can take some time to make new friends at college; be patient.

Stay open. You are going to meet so many different people every day. Just stay open.

—*Lina J.*
Georgia State University Sophomore

GOING HOME FOR THE FIRST TIME is a combination of the best and worst feelings you will ever have. Although it is fabulous to hook back up with the old crowd, party where you used to, and possibly rediscover that old flame, it is also very hard to realize that every one of your friends now has a life that is completely separate from your experience. Sometimes reuniting is not the celebration you thought it would be. Acknowledge your differences, and enjoy your friends for who they are. Look at photos, hear crazy stories, and go out and have fun together, but always remember that things have changed (which is not necessarily a bad thing). And never go back to the old ex; it only ends in trouble.

—*A.*
Princeton University, Freshman

I HANG OUT WITH ABOUT FIVE PERCENT of the people that I hung out with freshman year. You hung out with them because you had to spend time with them; they were on your floor. But then you figure out whom you like.

—ZAK AMCHISLAVSKY
GEORGETOWN UNIVERSITY, SENIOR

• • • • • • • •

" Don't spend too much time with your high school friends. Half my high school ended up going to my college. I was fortunate enough to live on the other side of campus. They're still hanging out with each other. They've never met other people and they all live together. "

—R.S.
UNIVERSITY OF MARYLAND, JUNIOR

• • • • • • • •

INVITE YOUR HIGH SCHOOL FRIENDS over for a couple of days. The ones who stay in touch are the ones worth keeping for a lifetime.

—KHALIL SULLIVAN
PRINCETON UNIVERSITY, JUNIOR

MAKE REAL EFFORTS TO BE WITH YOUR FRIENDS, even if you're just doing dumb stuff like watching a movie or painting your nails. This is the only time in life where you'll be living with all your friends, and you'll miss it when it's gone. One of my best friends and I make a date every week to do our nails and talk; it's something you need to do anyhow, and it's so much more fun if you get to spend quality time and gossip with one of your favorite people. College can get really hectic: it's nice to know that some things can stay constant.

> —JULIE
> PRINCETON UNIVERSITY, SOPHOMORE

I HAVE ONE LIFE BACK HOME, and now I'm starting up a new life. In the beginning it's hard; you want to maintain your old life. But you also have to realize that you're maturing and changing.

> —MATT MONACO
> GEORGE WASHINGTON UNIVERSITY, FRESHMAN

Consider

REMEMBER THAT YOU'RE NOT THE ONLY ONE who's starting from scratch with few or no friends. Most of the people there are in the same situation. And most colleges have events for freshmen, especially if you live in a dorm. They will usually involve free food or a movie. Go, even if you don't like the food or the movie. At least you'll have the opportunity to meet people. That's the whole point! It'll give you something to talk about with the person later ("Wasn't the food last night horrible?").

> —LAUREN TAYLOR
> UNIVERSITY OF GEORGIA, GRADUATE

3 WAYS TO STAY IN TOUCH WITHOUT TALKING

College can be truly overwhelming. If you have perfected the college experience, you should be busy from sun-up to long after sundown – classes, studying, extracurriculars, parties, more studying.

Time management is key. And in that realm, every student must learn how much time to "give" to staying in touch with family and old friends. Your time is precious: You don't want to spend hours on the phone with a talkative best friend from high school, or detailing your syllabus to your mother.

Lucky for you, we live in an era when we have ways of keeping in touch without always having to talk. Here are three common techniques to use to your time-management advantage.

1. **Texting.** A well-written but brief text can let someone know you're thinking of them and impart a tidbit of information – without committing to an entire conversation. Start off with, "Really busy right now, but just wanted you to know ..." End with an indefinite "Will call soon."

2. **Facebook "liking" or commenting:** Visit the page of a friend you've been meaning to call. Find something they've posted and hit the "Like" link (assuming, of course, that liking it is not insulting in any way). There. You just communicated with them. Feeling verbose? Write a brief comment. Now get back to your college life.

3. **Good ol' email.** Great to use with parents, an email doesn't have to be any longer than a text. And if you want to avoid long return emails filled with questions, start off with "really busy" and end with a vague reference to calling soon.

The Editors

FAMILY, FRIENDS AND YOUR NEW COLLEGE PALS

One of the trickiest things about your first year of college is balancing relationships. Not romantic relationships – we all know that finding love is tricky anytime. Your first year of college is going to be filled with your multiple relationships (family, friends from back home, friends/classmates/hall mates/roommates from college), each unintentionally pulling you in different directions at the same time. How do you maintain strong ties to all of these people?

Parents/Family

- Make sure you talk to your family at least once a week at first … not just your parents, but siblings too.
- From time to time, sit down and write your family a letter. It's a lost art; they'll appreciate the thought behind it, and they'll probably stick it to the fridge for a while. Plus, it sends a subtle hint that you want them to mail you things – like cookies and other snacks, gift cards to grocery stores and movie theaters, etc.
- Look at your course syllabi, your planner and any upcoming campus events that you want to go to, and pre-plan a weekend to go home. Your family may even enjoy the anticipation.
- Invite your family to come visit you on campus. Maybe your university has a Parents/Family Weekend event, or your family wants to go see the big game with you. You can give them a little taste of your life on campus. (Just clean your room first.)
- An even cooler idea: If you have younger siblings that may have a weekday off from school (and if they live nearby), have them crash with you overnight and bring them to class. All of your friends, classmates and hall mates will enjoy the guest, and your younger sister or brother will get to see what college is like.
- If your university has a Parents Association, plug your family into it. There may be some good incentives or benefits for doing so, like super-close seats at graduation when you receive your diploma, etc.

Friends from Home

- Invite them to come out for the big game, the campus concert/festival, or just to hang out and see the campus. Also make a trip to go visit them at their campus. You'll both appreciate the chance to swap stories, compare the campuses, and meet each other's friends.
- Connect to each other's friends via Facebook, to expand your networks and to give you more things in common.
- When you know you're going home for the weekend, connect with your friends from home and plan out time to hang out.
- Use your online social networking tools to keep up with all of your friends. Even just remembering to wish them a happy birthday and responding to an occasional status update will make a world of difference.

College Friends

- When you go home for the weekend, or even just a day, bring one of your college friends with you. It will be fun to show them around your hometown. They might even invite you to their house.
- Your college friends have families, too. Try to coordinate going home the same weekends.
- Plan a road trip with three of your closest college pals. A road trip is a must during every college experience!

Scott C. Silverman

WHILE MY HIGH SCHOOL FRIENDS are not as involved in what I am trying to do as my Curtis friends, they remain my truest of friends. They represent a place where I can come anytime and be comfortable.

—*N.*
CURTIS INSTITUTE OF MUSIC, SOPHOMORE

Save high school friends for drunk dialing. Or for face-to-face contact on breaks.

—J.V.
 THE COLLEGE OF
 WILLIAM & MARY
 GRADUATE

THE BEST THING ABOUT COLLEGE is that your friends are there. If you think that you're weird because you love Judy Garland, or superheroes, or the smell of books or whatever, your friends are still there. Your friends were probably there in high school as well, but this time there's more of them. And these friends are great, great people who are going to support you through everything, but are also going to sit you down if you're completely and utterly wrong.

—SHANNON KELLEY
 KENYON COLLEGE, JUNIOR

• • • • • • • •

IT'S FAR TOO EASY TO MAKE FRIENDS in college. What is difficult is weeding through the self-serving jerks and spending as much time as possible with your true crew. But make it your first priority. These select people are the key to eternal happiness and enlightenment.

—JOHN
 UNIVERSITY OF WISCONSIN AT MADISON, GRADUATE

• • • • • • • •

WHEN I MET MY BEST FRIEND, she was crying in her bed in our freshman dorm. She had a long-distance boyfriend. She was from the mountains of Georgia. I'm from St. Louis. I went to a private Catholic girls' school. She went to a public school with rednecks and people with gun racks on their cars. We couldn't be more different. But we had a class together and one day, after I found her crying, she overslept. So I was like, "Oh, I'll call you in the morning," and we started walking to class together, and we got breakfast after class. We became friends.

—J. DEVEREUX
 GEORGETOWN UNIVERSITY, GRADUATE

WHEN FRIENDSHIPS END

"We like all the same music."

"She's just like me!"

"We're best friends already."

"I wish there had been more people like him in high school."

One of the most exciting things about starting college is making new friends. And because of all the freedom you have—to go to the cafeteria together for every meal, to meet up for coffee between classes, to stay up all night talking or playing air hockey in the lounge—everything gets accelerated.

People get used to seeing you and your friends together. *You* get used to going everywhere together. You thought that starting college not knowing anyone would be scary, but now you're set!

But. The quick-blooming friendships of Welcome Week don't always last. Intellectually, you know that college is a time to reinvent yourself, try new things, shed some old habits. Still, it's incredibly painful when *you* are the "old" habit getting shed. Suddenly, your new BFF doesn't want to stay up talking about bands—she's got other plans. And it's not just the two of you anymore eating huge stacks of waffles on Sunday mornings; you're sharing a big table with 10 other kids from your hall.

So what can you do? Go ahead and feel the pain. Mourn the friendship just like any other breakup, and know that things will never go back to the way they were with that person. Write a bad poem if you must, then get rid of it (not much privacy in the dorm).

And open yourself up to new friends.

Frances Northcutt

ONE OF MY BIGGEST MISTAKES was trying to keep in touch with everyone from my small high school graduating class. Bill Cosby once said, "I don't know the key to success, but the key to failure is trying to please everybody." If I could go back and change one thing, I would not try as hard to keep in touch with everyone. I would have focused more on securing more meaningful relationships in college and on my studies.

—*DAVID*
ANDERSON UNIVERSITY, SENIOR

• • • • • • • •

IT'S VERY EASY FOR A GIRL to find guy friends. My freshman year all my friends at first were guys. I loved the attention and they were cool to hang out with. But while other girls were making friendships with girls that were solid, I was not. So when I hit a rough time and needed a female shoulder to cry on, it was not there. This was a big mistake I paid for dearly.

—*KAROLINE EVANS*
CARNEGIE MELLON UNIVERSITY, JUNIOR

• • • • • • • •

I WENT TO COLLEGE PLANNING ON STAYING in close contact with all my "friends" in high school – all 200 of them. I had to learn that being a social person did not mean I had to talk to everyone I was friends with in high school on a regular basis. With my true friends, I found the best thing to do was send an encouraging or "just saying hi" text message or email to those I really cared about when I didn't have time to have a long conversation.

—*MERELISE HARTE ROUZER*
GEORGIA INSTITUTE OF TECHNOLOGY, SOPHOMORE

WALK TO CLASSES WHEN YOU CAN. It's good for you
and it will give you a chance to get to know the
campus. Notice the people around you. Take time
out of your day to sit on a bench and look at your
surroundings. Be friendly; make the effort to say
hello, even if the other person looks grumpy.

—*J.S.*
UNIVERSITY OF GEORGIA, GRADUATE

• • • • • • • •

TRY AND FIND A FEW UPPERCLASSMEN FRIENDS, who
can help you find new classes, meet new people,
and broaden your perspective from the typical
freshman experience. I had one guy on my hall
who would talk to me every night when we
would brush our teeth, and he would always
invite me to things, or just ask me about school
and stuff. It was good to have someone like that.
Some people use RAs, bible study leaders, group
presidents - whatever it is, it's important to realize
that you're here with 3 other classes of awesome
and successful Tar Heels, not just your own
year. College is less about those kinds of cliques,
and until you realize that it can be a bit nerve
wracking.

—*BEN MILLER*
UNIVERSITY OF NORTH CAROLINA AT CHAPEL HILL, SENIOR

• • • • • • • •

MAKE FRIENDS WITH PEOPLE WHO ARE NOT FRESHMEN.
Doing organizations on campus helps you meet
older students. Now that I'm a senior, I have a big
network of friends outside of college, that I can
ask for advice about things I'm about to do.

—*CATIE*
HARVARD COLLEGE, SENIOR

WHO YOU HANG OUT WITH IS IMPORTANT. You have to look at it as an extension of high school: there are still going to be different groups and cliques, and you have to make sure you don't hang out with the partyers too much. It's good once in a while, but I suggest having a core group of friends that are motivators and that really help you stay on track and go to class. The freedom in college can be great, but it can also get you in trouble. You need to stay motivated.

—JESSICA DOSHNA
UCLA, GRADUATE

• • • • • • • •

I MADE A BUNCH OF FRIENDS that, coming out of high school, I wouldn't have expected to be my friends. And that was great. You gotta go to clubs, take risks, talk to people. Really anyone can be your best friend but you gotta say hi.

—MATT
TUFTS UNIVERSITY, SOPHOMORE

• • • • • • • •

RATHER THAN LOOKING FOR COOL KIDS to be friends with, find people you just really get along with. I ended up being friends with people across the hall – they were nice, and really into music. They didn't go out every night but that was better. I haven't heard of a lot of people who go out every night who have a good academic standing!

—MATTHEW GUTSHALL
ST. JOSEPH'S, JUNIOR

• • • • • • • •

INTRODUCE YOURSELF TO EVERYONE; it makes a difference. If you continue to say hi to people, you'll get to know people. Not everyone will be your best friend, but you'll get there. You'll have new friends.

—J. DEVEREUX
GEORGETOWN UNIVERSITY, GRADUATE

THE BEST WAY TO MAKE FRIENDS IN COLLEGE is to cling to them and never, ever let them out of your sight. You might think I'm kidding, but I'm not. The first time I hung out with my closest friend in college, we just ate ice cream and watched "Doogie Howser". Neither of us particularly enjoyed the show, and we didn't seem to have much in common, except that we were both nervous and desperate. Bam! Friendship. Before long, we texted each other before every meal and hung out in each other's room every night.

Obviously, we needed to make more friends, but we were both at a loss as to how to find them. Fortunately we figured out the eating schedule of a group of kids we liked and stalked them mercilessly, pretending that we just happened to run into them every day (my school is really small, so that's not too unbelievable). And to everyone's surprise, it didn't end in a restraining order but in real friendship. I still consider my friends in college to be the coolest people I've ever met.

—SHANNON KELLEY
KENYON COLLEGE, JUNIOR

DEFINITELY KEEP IN TOUCH with your high school friends. You can always count on them for support and good laughs. This may be stating the obvious, but when you return home, they'll be the first ones (aside from your family) who will want to spend time with you and with whom you will most likely socialize, so why fall out of touch?

—ARIEL MELENDEZ
PRINCETON UNIVERSITY, FRESHMAN

DON'T LET THINGS THAT BOTHER YOU linger too long. My friend went out with a guy that I had been seeing. That hurt my feelings. Instead of resolving the problem immediately, I waited until I was too angry to discuss it like a rational adult. I learned later that she honestly never intended to hurt me. But since I waited until I was furious, her feelings got hurt and she never got over it. Our friendship never fully recovered.

—*ERIN*
CENTRAL BIBLE COLLEGE, GRADUATE

. . . .

IF YOU'RE THE KIND OF PERSON who studies alone, you're not going to be finding a support system by focusing on classes. You need to make sure you're finding a support system in your new environment.

—*EMILY*
HARVARD COLLEGE, SENIOR

. . . .

A LOT OF MY FRIENDS have been unhappy with me since I went to college because I haven't been able to keep in touch as much as they'd like. It's tricky because I have a completely new life and am constantly busy, but a lot of the time they don't understand that. It's still something I'm grappling with, and it even makes me a little uncomfortable when my old friends come onto campus. There's always that feeling that they don't really fit into this new world. I try to call when I can, but it's strange— out of sight, out of mind.

—*SETH*
OGLETHORPE UNIVERSITY, FRESHMAN

Going Out, Getting Serious: Dating & Sex

Should you hang on to that high school boyfriend or girlfriend as you enter college? Should you get serious with someone within a month of starting your freshman year? Is hooking up acceptable now, or will it spark high-school-like drama? And is it okay to date someone in your dorm? You'll be faced with a lot of questions regarding dating and love in college. You will make mistakes. One thing's for sure: You will never again witness a dating scene like the one you'll find on your college campus. Here are some tips to help you make the most of it.

USE REQUIRED **P.E.** CREDITS to your advantage in meeting potential dates. Girls, try bowling or weight lifting. Boys, go with ballroom dancing or walking.

—WENDY W.
UNIVERSITY OF GEORGIA, GRADUATE

WHEN YOU'RE NOT PAYING ATTENTION, THAT'S WHEN SOMEONE WILL BE LOOKING AT YOU.

—SARAH
GEORGIA INSTITUTE OF TECHNOLOGY GRADUATE

HEAD**LINES**
Best Advice and Top Tips

- Don't leave a high school sweetheart waiting at home—you'll miss out on a lot of dating.
- Frat parties are not the best places to look for long-term relationships.
- Avoid dating someone in your dorm—breakups can be very messy.
- Ladies: be smart, use good judgment, and always keep yourself safe.

I'M REALLY HORRIBLE at talking to a hook-up afterwards. I just avoid them because I feel it would be awkward. I always kind of want to talk to them and apologize for avoiding them, but I never get around to it. To avoid this, just think before you act.

—*NATHANIEL SCHIER*
POMONA COLLEGE, SOPHOMORE

. . . .

YOUR FIRST SEMESTER, DON'T DATE. You're still trying to get settled in college, you're making some new friends, you're dealing with all the anxiety of being away from your family and high-school friends, you're trying to get into classes that are much harder than you've had before. There's a lot of stress that first semester. Whether you're a guy or girl, you've got four or five years, and maybe after college, to meet the right person. Enjoy the freedom and you'll have a lot more fun that way.

—*C.W.*
RHODES COLLEGE, SENIOR

DON'T BELIEVE THAT AN UPPERCLASSMAN is going to call you for a date, like he says he's going to. Don't wait by the phone. He gets drunk at frat parties and hooks up with the first thing he sees; that's how guys "date" in college.

—*K.E.R.*
FLORIDA STATE UNIVERSITY, GRADUATE

. . . .

❝ Our dorm was arranged in suites; there were 18 people sharing a living room and a restroom. It was pretty much understood that you don't have a relationship with a suite mate because that was bad. That would cause horrible conflicts for everybody else in the group. ❞

—*D.H.*
UNIVERSITY OF CALIFORNIA AT BERKELEY, GRADUATE

. . . .

LADIES, BE SMART, be safe, and remember that the university health centers are a great place to go in situations of need.

—*ERIN*
SUFFOLK UNIVERSITY, GRADUATE

You need to go out and party and meet lots of people.

—*ANONYMOUS*
  YALE UNIVERSITY
  SOPHOMORE

AS A FRESHMAN you can still get women to hang out with you despite the competition from the older guys. I talk to the woman to get to know her—you have to know about the person you want to go out with. Most guys try pick-up lines and the like, which women can see right through. When I know what they are like, I can go further and ask to be with them in a more private setting. My method is mainly to get a woman to get acquainted with me, and I with her, before we hook up.

—*Y.H.*
  UNIVERSITY OF VIRGINIA, JUNIOR

• • • • • • • • •

I HAD A BOYFRIEND FROM HOME, which was a big mistake. It kept me tied to home a little too much. I went a full year before we broke up. And I didn't party that much because of the boyfriend. I didn't drink at all in high school and that took a year to kick in, too. Then I was just like, screw it, I'm going to go out and have fun.

—*LYNN SNIFFEN*
  BOSTON COLLEGE, JUNIOR

• • • • • • • • •

I WASN'T A VERY PROMISCUOUS GUY in high school so the thought of going to a frat party with two kegs, tons of twenty-one year old frat guys who knew what they were doing and a bunch of scantily clad women was terrifying. I went though, and eventually got used to it. You have to be proactive or else you won't get what you want. Do anything—talk to girls, talk to guys, dance, or have a drink. I swallowed my pride and accepted that there is nothing wrong with someone saying to you, "I'm not interested." If you can't accept that, you might as well not even bother.

—*MICHAEL*
  NORTHWESTERN UNIVERSITY, SOPHOMORE

A GREAT PLACE TO MEET GIRLS is at the bookstore. Upon receiving the class syllabus, you have to buy books. If you're in the bookstore and you see a girl buying books, it's an easy entrance: "Oh, are you taking history?"

—*J.R.*
COLUMBIA UNIVERSITY, GRADUATE

• • • • • • • •

TURKEY DROP: This is the time around Thanksgiving when freshmen break up with their significant others they "promised" to date for life. This is typical. Expect it.

—*RAE LYNN RUCKER*
BIOLA UNIVERSITY, GRADUATE

• • • • • • • •

DON'T EVER LISTEN to what any college guy says. They all lie—about everything. Especially if they say, "Let's go for a walk." That's the worst: Run screaming.

—*JENNIFER SPICER*
FOOTHILL COLLEGE, GRADUATE

• • • • • • • •

DON'T COME WITH A GIRLFRIEND from home. There are several reasons. First, this is the first time you will really taste freedom and you do not want to be limited and restrained by someone from home. Second, there is booze and parties everywhere. You will feel like you are in a candy store. And you will see girls who are not the girl you grew up with. Everyone is insecure and looking for a connection.

—*DEREK LI*
CARNEGIE MELLON UNIVERSITY, JUNIOR

Roller-skating, bowling, and getting ice cream cones are still great dates in college. In fact, you get major points for being bold enough to do them with gusto.

—*BRIAN TURNER*
UNIVERSITY OF GEORGIA GRADUATE

ADVICE FOR THE DATELORN

IT'S A MISTAKE TO START DATING the first few weeks of college. I mean, compared to high school, college is paradise for dating: you're surrounded by people with your interests, you can stay up late, go to parties whenever you want, you can sleep together and not worry about parents—it's amazing. But be patient. There's this huge rush to date someone, but it's important to make friends first. That way, when you break up with someone, you still have your friends. If you start dating someone right away, you may miss out on making real friends, and that's more important.

Date someone who is also a freshman. In the first few months of school, it's hard to really relate to someone who's older. Plus, if you date someone who's older, it takes you away from your dorm and first-year activities; it almost makes you skip your first year. If you date someone who is also a freshman, you can go through freshman year together.

> —SUMMER J.
> UNIVERSITY OF VIRGINIA, SENIOR

. . . .

DON'T DATE SOMEONE IN YOUR HALLWAY; I did. Not only are you living together, but you also have shared counselors and shared activities; you can't escape them. Anytime I went anywhere, or anytime he went anywhere, we would know about it. We'd have fights over IM, and sometimes we'd have to run down the hallway to go yell at each other. And even if we were to break up, there was no chance of having our own lives without the other person knowing about it. So I basically continued to date him for the whole year, regardless of how happy I was, in order to not deal with the issues involved with having him around.

> —CATE
> BROWN UNIVERSITY, JUNIOR

SOME GUYS ARE GREAT; some guys are not so great. Coming to school, no one has a past; people are going to be pushing the image they want you to see. So many people put up a front. They are who they're not. You can't possibly trust someone if you've just met them, so take time to get to know people. And don't have a relationship your first semester.

—*KERRY*
GEORGETOWN UNIVERSITY, GRADUATE

. . . .

"If someone gets you alone, and gets the room all comfy and dim, and asks if you like Beefeater, please run screaming for eight miles in the opposite direction. They don't just mean gin, no matter what they say."

—*KARLA SAIA*
SAN DIEGO STATE UNIVERSITY, JUNIOR

. . . .

BE PREPARED TO MEET NO WOMEN your freshman year who want to date you. They are just not available. Either they have boyfriends, or hang-ups, or they like girls. Whatever the reason, as a freshman you will have no girlfriend. If I knew why, I would not be alone.

—*JOE MAYAN*
CARNEGIE MELLON UNIVERSITY, SOPHOMORE

YOU WANT TO KNOW HOW TO GET GIRLS? Respect them. Be nice to them; it's that simple. Forget pickup lines or getting them drunk. In fact, warn them about guys like that. It sounds silly, but be their hero by being nice and thinking of them. Also, never, ever, ever try a pickup line, unless you're just kidding around. They never work. The only pickup line that works is, "Hi. How are you?" It's a legitimate start to a conversation.

—R.B.
MASSACHUSETTS INSTITUTE OF TECHNOLOGY, JUNIOR

" Be friends until you know you really want to take it to the next level. I see so many girls having sex right away because they need reassurance. They later regret it. "

—SARAH LOLA PALODICHUK
RIVERSIDE COMMUNITY COLLEGE, GRADUATE

I LEFT A SERIOUS RELATIONSHIP hanging when I left high school, so I didn't date anyone seriously my whole freshman year. I just hooked up and had one-night stands. I enjoyed being single in college—true love will come eventually, and until then, you should have some fun.

—P.
PRINCETON UNIVERSITY, SOPHOMORE

DON'T DATE SOMEONE you're good friends with. If you go to a small school, it becomes a thing where everyone knows about your business, everyone knows everything about your relationship.

—CONOR MCNEIL
EMORY UNIVERSITY, SOPHOMORE

• • • • • • • •

THE BIGGEST THING I TOLD MYSELF was to put the whole boyfriend thing on hold. I figured it would be too much of a distraction to have a significant other. That helped.

—JERI D. HILT
HOWARD UNIVERSITY, SENIOR

• • • • • • • •

IN THE FIRST TWO WEEKS OF MY FRESHMAN YEAR, I met a senior. We started dating and were soon an official couple. It was good while it lasted, but a year later, after he graduated, we broke up. All of the friends I had before going out with him had already moved on to hang out with other friends. They all had their own groups, and I wasn't included because I thought that I was so cool going out with a senior. Yeah, right! I was left in the dust.

—LYNDSEY WENTZ
KUTZTOWN UNIVERSITY, JUNIOR

Be careful about dating too many older men when you're 18. Make sure they're actually going to your school.

—ANONYMOUS
CALVIN COLLEGE
GRADUATE

WHERE THE HOT GUYS ARE

What male student body gets the best grade in looks? According to Collegeprowler.com, Pacific Union College in California is the only school in the country that scored 10 out of 10.

Avoid meeting
people at frat
parties when
you're look-
ing to date.
It's hard to tell
how sincere
they are when
you're a fresh-
man.

—ANN MALIPATIL
EMORY UNIVERSITY
SENIOR

THE SINGLE-ROOM BATHROOMS in the college library are the best place to have quickie sex on campus.

—J.
UNIVERSITY OF GEORGIA, GRADUATE

• • • • • • • •

IT MAY LOOK LIKE THE GIRLS who are out partying, and doing who knows what with who knows who, are the girls getting the guys. But they're not, really. Also, the nice boys are not on sports teams. I don't know where they are, but they're not on sports teams.

—EBELE ONYEMA
GEORGETOWN UNIVERSITY, SENIOR

• • • • • • • •

I'VE SEEN THE MISTAKE OF PEOPLE staying with their high-school boyfriend or girlfriend, then break-ing up with them senior year. That's a terrible experience. You lose the entire novelty of being in college. I would recommend meeting new people and going out with different types of people, whether they're from other states or countries, or whatever.

—MIKE
UNIVERSITY OF TEXAS AT AUSTIN, GRADUATE

• • • • • • • •

HOOKING UP—DON'T DO IT on Halloween unless you really know who is behind that costume. I had a lot to drink and ended up with a very big surprise once we got com-fortable. I ran out of there quick-ly: it was a very homely girl.

—JAMIE JASTA
CARNEGIE MELLON UNIVERSITY, SENIOR

SADDER BUT WISER

I met my girlfriend in my freshman year. All year long I had been active with my dorm. It was coed and very community-oriented. Then my friend moved into my dorm, and things changed. We started dating and did the whole isolation thing, and it was especially dumb because of the community feeling on our floor. As it turned out, I dated her until spring of senior year, and in the process, I stopped really doing the whole college scene thing; this is something one should definitely not do.

Breaking up with my girlfriend was the hardest thing I have ever done: Basically, you grow up with the person in college, and you go through your whole college experience with just them. I found myself almost at the beginning of the cycle; having to develop friends and cultivate relationships, and trying to bring back friendships with people I had deserted over the years.

—*D.*
AMERICAN UNIVERSITY, GRADUATE

ALWAYS GO TO PARTIES WITH A BUDDY. At one point my freshman spring, my friend had left the party and there was this guy who wouldn't leave me alone and was being really aggressive - but luckily the fire alarm went off and the whole building had to evacuate so I got out of that situation! Just try not to let yourself get isolated.

—*CATIE*
HARVARD COLLEGE, SENIOR

MY SISTER IS A FRESHMAN. I told her not to hook up with a lot of guys, not to get a bad reputation, because you can't shake it; it follows you everywhere. I'm a senior now, and some of the people that in my opinion have had bad reputations for whatever reason, when I look at them now, that's what I think of. Some people have been away for a year, studying abroad; some people, I haven't seen them since freshman year. But the reputation sticks.

—*TIM JOYCE*
GEORGETOWN UNIVERSITY, SENIOR

● ● ● ● ● ● ● ●

" Try to avoid feeling committed to anyone the first year. Don't get too serious about dating any particular person. Spend some time. And I wouldn't go in with too much baggage from high school, either. "

—*RYAN A. BROWN*
UNIVERSITY OF NORTH CAROLINA AT CHAPEL HILL, GRADUATE

● ● ● ● ● ● ● ●

DON'T DO ANYTHING WITH A GIRL who's not making rational decisions; that's a good way to get thrown in jail. It's better to be extremely modest in that situation. If a girl wants to do something with you, you can do it the next time or three times down the road.

—*NICHOLAS BONAWITZ*
UNIVERSITY OF ROCHESTER, GRADUATE

TIS THE SEASON . . . FOR LOVE

Take full advantage of all of the social opportunities that college offers a freshman, and avoid any serious relationships that may hamper or deter you from enjoying all of the rites of passage of being a college freshman. There is no better time than fall on a college campus, with fraternity/sorority rush, parties, and football games to enjoy and revel in. If you have a significant other, or meet someone who could quickly become a significant other, find any reason to put that relationship off until winter when it gets cold and the social life slows down a bit. Keep in mind, however, that after winter comes spring break, when once again, all ties must be broken.

I learned this lesson the hard way; I had a serious girlfriend who attended Auburn while I was attending Georgia Tech. Not only did I put many unnecessary miles on my car, I also missed the opportunity to meet many other interesting coeds with a lot to offer. While my fraternity and college experience was certainly not without its share of fun, a serious long-distance girlfriend did not enhance it. And to make matters worse, I actually dropped a Naval ROTC scholarship (and an opportunity to become a pilot) after my freshman year because I thought I would rather marry the Auburn coed than cruise the Mediterranean on an aircraft carrier. Needless to say, we broke up less than a year after this very forward-looking decision. That's another reason for stalling those serious entangling relationships early in college; they hamper logical decision-making.

—*S.A.H.*
GEORGIA INSTITUTE OF TECHNOLOGY, GRADUATE

ASK PEOPLE OUT. It takes guts but you'll never know unless you try. And everyone appreciates a little more courtship and a little less of the senseless hookup culture.

—SEAN CAMERON
PRINCETON UNIVERSITY, SOPHOMORE

• • • • • • • •

I HAVE A FRIEND WHO STARTED DATING her boyfriend about a week after they got to college. She never really did freshman year like some people do, and it's affecting her now. She feels like she didn't go through the crazy freshman stuff before getting into a serious relationship.

—HANNAH
EMORY UNIVERSITY, JUNIOR

• • • • • • • •

I TRANSFERRED TO ANOTHER SCHOOL because my girlfriend couldn't get into my school. After I transferred there, we dated for another six months, then broke up. I felt like an idiot, because I had transferred to an easier school.

—JUAN GONZALEZ
CLEMSON UNIVERSITY, GRADUATE

• • • • • • • •

AS A FRESHMAN, a male friend of mine invited me to his room to "watch a movie." I had a boyfriend back home and was not promiscuous at all, so I honestly thought this guy was a friend. Halfway through the movie, I turned around to realize he had pulled out his penis and was sitting there looking at me. After a few confused and startled words, I got my stuff and left. He later apologized and said he thought we were on the same page when he invited me to his room. He thought I knew what the words "watch a movie" meant in college, especially at 10 p.m. on a Friday night. I did not!

—CHAVON
XAVIER UNIVERSITY, GRADUATE

Advice to the guys: know that she's just waiting for you to come up to her and say hi. I'm now in grad school; it took me seven years to figure that out.

—KAMAL FREIHA
UNIVERSITY OF OREGON
GRADUATE

STAY AWAY FROM THE BOYS on the athletic teams; they're players in the dating scene. They think they're really cool, and they take advantage of the freshman girls. The freshman girls come in and they're in awe, and the athletes hit on them and take advantage of them. Beware.

> —A.
> GEORGETOWN UNIVERSITY, SOPHOMORE

If you're looking for love, be patient.

> —KHALIL SULLIVAN
> PRINCETON
> UNIVERSITY, JUNIOR

" Advice on dating: Don't. It costs too much. Go out with friends and meet new people. If you do date, don't date one person exclusively. It only leads to trouble. "

> —JIMMY LYNCH
> AUBURN UNIVERSITY, GRADUATE

YOU DON'T EVER WANT TO MOVE IN with a girlfriend. If you do, your lifestyle becomes limited; you always have to come home with her and you always have to deal with her. I had roommates who were a couple living together in my house and I saw them fighting all the time. The reason was that they were together too much, and the expectations grow and grow and if they don't meet those expectations for one moment, they get in a fight.

> —STEPHAN
> UNIVERSITY OF CALIFORNIA AT SANTA BARBARA
> GRADUATE

You come to college and there are women everywhere; that's probably the best thing about it. But you have to have your act together. If you don't have your obligations in order, you're never going to make it. I've seen people fail out of college in the first year. But if you have your time managed right, there's nothing you can't do.

—*Chris McAndrew*
University of Delaware, Junior

• • • • • • • •

" College is when dating really begins. In high school I had boyfriends, but I never really dated. It was in college that I began to better understand the concept. "

—*Heather Pollock*
California State University, Graduate

• • • • • • • •

The summer after my freshman year, I met this guy who lived hundreds of miles from my school. We dated for a year and a half: I drove to his town, five hours away, almost every single weekend of my sophomore year; it really got old. Long-distance relationships suck. Don't try it.

—*Katherine*
Auburn University, Graduate

LATE-NIGHT HANGOUT: top of the parking deck at the medical center. Great views, quiet, good for making out. For the thrill factor: the 50-yard line in the football stadium.

—MARGOT CARMICHAEL LESTER
UNIVERSITY OF NORTH CAROLINA AT CHAPEL HILL, GRADUATE

• • • • • • • •

DON'T TRUST PEOPLE as quickly as you might want to. As a freshman girl, you could get in a lot of trouble if you don't watch yourself. Listen to your friends when they say you shouldn't do something. They probably know something more than you. You probably won't listen to them; but you should.

—LAUREN
GEORGETOWN UNIVERSITY, SOPHOMORE

• • • • • • • •

I DIDN'T REALLY DATE. I went to clubs a lot; danced and partied, but all for fun. I gave guys fake phone numbers (*that* was fun). Just remember, dancing with a guy and going home with a guy are two different things. Kissing a guy at a club and going home with a guy are two different things. One thing does not always need to lead to the other. Be patient. And no, boys will not die if you don't "help them out."

—LESLIE M.
UNIVERSITY OF FLORIDA, GRADUATE

• • • • • • • •

IF YOU HAVE A BOYFRIEND AT HOME, get rid of him: You're going to stay in your dorm, you're not going to do anything, you're not going to meet new people; you're not going to live your life.

—AMBER WITTEN
LOS MEDANOS COLLEGE, SOPHOMORE

Don't give in to pressure. I am glad that I didn't and stayed true to myself.

—ALLISON
UNIVERSITY OF
NORTH CAROLINA
AT GREENSBORO
SOPHOMORE

UNIVERSITY HEALTH CENTER

It's not just for treatment of minor cuts and sprains. Your college's health center may provide some or all of the following services:

Advice nurse
Alcohol and drug treatment, counseling, prevention
Allergy injections
Birth control
Emergency contraception (the morning-after pill)
Ergonomic evaluations (especially for computer setup)
Flu shots
Health classes
HIV testing/prevention/care
Nutritional counseling
Physical exams
Physical therapy
Rape/sexual assault prevention/response
Referral to medical services in the community
Sexual health education
Smoking cessation assistance
TB testing

Various other vaccines and immunization, such as:

Gardasil (for HPV)
Hepatitis A
Hepatitis B
Meningitis
Travel shots
Weight management

Services are confidential, and are typically offered at no or low cost to you (other than the health fee typically built into the cost of college).

Frances Northcutt

IF YOU GENUINELY WANT TO BE SINGLE so you can party hard your freshman year, that's great. However, if you're in a serious relationship that you don't want to lose just because you're going to college, don't let anyone pressure you into ending it. Yes, many high school relationships fail during the freshman year of college, but the good ones can stand the test of time and distance. I have two friends who are now married to their high school sweethearts, and two more who are engaged.

—ANONYMOUS
ILLINOIS WESLEYAN UNIVERSITY, JUNIOR

IF YOU KEEP YOUR BOYFRIEND BACK HOME, you must learn to trust each other. My boyfriend lives in Maryland and I'm at school in North Carolina. My freshman year, we talked on the phone every night, and he would always tell me how much he missed me and how hard it was to be that far away. We visited each other, but he would complain that it wasn't enough. It was also hard to see the other girls go to parties and dance and kiss other boys. But I didn't want to break up; I love my boyfriend. Over the past year, he has learned to trust me. I have told him a million times that I would never do anything to hurt him; he finally believes me.

—ALLISON
UNIVERSITY OF NORTH CAROLINA AT GREENSBORO, SOPHOMORE

TWO RULES: Don't date three guys at the same time who are all on the soccer team together. And don't date anyone on your dorm floor.

—HEATHER POLLOCK
CALIFORNIA STATE UNIVERSITY AT FULLERTON, GRADUATE

Guys, be aggressive meeting girls. It's not going to come to you. You've got to make it happen yourself.

—ALEC
BOSTON COLLEGE
JUNIOR

DO NOT GET INTO A SERIOUS RELATIONSHIP your fresh-man year. I started dating a girl in October. We had a very passionate, exclusive relationship, which was great until we broke up at the end of the year. I realized that I did not meet any new people after meeting her and I was left with no new friends, only acquaintances.

—GREGORY MOGILEVSKY
UNIVERSITY OF NORTH CAROLINA AT CHAPEL HILL, GRADUATE

. . . .

DON'T DATE PEOPLE IN YOUR DORM, especially if you're just hooking up after a party, because there will be a breakup and, therefore, awkwardness in the dorm. It's impossible to avoid someone in your building. You'll step into the elevator and they'll be there and everything gets silent.

—REID ATTAWAY
JAMES MADISON UNIVERSITY, FRESHMAN

. . . .

DO NOT HAVE SEXUAL RELATIONS with anyone in your dorm, because if you have a one-night stand, you don't necessarily want to see them the next day; that creates tension. Dating isn't a bad idea; it just depends on whether you can handle a rela-tionship. I recommend dating; it's healthy.

—N.
EMORY UNIVERSITY, JUNIOR

. . . .

FOR SOME REASON, I thought that I was going to find my husband in the first month of college. I was wrong. This belief was my biggest miscon-ception about college because in terms of dating, it gave me tunnel vision. College is about experi-ence and experimenting. Work on building friend-ships; relationships will come later.

—E.S.
DUKE UNIVERSITY, GRADUATE

Don't be afraid to be alone; take a class, meet strangers, join a club by yourself.

—WENDY W.
UNIVERSITY OF GEORGIA GRADUATE

HOOKUP ETIQUETTE

Keep condoms readily available. If the time comes, you'll have them local. And your RA should have condoms, if it comes down to it. Ultimately, it's up to the couple to use them. If the thought of sex is out there, it is important to talk about condoms. The last thing you want to happen is there to be a "miscommunication" mid-hookup.

After hooking up, stay awhile. Spend some time after talking. Don't zip up and run.

How you meet usually determines how your relationship will go. If you meet one drunken night, most likely it's a one-night thing. If you met in class while discussing the last lecture, you most likely owe the girl a call after the hookup, since the relationship began on something less superficial.

—E.F.
CLAREMONT MCKENNA COLLEGE, SOPHOMORE

DURING MY ORIENTATION, I met a girl who ended up on the same floor in the dorms. We became best friends and a month later we started dating. We're about to celebrate our fourth year of that. I strongly advise incoming freshmen to look for friends, not dates. You'll want them as you make the transition into and eventually out of college. Also, the connection that comes from being intimate with someone you're friends with makes being in a relationship worthwhile and takes away what might otherwise be awkward or even dangerous.

—RON Y. KAGAN
CUNY/MACAULAY HONORS COLLEGE, SENIOR

I advise against dating anyone exclusively as a freshman.

—*J.V.*
THE COLLEGE OF WILLIAM & MARY GRADUATE

ENJOY COLLEGE AND DON'T DATE TOO SERIOUSLY. I entered college with a boyfriend. We met in high school at the Model U.N. conference, and then he went on to Tufts University in Boston, while I came to the Macaulay Honors College at CUNY. While I did enjoy my frequent trips to Boston and to a "real" college campus (CUNY is urban), I feel that I could have experienced more in college. It is now senior year and we just broke up. We were together all through this time when we both should have been dating and experiencing life, without being bogged down in a long distance relationship. This is not the time to settle down, so just enjoy getting to know yourself and who you are. The more you date, the better. See what's out there.

—*GERALDINE SARAH COWPER*
CUNY/MACAULAY HONORS COLLEGE, SENIOR

• • • • • • • •

DATING IN COLLEGE CAN BE ONE of the most fun and confusing experiences. I had a boyfriend for a year, and I loved every minute of it. Getting to know someone outside of their high school "label" allows you to make your own refreshing decisions about them. You get to know them on a deeper level and you get to experience really fun, new and challenging things together. However, college is the one time in your life when you're surrounded by a million different people your age. Meet as many boys or girls as you can. It's really fun! It's so important to also experience being single. It can be painful at first, but college helps to form, create and shape independence. More importantly, you try more things when you are single. It is just a fact of life. You are out more, meeting more people and having different experiences.

—*A.T.*
UNIVERSITY OF MICHIGAN, SENIOR

WHERE THE HOT GIRLS ARE

Guys, we all know that while academics and a career may have some importance, the most critical factor when choosing a college is the women. Here are the top five hottest female student bodies in the country – in the eyes of the careful reviewers at Collegeprowler.com:

1. Miami University, Oxford, OH
2. James Madison University, Harrisonburg, VA
3. Chapman University, Orange, CA
4. University of Southern California, Los Angeles, CA
5. Brigham Young University, Provo, UT

DON'T SERIOUSLY DATE ANYONE your first semester. Or even your second semester, honestly. Use this time to seriously think about what you want in a romantic partner and what you need to be happy in a relationship. This the perfect time to mess around and be trashy, so take advantage of it. You're too young to be looking for your soul mate.

—SETH
OGLETHORPE UNIVERSITY, FRESHMAN

• • • • • • • •

AT THE BEGINNING OF COLLEGE, everyone is a stranger (which means random hookups aplenty). Get to know people and learn how the social scene works before even thinking of "doing anything." I saw two of my roommates get involved with guys they barely knew during the first month of school.

—LIZZIE
BOWDOIN COLLEGE, FRESHMAN

THE FACEBOOK BREAK-UP

ONE THING THAT I would totally steer clear of (and I think many of my friends would agree) would be being in "Facebook relationships" – or putting your relationship status on Facebook. When my boyfriend and I broke up, we decided I would be the one to take it off Facebook first. It was really upsetting. It is so weird to go from looking at that on your Facebook page to it suddenly not being there. Not to mention the fact that if you haven't set your privacy settings, everyone on your newsfeed will find out about it and suddenly you are explaining your situation to people who didn't even know you were in a relationship in the first place!

—ANNIE THOMAS
UNIVERSITY OF MICHIGAN, SENIOR

16

Parties 101: How to Have Fun & Be Safe

Y ou don't see them on the college website or featured in the glossy
viewbook, but you and your friends know that parties are a crucial
part of the college experience. And everyone else in your life knows it too:
your parents, your RA, your high school principal, your professors. You
know they know because they've all been giving you advice on how to have
a great time without getting yourself into too much trouble. So be honest—
did you really pay attention? Just in case you didn't (and even if you did),
read this chapter. Disclaimer: Some of this 'advice' will get you into trouble.
Be smart and safe.

WHEN YOU'RE AT A PARTY, TRY TO THINK about the
next morning. Ask yourself the question: Will I be
able to look at myself in the mirror?

—G.
UNIVERSITY OF NORTH CAROLINA AT CHAPEL HILL
SOPHOMORE

DON'T PARTY
BEFORE TESTS.

—H.K.S.
OXFORD COLLEGE
JUNIOR

HEAD**LINES**
Best Advice and Top Tips

- In college the words "party" and "beer" go hand in hand.
- If you set your drink down and walk away, don't go back for it—it's too risky.
- Never drink and drive—DUIs go on your permanent record.
- As long as you're staying on top of your work, you're not partying too much.

Don't drink the punch. There's a lot more alcohol in there than you think.

—ANONYMOUS
YALE UNIVERSITY
SOPHOMORE

GO TO PARTIES. I didn't party at all in high school. When I went to college, my R.A. took me to a frat party the second night I was there. I wouldn't say overdo it, but you should experience that part of college life.

—ERIC FRIES
BOSTON UNIVERSITY, GRADUATE

. . . .

IF A MAN APPROACHES YOU and your friends at a garden party offering strange-looking mushrooms in a baggie, tell him you're not hungry.

—D.D.
UNIVERSITY OF PENNSYLVANIA, GRADUATE

. . . .

A LOT OF PEOPLE COME IN HERE and they don't have experience drinking, and they just sort of explode. My friend had a freshman roommate who failed out the first semester because he had spent all his time drinking. Don't get in over your head.

—LEE ROBERTS
UNIVERSITY OF NORTH CAROLINA AT CHAPEL HILL, SENIOR

IF YOU WANT TO DRINK FOR FREE, head to a bar and pretend you don't want to drink alcohol. You'll suddenly be everyone's pet project. As the efforts to convert you mount, give in slowly; not only will everyone have a good time, but you'll have a good buzz to match.

—*BRIAN TURNER*
UNIVERSITY OF GEORGIA, GRADUATE

· · · · · · · ·

DON'T DRINK HARD LIQUOR—stick to beer. You have better control with beer. I had bad experiences with liquor. If you wake up the next morning and you don't remember what you did, you've had too much to drink.

—*REID ATTAWAY*
JAMES MADISON UNIVERSITY, FRESHMAN

· · · · · · · ·

IF YOU'VE NEVER FUNNELED THREE BEERS after going shot for shot with some guy in your bio lab, don't do it the first night on campus; you will end up throwing up in the washrooms, and it is just not pretty. Yes, college is a time for experimentation and partying, but don't screw up what you worked 12 years for just because the opportunity is there.

—*AMY*
PRINCETON UNIVERSITY, FRESHMAN

· · · · · · · ·

GOING OUT TO PARTIES WAS GREAT but it wasn't the social life I really needed -- the work/play balance I needed was finding those close relationships and support so that I had a support system at school.

—*EMILY*
HARVARD COLLEGE, SENIOR

YOU HAVE TO LEARN that the week is for studying and the weekend is for partying. You can't think that you just party every day. That's what I thought: I thought that college was a never-ending party, without work. I thought it was going to be easier than high school, without busy work. But it's overwhelming.

—AMY HOFFBERG
UNIVERSITY OF DELAWARE, FRESHMAN

• • • • • • • •

THE FIRST WEEK OF SCHOOL, I went out partying with my friends and next thing I remember, I was locked outside my room with no key, naked and soaking wet at five in the morning.

—S.
HARVARD COLLEGE, SOPHOMORE

• • • • • • • •

FOOTBALL GAMES ARE SO MUCH FUN HERE—everyone is drunk in the stands. On game day, the whole campus is up by 9 a.m. You can't get students up at 9 a.m. for school, but they'll get up early to start partying before a game.

—M.M.
BOSTON COLLEGE, JUNIOR

• • • • • • • •

ONCE I WENT TO A PARTY OF ALL INDIANS. Everyone in the room was Indian except me. The food, the conversations, the dress—everything was Indian. By the end of the night I thought I was Indian and was ready to give up beef forever.

—JOE MAYAN
CARNEGIE MELLON UNIVERSITY, SOPHOMORE

No matter how desperate you are for a daiquiri, do not use blueberries.

—MARGOT
CARMICHAEL LESTER
UNIVERSITY OF
NORTH CAROLINA
AT CHAPEL HILL
GRADUATE

ALCOHOL IS A REALLY BIG FACTOR in what goes wrong with freshmen. Everything is new, you're getting a lot of attention from other people, and when you're under the influence of alcohol you don't make the best decisions. And there's peer pressure: A lot of people think they're above peer pressure, but when you get in a scene with a hundred other people having a good time, you don't do things you would normally do.

—*A.G.H.*
UNIVERSITY OF VIRGINIA, SENIOR

• • • • • • • •

" Don't try to drink all the beer on campus. You can't, trust me. And not having a car your freshman year is a good safety measure. "

—*STEVE DAVIS*
FLORIDA STATE UNIVERSITY, GRADUATE

• • • • • • • •

DON'T FEEL LIKE YOU NEED to funnel beers to have a good time, and know that if you choose not to drink, there are tons of other people who don't either. But don't lecture other people—if they wanted you to be their mom, they would've asked. Exceptions: your close friends, people who are being offensive to you, people you are close to, and girls who are about to be taken advantage of because of their state.

—*JULIE*
PRINCETON UNIVERSITY, SOPHOMORE

ASK THE ADVISER

Everyone knows that college students drink. Am I really going to get into trouble for having a couple of beers in the dorm?

You're half right—all college administrators know that *some* college students drink. Plenty of students don't drink at all, or drink very moderately. But your question is about getting into trouble.

The answer depends on your college. Some colleges have almost supernatural powers when it comes to sniffing out that kind of rule breaking, whereas others operate on a purely human skill level. The second half of the story is what happens to students who are caught drinking. There will always be consequences, but they may vary in type and severity. Read your dorm handbook to find out your college's policy, and don't be fooled by other students who tell you that "they don't really mean it;" if it's on the books, it could happen to you.

Frances Northcutt

MAKE SURE YOU GO OUT with reliable people. When you party and get trashed in college, you need a support system. If you're passed out, you need someone to drag you home. Always party with people you trust.
—KYLE
UNIVERSITY OF TEXAS AT AUSTIN, GRADUATE

. . . .

JUST BECAUSE YOU can do every drug and drink everything, it doesn't mean you have to or you should. It'll take you a while to figure that out.
—A.W.D.
GEORGIA STATE UNIVERSITY, GRADUATE

HOUSE PARTIES ARE THE WAY TO GO! Forget frats, clubs, or fancy bars. Drink cheap, fast, and with friends. It's all about the people, not the place. The most fun I had was spending the night at a friend-of-a-friend's house partying, and then taking the party back to my apartment. We hung out until the wee hours of the morning. The fun is right where you are.

—JACKIE
STATE UNIVERSITY OF NEW YORK AT BINGHAMTON, GRADUATE

" If you're a bunch of girls and you go to a frat party, which you will, be aware of your surroundings and keep track of each other. Be in charge of yourself, and keep track of your girls, and they'll keep track of you. "

—TRACY
UNIVERSITY OF COLORADO, GRADUATE

IF YOU'RE GOING TO DRINK, drink *before* you go out. It saves tons of money. Use the money you save to buy a video game system to keep you occupied.

—JIMMY LYNCH
AUBURN UNIVERSITY, GRADUATE

I DON'T DRINK. It's not hard to socialize if you don't drink, because everyone needs a designated driver. If I go, they usually buy my dinner. So it works for me.

—*B.M.*
UNIVERSITY OF MARYLAND, JUNIOR

• • • • • • • •

" Alcohol makes some people seem more attractive than they will look the next morning. So, think a little more about your decisions at frat parties. "

—*H.K.S.*
OXFORD COLLEGE, JUNIOR

• • • • • • • •

YOU'RE AHEAD OF THE CURVE once you accept that the upperclassmen get all the hot girls at parties. The football players do, too. Instead of worrying about this, work on building friendships.

—*MICHAEL*
GRADUATE

• • • • • • • •

HERE'S SOME ADVICE that my brother left me on my answering machine the first week I was in college: "If you smoke pot in your room, make sure to put a towel under the door."

—*B.K.*
CORNELL UNIVERSITY, GRADUATE

Stay on top of your stuff, and regulate your drinking habits.

—*BRETT STRICKLAND*
GEORGIA STATE
UNIVERSITY
FRESHMAN

AS FAR AS DRINKING GOES, I had a closed mind. I thought, I don't want to go through four years of school drunk and not experiencing everything. I didn't realize you could balance those things. So I didn't drink at all. Then I gradually started with friends here and I was like, you know what? Going out with friends on Friday night and partying doesn't mean you're wasting four years. It just means you're experiencing different things.

—*LYNN SNIFFEN*
BOSTON COLLEGE, JUNIOR

* * * * * * * *

I DON'T DRINK. When I go to parties, people ask why I'm not drinking and I'll just tell them I decided I don't want to do it. Ninety percent of the people I talk to about it—even the people who are completely drunk—think it's cool and say I should stick with it.

—*REID ATTAWAY*
JAMES MADISON UNIVERSITY, FRESHMAN

* * * * * * * *

THERE ARE LOTS OF PARTIES THE FIRST YEAR and you meet a lot of eager goofs: people who want to make a bold statement and show you who he/she is. It seems like they're in high school again, trying to compete to be cool. Take these poseurs with a grain of salt!

—*MICHAEL ALBERT PAOLI*
UNIVERSITY OF TORONTO, GRADUATE

* * * * * * * *

TRY TO LIMIT THE DRINKING to three times a week. Work hard Monday through Thursday, and party Thursday, Friday, and Saturday nights; that's what worked for me.

—*NICK DOMANICO*
UNIVERSITY OF CALIFORNIA AT SANTA BARBARA
SENIOR

How can you tell if you're partying too much? If you're doing fine in classes, you're not partying too much. If you don't do well in classes, you're partying too much.

—*NOURA BAKKOUR*
GEORGETOWN
UNIVERSITY
SENIOR

I DON'T PARTY A LOT NOW. The first couple of years, I partied too much. I realized, this is a lot of work, trying to party and go to school, and it's expensive. So, I decided I didn't need it; it's too much effort.

—ADAM PENA
AMERICAN REPERTORY THEATER AT HARVARD, JUNIOR

• • • • • • • •

YOU'RE GOING TOO FAR with the drinking when you have to drink every time you want to go out. When you "pregame" for everything: "Let's go to the diner, let's pregame first!"—that kind of thing. Some people have an obsession with it.

—DANIEL RUSK
UNIVERSITY OF MARYLAND, SOPHOMORE

• • • • • • • •

DON'T DRINK TOO MUCH; at this school, it can cost you a lot of money. My freshman year, my roommate got alcohol poisoning. She came home early one morning and passed out. We couldn't wake her up so we called campus security and an ambulance came and took her to the hospital. She was fine afterwards, but the school fined her $2,000; plus, she had to pay her hospital bill.

—LIANA HIYANE
SANTA CLARA UNIVERSITY, JUNIOR

• • • • • • • •

QUITE A FEW FRESHMEN, me included, got way too drunk during orientation week before classes began and did something stupid. Those stories spread and stay alive. It took about a year for me to live mine down, and I got lucky because other people involved in the story left the school, making it a lot less interesting to tell. If I had known this would happen before I started school I could have saved a year of embarrassment.

—ANONYMOUS
WASHINGTON AND LEE UNIVERSITY, JUNIOR

GIRLS, BE ESPECIALLY CAREFUL of what you drink while at clubs or house parties, because an uncovered drink could mean a lost night and a trip to the gynecologist the next day.

—*ANONYMOUS*

WISDOM FOR WOMEN

WHEN YOU GO OUT, HAVE SOMEONE WITH YOU that you trust—I don't care if you're just going over to a guy's house, you don't want to be left alone. You need a friend who knows when to take you home. I have a friend and we do that for each other; we don't let each other out of sight. Sometimes I'll get pissed off and get in a full-on fist fight, saying, "No, I can handle this!" and she's like, "No, I'm taking you home right now." We have to be strict with each other, but it's good to have someone looking out for you.

> —*MOLLY SELMER*
> *SONOMA STATE UNIVERSITY, GRADUATE*

WHEN YOU'RE DRINKING, know your limits. Girls don't know how much they can drink, because they don't drink as often as guys. So girls will play drinking games with guys, thinking that they're cool and tough; then all of a sudden they're messed up, throwing up, or passed out.

> —*JENNIFER SPICER*
> *FOOTHILL COLLEGE, GRADUATE*

THERE ARE A LOT OF SCUMBAGS OUT THERE who try to take advantage of girls, especially freshmen. Don't put your drink down or let someone else get you a drink, because they could put something in it. Never walk around campus alone at night. Be careful.

> —*KATHERINE*
> *AUBURN UNIVERSITY, GRADUATE*

DRINKING: I GOT WRITTEN UP BY THE POLICE multiple times for stupid reasons. It caused me some problems with housing for my sophomore year. And I lost housing for my senior year. I'm pretty liberal about drinking, but you've got to watch yourself. Blackouts are never too good.

—*M.M.*
BOSTON COLLEGE, JUNIOR

" I worked in the bars on the weekends, which was cool because you're still in the social scene and you can see everyone, but you're making money instead of spending money. "

—*STEVEN RILEY*
STATE UNIVERSITY OF NEW YORK AT BINGHAMTON, GRADUATE

IF YOU GO TO A SCHOOL WHERE IT GETS COLD, get a somewhat fashionable jacket that can stand the wear and tear of a party. You'll want a jacket that's cheap, that will stand up to dirt, spit, beer, the weather, and your friend's drool.

—*JOSEPH S. SMITH*
PENNSYLVANIA STATE UNIVERSITY, GRADUATE

DON'T GET TOO CAUGHT UP IN ALCOHOL. I personally believe that college is the time to experiment with stuff like this; but if you do plan on getting drunk, try to set a reasonable limit and abide by it. If you pace yourself, this isn't too hard to do. And definitely try to confine it to the weekend. If you start drinking Thursday or even Wednesday nights, your studies and your grades will suffer. There's nothing like coming home inebriated at 2 a.m. and still having homework to do for the next day, especially when your responsible friends already did it together as a group and have gone to sleep.

—ANONYMOUS
UNIVERSITY OF VIRGINIA, SENIOR

. . . .

IN MY FRESHMAN YEAR I would go out every night on weeknights and stay out until 5 a.m., when I had to be in class at 9 a.m. I wasn't making it. That was the last semester I didn't live at home.

—ODELL
HUNTER COLLEGE, SENIOR

. . . .

MAKING FRIENDS WAS MY NUMBER ONE worry before going to college. I'm incredibly shy; during orientation week, I didn't go to half the planned activities for my dorm. Before I knew it, everyone had settled into their own groups. One day I was talking to my mom about a bench-painting event going on at my dorm; she encouraged me to just go outside. So I did; by the end of the day, I had a dinner date with the girl who is now my closest friend. Talk to random people because you'll find something you have in common to bond over. With my friend Carrie it was a love for Cosmic Cantina chicken burritos.

—SAMANTHA STACH
DUKE UNIVERSITY, JUNIOR

Go meet new people; they won't bite!

—*Janelle*
University of Georgia, Junior

FRESHMAN FACTOID

40 percent of college students "binge-drink" (defined as drinking at least 5 [for men] or 4 [for women] drinks in a row, at least once in the previous two weeks).

Try to steer clear of the drinking as much as possible. It's easy to get too fixed on the drinking of beers each night. That usually ends up causing trouble.

—*David Blaney*
Williams College, Graduate

• • • • • • • •

Looking back now, I wish I could change some of the partying to more studying.

Don't get stupid; people remember that. People will say, "Oh, I remember that party when you were passed out on the stairs." Whatever you do, it will follow you around the rest of your life. You want to have a good time, but you don't want to get carried away.

Everyone does stupid things, but don't get caught doing something illegal. You pick up habits in your freshman year where you say, "Oh, I didn't get caught then, so I might as well do it now." Then you get caught, and you're like, "Oh, that's how the real world works."

—*Josh H.*
Purdue University, Graduate

• • • • • • • •

When I first got to Temple I wasn't super outgoing or into the party scene, because I didn't have any close female friends yet to go out with, and a lot of people I met weren't into that scene. Don't feel pressured to experiment with partying and going out right away; you can take your time and meet some good friends. Don't feel obligated to do anything you're not comfortable with.

—*Nina*
Temple University, Junior

GO TO FRAT PARTIES with a bunch of girlfriends, and make sure you all go home together. Don't listen to any of the crap the guys try to hand you. They're looking for freshmen; they're waiting for them. Freshmen are so naïve and gullible and they think everything the guys say is true, and it's not. The guy will say anything: he'll say all these nice things and make a girl feel special, but it doesn't matter. He won't know your name the next day. He probably doesn't know your name right then.

—*KRISTIN THOMAS*
JAMES MADISON UNIVERSITY, JUNIOR

" Never, ever drive after drinking any amount of alcohol at all. A DUI will give you a police record and cost you thousands in legal fees and fines; don't even chance it. "

—*WENDY W.*
UNIVERSITY OF GEORGIA, GRADUATE

IF YOU GET DRUNK, don't throw chairs at your dorm neighbor. My neighbor had the same major as mine and I saw her for the next four years. She remembered that.

—*CASEY*
GEORGETOWN UNIVERSITY, SENIOR

MORE WISE WOMEN

THERE WERE A LOT OF FRESHMAN GIRLS that I took home from bars; they thought they had friends. They got too drunk, and their friends left. We used to find girls drunk in the bathrooms of bars all the time. They didn't know where their friends were and they would need someone to take care of them.

Girls, don't put down your drink. I think I went to a great school, but you don't know who is around. I had a friend who was drugged her sophomore year. She had two beers and all of a sudden she's out of her head and can't stand. And we thought she must have done shots and we didn't know about it. But the next day, she was in bed and couldn't get up. And she'd had hardly anything to drink. You don't know who's out there; you have to be careful.

You don't want to go to bars when you're a freshman, anyway. You're not going to meet anyone that you want to meet. I mean, who do you meet at a bar? Alcoholics and weirdos.

—*J. DEVEREUX*
GEORGETOWN UNIVERSITY, GRADUATE

• • • • • • • • •

YOU HAVE TO BE CAREFUL. We went to frat parties where they kept trying to give us drinks and beers. They went into the bathroom and then came out with a cup of beer. We were like, "Wow, no. Can I watch you pour it, please?" Some girls don't know better.

—*CHRISTINE*
UNIVERSITY OF RHODE ISLAND, SOPHOMORE

• • • • • • • • •

YOU KNOW YOU'RE AT A GOOD PARTY when you get slammed against the wall trying to get to the keg in the corner. And guys try to get girls to go in for them. Girls get alcohol more easily than guys do.

—*WHITNEY*
YALE UNIVERSITY, FRESHMAN

As much fun as it might seem, do your best to not get black-out drunk to the point where you cannot find your way home. First of all, no one likes to take care of the person who can't stand up or find their way home. They will, but they don't like to. Recognize when enough is enough. You will still have a great night, you will get home safely, you will not get yourself in possibly dangerous situations, and most likely, your tomorrow will be *much* better!

—*Elizabeth*
University of Illinois at Urbana-Champaign, Graduate

. . . .

" Don't drink to get drunk. You're not cool if you're drunk. Better to get a social buzz that keeps you in a jovial and rhythmic mood all night. "

—*Richard*
Georgia Southern University, Graduate

. . . .

Always go to parties with people you know, and be careful with your alcohol, wherever you put it down. And don't drink so much, because there are cops around. And don't do anything stupid, if you can help it.

—*Anonymous*
James Madison University, Sophomore

. . . .

If you're going to buy weed, don't buy it from the drunk on the street. What you'll end up with is oregano held together by glue.

—*J.G.*
Florida State University, Graduate

DON'T BE SO DRUNK that you can't enjoy sex. Bad things happen. Just make sure you know your limits and that you're not afraid to say no. You have to know what kind of person you are and what works for you.

—*MATT*
TUFTS UNIVERSITY, SOPHOMORE

. . . .

MY FRIENDS AND I HAVE A BUDDY SYSTEM where you stick with three or four people the whole night and then those friends can help you out. When we go to a party, the first thing we do is tie all the sleeves of our jackets together. Why? Because people sometimes steal or accidentally take jackets at parties! I lost my North Face that way!

—*TAYLOR WHITNEY PETTIS*
BLOOMSBURG UNIVERSITY, JUNIOR

ADVICE ON STAYING DRY

IF YOU DON'T WANT TO DRINK, then it's all about the people you find. If you surround yourself with people who drink and who will pressure you, it will be a difficult situation. If you surround yourself with people who are hesitant to drink or who are responsible, it won't be such a problem.

—*ANONYMOUS*
UNIVERSITY OF VIRGINIA, SENIOR

. . . .

DON'T FEEL THAT YOU NEED to be at every party all the time. It's perfectly OK to be at home sleeping on a Saturday night; there's nothing wrong with that. More people do it than you think. If you get too caught up in the social scene, you lose sight of other things.

—*HANNAH SMITH*
HARVARD UNIVERSITY, JUNIOR

WORDS OF WARNING

DON'T MAKE DRINKING A COMPETITIVE ACTIVITY. If you find yourself trying to prove how much you can drink to impress others, then it's going to end badly. You'll get alcohol poisoning, whether you believe you're immune or not. Or, you'll end up puking your guts out in front of your friends and people you don't even know. Also, drinking should not be the main activity of your night. If you go out just to drink, you're going to get drunk. If you go out to meet people at a party, or to dance, play a game, or bowl, focus on the main activity first, and then just let the drinking be an additive; it should never be the focus of your night. The funny thing is, the people who make it the focus of their night can't understand why everyone else might not want to do the same thing. But watch those people; they're cool when they're playing quarters and making jokes and doing shots, but they'll end up puking or acting like idiots.

—ANONYMOUS
VILLANOVA UNIVERSITY, GRADUATE

IF YOU DO DECIDE TO EXPERIMENT WITH ALCOHOL and drugs in college, be prepared to accept the consequences of your actions; what you're doing may be illegal and, as such, a poor decision. Alcohol and drugs are only a temporary escape from the dullness of life. If you find yourself consumed by these substances, you may need to reevaluate the directions your life is going in and realign yourself. If you're drinking to be more social, then maybe you're too self-conscious. If you're smoking marijuana to relax and be happy, then maybe you need a hobby. There are plenty of people and activities on campus to keep you busy without having to resort to drugs and alcohol on too regular a basis.

—ARIEL MELENDEZ
PRINCETON UNIVERSITY, FRESHMAN

> Just because the beer is being served in Dixie cups doesn't mean you can drink 40 cups and still drive home.
> —SCOTT WOELFEL
> UNIVERSITY OF MISSOURI, GRADUATE

ALWAYS PUT YOUR HAND over your drink, to keep people from putting something in your drink. Obviously, you shouldn't just leave your drink and come back to it. But also, cover your drink when you carry it. That was the overwhelming advice I got from everybody when I came to college.

> —BETHANY
> JAMES MADISON UNIVERSITY, SENIOR

A FRESHMAN GUY FINDS A GOOD PARTY by finding some hot freshman girls and going where they go. Or, you can hook up with an upperclassman; they know where the good parties are.

> —DAVE
> UNIVERSITY OF RHODE ISLAND, JUNIOR

WHEN YOU FIRST START COLLEGE, the phrase "three-day weekend" takes on a whole new meaning. The more social students tend to go out on Thursday night for the sole purpose of drinking themselves into a stupor. Friday night is a rest-and-recuperation night, and then the partying resumes Saturday night. By the time you wake up on Sunday it's already mid-afternoon. This trend fades by the time you start sophomore year. If it doesn't, you are officially an alcoholic and/or a stoner.

> —JOSHUA BERKOV
> BROWN UNIVERSITY, JUNIOR

BOOZE OVER BOOKS?

According to a recent survey, freshmen who said they had at least one drink in the past 14 days spent an average 10.2 hours a week drinking ... and only 8.4 hours a week studying.

SCARY STORY

It was Halloween of my freshman year. We were having a party in the dorm—not a costume deal or anything, just partying in random rooms. I was drinking mainly screwdrivers out of one of those 42-ounce, McDonald's cups. A friend of a friend, who came up to visit with her meathead boyfriend, got into a fight with him and ran away. She was about to get us written up—at Westfield State, "written up" means getting kicked off campus for five weekends—so my friend and I split up to find her. I found the psycho tucked under a stairwell, crying. I put my hand out to help her up, and the crazy girl bit me really hard. The mark she left looked like ringworm!

I said, "Whatever," gave up on that problem, and proceeded to get fizzled for rizzle—drunk, that is. The vodka I was drinking was good old Poland Springs vodka, the cheapest form of the stuff around. Let's just say that at the end of the night I puked in my roommate's garbage and passed out face down on my rug. It does not end there: I woke up outside, crying, to the sound of a fire alarm. My friends told me they had come into my room, where I was just walking around in circles; they put my jacket on me and brought me outside. This is where I allegedly was crying to call my mother. Fortunately, I don't think that many people saw my scene. Anyway, my friends ended up bringing me to my other friend's dorm and putting me to sleep. That is what I like to call Alcoholism.

Lessons learned: 1) Screw your friend who is about to get written up, and 2) Drink beer—it could save your life.

—B.
WESTFIELD STATE COLLEGE, GRADUATE

FRESHMAN DRINKING PRIMER

1. Every college student needs to know the old mantra, "Liquor before beer, never fear. Beer before liquor, never sicker."
2. It helps to have a glass of water with, or in between, drinks. And don't drink on an empty stomach.
3. If you close your eyes and you can't keep your balance, it's probably time to stop drinking for the night.

> —D.R.
> UNIVERSITY OF NORTH CAROLINA AT CHAPEL HILL, GRADUATE

. . . .

TO PREVENT SERIOUS TROUBLE—and perhaps even death—you must follow some simple rules. First, you need to do the stand-up test: The first time you drink a lot of liquor, don't do it all sitting down. You won't feel what it's doing to you. But the first time you stand up, hit the floor, and eat some carpet, you will suddenly feel what it is doing to you. So, stand up often while drinking liquor, to better measure the effect. Also, drink a lot of water when drinking alcohol; you've got to dilute that stuff.

> —R.S.
> GEORGETOWN UNIVERSITY, GRADUATE

. . . .

THE BEST WAY TO GET OVER A HANGOVER is water and bread. Bread is your best friend: It helps take care of your stomach, and it fills you and soaks up anything. The water makes you not dehydrated anymore. The next day, just make it a Blockbuster night; that's all you need to do.

> —BETH
> DIABLO VALLEY COLLEGE, FRESHMAN

. . . .

DRAMAMINE is an incredible cure for a horrible hangover.

> —J.
> UNIVERSITY OF GEORGIA, GRADUATE

Animal House: Fraternities & Sororities

*I*n days of old, every college student knew Greek and Latin. Today, you just know enough Greek to tell Psi Chi from Alpha Delta. But what do fraternities and sororities really do, besides throw parties? You know there's more to the whole Greek thing than what you've seen in movies. In this chapter, Greeks and non-Greeks tell the story behind the letters.

BE A PART OF THE GREEK SYSTEM. It is a great place for networking down the road. People get hired because they were in the same sorority as the boss.

—HEATHER POLLOCK
CALIFORNIA STATE UNIVERSITY AT FULLERTON, GRADUATE

IF YOU DECIDE TO RUSH, TAKE IT WITH A GRAIN OF SALT.

—D.
DUKE UNIVERSITY
SENIOR

HEADLINES
Best Advice and Top Tips

- The majority of people involved in Greek life generally love it.
- When deciding whether to "go Greek," first figure out what you want from college; then check which organizations offer this.
- Got free time? Greek life will fill most of it with socials, volunteer events, sports, and more.
- Fact: People who don't take part in Greek life also enjoy college.

I JOINED A FRAT THE SPRING SEMESTER of my freshman year. It was a great experience; the best thing I ever did. I was against fraternities completely, I got dragged into it, and now the brothers are my best friends. I was that guy who said, "Frat guys suck!" But things change.
— *CHRIS MCANDREW*
UNIVERSITY OF DELAWARE, JUNIOR

. . . .

I WENT TO A LARGE SCHOOL where you didn't have to be Greek to have a life. But I wanted both, so during my sophomore year I decided to pledge. This gave me time to make other friendships with people who weren't necessarily going Greek. And as it turned out, not all of my closest friends from freshman year decided to go Greek. My advice: Don't jump into pledging. Get to know the campus, get to know friends outside of Greek life, and get used to what life is like without it. That way you can decide if it's right for you. At my school, sororities were very competitive, and many women never got invited to join any sorority. So this was tough for some people.
— *ANONYMOUS*
INDIANA UNIVERSITY, GRADUATE

FRESHMAN GIRLS SHOULD GO through sorority Rush, but don't take it too seriously. If you take it to heart, people can tell. You run the risk of getting really hurt. It's just a group of girls; there are other things in life.

—ANONYMOUS
UNIVERSITY OF VIRGINIA, SOPHOMORE

JOIN WHATEVER FRATERNITY ATTRACTS THE HOTTEST chicks—that's all frats are good for, anyway.

—J.G.
FLORIDA STATE UNIVERSITY, GRADUATE

“ At least try Rush. You don't have to pledge, but going through Rush is a really good time to meet other girls who are going through what you're going through. It's a really great bonding time. ”

—DENISE O.
UNION COLLEGE, JUNIOR

THE STUFF YOU HEAR about wild frat hazing is mostly college lore; in fact, some of the pranks or "rituals" are most likely obsolete. Like, you hear about the "ookie cookie," but again, it's a myth— it's not all like *Animal House*.

—JAMES WILLIS
UNIVERSITY OF CALIFORNIA AT DAVIS, SENIOR

Consider

Even if you don't want to be in a frat, you should do Rush; you'll get free drinks and have fun.

—*J.D.*
EMORY UNIVERSITY
SENIOR

I'M IN A SORORITY, and it's the best thing I've ever done in my life. I'm such a better person for being in a sorority. But it's way too early to pledge freshman year; I pledged sophomore year. You need to establish yourself at your college first. You meet your freshman group of friends; then you can pledge sophomore year. I did, and I didn't feel like I was pledging too late. The year I pledged, there were 450 sophomores, versus like 50 freshmen. It's just too much for freshmen.

—*KRISTIN THOMAS*
JAMES MADISON UNIVERSITY, JUNIOR

• • • • • • • •

THE FIRST FRAT PARTY I went to as a pledge, they told us not to wear anything nice. First thing that happens when I walk in, a girl throws an entire beer on me. It was called Beer Splash. I was like, "This is where I want to be."

—*A.G.S.*
UNIVERSITY OF TENNESSEE, DID NOT GRADUATE

• • • • • • • •

THE WHOLE PROCESS TRULY IS SUPERFICIAL. Sorority members judge rushies based slightly on appearance and primarily on a five- to 10-minute conversation that takes place within the most fake and uncomfortable environment. With all this in mind, if you want to join a sorority, you take it for what it is. Don't go into Rush believing that the girls you meet have the final say (or any say, for that matter) on who you are, or how "cool" or desirable you are. They're judging you based on a glimpse of who they think you are.

—*D.*
DUKE UNIVERSITY, SENIOR

SCIENCE EXPERIMENT?

In my fraternity house, we had a very old iron stove in the kitchen, which was original to the house. The stove was huge, and completely useless—it hadn't worked in decades. But nobody could move it because it was so heavy, and no trash disposal company or dumping ground would accept it—not even if we paid them to take it! It seemed as though our house was stuck with this old relic for another 80 years.

Then one night we had a brainstorm. In the middle of the night, about 10 of us hoisted this piece of useless iron onto a dolly, and rolled it across campus to the Science Center. Now, in the lobby of the college's Science Center was a small museum of scientific artifacts (you know, like a 200-year-old microscope, or a skeleton of a 1 million-year-old small rodent). So, we found a nice little nook for the stove (right in between some relics) and placed a professional-looking sign on the stove which said: "Random Kinetic Energy Enhancer, circa 1842." Only a science geek would know that that is another way of saying: "This is an old stove."

The relic stayed for about a week, then was hauled off by the university. We didn't pay a dime.

—*I.L.S.*
WESLEYAN UNIVERSITY, GRADUATE

GREEK 101

Choose one from Column A and one from Column B to find the group that's right for you.

A: WHAT	B: WHO
Social—If you want to make friends	**Fraternity**—All guys
Service—If you love volunteering	**Sorority**—All ladies
Professional—If you're looking to do some career networking	**Coed**—You know what this means
Academic/Honor—If you're smart, want everyone to know you're smart, and prefer hanging out with other people who are just as smart as you are	

Frances Northcutt

I ENDED UP GOING GREEK in the spring semester of my freshman year. I had never planned on it in the past, but you really just have to try it out and see if it's right for you.

—MELANIE
PENNSYLVANIA STATE UNIVERSITY, SOPHOMORE

AFTER A WHILE, YOU GET KIND OF BORED with college, and it's good to meet people and network through fraternities. I've met a lot of people from different walks of life. I've learned a lot about people. There were some people that I met while pledging, and I had a feeling I might not like them. But then I got to know them and I ended up liking them.

You shouldn't rush frats the first semester. Get acquainted with the university. The second semester, it's a good thing to do. It's something to complement your academics. It helps keep you focused.

—RON SILVER
UNIVERSITY OF MARYLAND, JUNIOR

If you're in a frat or sorority, be prepared for people to put you down for being Greek.

—SHEILA CRAWFORD
NORTH CAROLINA
STATE UNIVERSITY
SOPHOMORE

· · · · · · · ·

DON'T PLEDGE YOUR FIRST YEAR. You will limit your experiences as a freshman. And it takes up a lot of time. I pledged my sophomore year, and I know people who did it their junior year. Don't be in a hurry: Greek life isn't going any- where!

—NIROSHAN RAJARATNAM
UNIVERSITY OF MARYLAND, GRADUATE

· · · · · · · ·

I DID NOT JOIN A FRAT because I did not want to do chores. I did chores at home and left that behind; who needs it? But to meet girls, the frat guys do have an advantage.

—INSU CHANG
CARNEGIE MELLON UNIVERSITY, JUNIOR

'GREEK' MYTHOLOGY 101

Thinking of joining a sorority or fraternity? Here are common myths about Greek life in college – and the facts.

1. *"A fraternity/sorority just means I have to pay to make friends. I don't need to do that."*
   ▷ FACT: Joining a sorority or fraternity is not paying for friendship. The point of these organizations is to form lasting bonds with a wide variety of individuals with whom you share some common interests and goals, and to provide meaningful college experiences. This is no different from you and a group of friends deciding to go rock-climbing or camping, but the dues help cover the expenses up front.

2. *"Greek organizations are all about binge-drinking, drug-use and partying."*
   ▷ FACT: While there are parties, and alcohol, it's a personal choice of how often you go to parties and what you do there. A high percentage of Greeks do not drink and alcohol consumption has never been a prerequisite for membership. Most Greek organizations conduct themselves responsibly much of the time, and all of them engage in some form of community service on a consistent basis. Some even raise tens of thousands of dollars for charity each year. Many Greek organizations have a higher chapter-wide GPA than that of the entire student body, and a lot of their members may be involved in leadership roles on campus.

3. *"Greek life has nothing to offer me. I already have a great social life."*
   ▷ FACT: As stated above, there are plenty of community service opportunities that the Greeks participate in - from carnival-type events and Greek Weeks to sponsored walks and neighborhood clean-up projects. The leadership potential is also great with countless committee chair, program coordinator, and executive officer positions in each organization, and the skills you gain in your chapter will help you explore possible campus-wide leadership opportu-

nities. An astounding number of government and corporate leaders were involved in the Greek system. Finally, studies have shown that a higher percentage of fraternity/sorority members graduate than those who are not involved in Greek life.

4. *"Greek life is exactly as you see it on TV and movies."*
   - FACT: Pop culture, and the media, tend to focus on the sensationalized or well-known elements of Greek life (i.e. drinking, partying and goofing off), even if these are far less prevalent than strongly positive elements (i.e. community service, filling campus leadership roles and strong friendship bonds).

5. *"Fraternities are discriminatory and intolerant of people's differences. Sororities are catty and mean-spirited. They're elitist, homophobic and racist."*
   - FACT: Fraternities and sororities are open to all people and are actually comprised of a variety of people from different ethnic and economic backgrounds. To operate, a fraternity or sorority fundamentally needs members and is looking for men or women that represent their values not a specific mold. The ideals they generally look for include scholarship, friendship, leadership, and community service, among others.

6. *"Sorority women prefer fraternity men, and vice versa."*
   - FACT: This isn't true, but sorority women happen to know more fraternity men, and vice versa. Members of the Greek system do spend ample amounts of time together because of their shared values and beliefs. However, they also co-host events with organizations outside of the community and most have friends not in the Greek system.

7. *"You lose your individuality when you join a Greek organization."*
   - FACT: The reason Greek organizations are so successful is that each member brings something different to the table. Different experiences, different approaches and different ideas help the organization to thrive.

8. *"Greek life takes up too much time, and will affect my academics."*
   > FACT: Most organizations will help new members learn how to balance their fraternal obligations with critical things like classes and homework, jobs, and spending time with family and other friends.

9. *"Hazing is a common occurrence amongst all Greek organizations."*
   > FACT: Every Greek organization has a strict policy prohibiting hazing, and it's illegal throughout the country. Hazing is an infrequent occurrence in Greek organizations, but it's reported on more often than the positive things Greeks contribute to the community. Your university likely has a "No Tolerance" policy on hazing. Your campus's student activities and student conduct offices will follow-up on any legitimate reports of hazing in any organization (Greek or not). Offenders will not only face campus sanctions that could include suspension or dismissal, but oftentimes their membership privileges in the Greek organization are completely and permanently revoked.

10. *"The membership fees for a fraternity or sorority are too expensive. I don't have money for that."*
    > FACT: The fees associated with membership, often called dues, cover a lot of expenses you would otherwise have to cover out-of-pocket on a regular basis. The dues you pay will go to cover: 1) home office (to cover services and resources they provide to the local organization), 2) insurance (required for most organizations to cover the activities that you hold), 3) food for any events or meetings that you host, 4) a budget to cover the costs of a trip to the amusement park, or movies, 5) supplies and other expenses, and more. Essentially, the dues you pay will go towards a budget that your organization will use to hold activities. Many organizations even have assistance programs for members who may not be able to fully pay their dues from time to time, and possibly even some scholarship funding.

Scott C. Silverman

"I HAVE TO PAY TO BE YOUR SISTER?" That was the first question that popped into my head after accepting an invitation to join my dream sorority house. My whole family had been Greek in college, but I couldn't get past the fact that I was paying to have friends. Now, I understand that the friends I made in my sorority are forever, and even when I no longer pay for room and board and T-shirts, my sisters will still be there. I never bought my friends—I just put down a deposit.

—AMANDA SOUKUP
UNIVERSITY OF NEBRASKA, SOPHOMORE

" I avoided frat parties until I was a senior. That's when I knew better. "

—ANONYMOUS
UNIVERSITY OF RHODE ISLAND, SOPHOMORE

SORORITY SISTERS

I JOINED MY SORORITY on a whim—I was in a suite of eight girls my freshman year, and a lot of them were rushing. They encouraged me to come along for the fun experience. They said it's a great way to meet people, etc. And I went, but I didn't think I would join. But I found one sorority where I met a bunch of girls and had a lot of great conversations, so I figured I'd try it. I don't think it's right for everyone, or that everyone would feel that it's worth the time commitment. But I've had a great experience.

—COLLEEN
PRINCETON UNIVERSITY, JUNIOR

THE CAT IN THE FRAT?

Dr. Seuss (Theodore Geisel, class of 1925) studied at Dartmouth. Internet legend has it that he decorated his fraternity house walls with drawings of his strange characters; we're not sure it's a true story, but who cares?

FRATS ARE FOR IDIOTS. But if you really feel like you have to pay dues to make friends, or spend a month scrubbing toilets and performing idiotic stunts so people will like you, then I guess frats are for you. If you don't care about individuality, or respect for yourself or for women, sign up. If you want to bypass all opportunity for meaningful relationships and skip right to drinking buddies and one-night stands, go for it. Don't get me wrong: I was good friends with some frat boys and sorority girls in college, just like I'm friends with some Republicans now. But it was despite their affiliations, not because of them.

—*EAMON SIGGINS*
STATE UNIVERSITY OF NEW YORK AT BINGHAMTON, GRADUATE

• • • • • • • • •

WHILE I DIDN'T JOIN A FRATERNITY, I did decide to join an engineering society at my school. This one was pretty hell-bent on getting drunk every weekend, like most fraternities at my school. This naturally became my attitude in my freshman year, and even continued into my second year. Try to keep school your priority during the week (as much as possible) so that your weekend social life doesn't intrude on your studies, when drinking affects grades. Also, ask yourself if it's worth $1,000 a semester to be in one of these groups. (Mine was only about $160 a year, which was very appealing.) You'll probably also come to a point when you're a senior and you realize that these groups aren't as exciting as they were when you were a freshman.

—*ANONYMOUS*
UNIVERSITY OF VIRGINIA, SENIOR

IF YOU'RE GOING TO JOIN A SORORITY, bail after the first year—two years at most. The whole sorority-fraternity thing inhibits having a rich and diverse college experience. You're lumped together with a small percentage of the campus population, and you cheat yourself of the opportunity to meet interesting people who wouldn't be caught dead on Greek Row. At first, a sorority or fraternity can be comforting. You just left home for the first time, and being around people who are like you can put you at ease; that's OK. But after the first year or two, it's not doing you any favors. Get out. Find the best in the bunch, keep them as friends, then bail. You may catch flak, and you won't be a lifetime member of your frat or sorority. But you will be better off, finding your own way on your own terms.

—*B.P.*
FLORIDA STATE UNIVERSITY, GRADUATE

PLAY TIME

According to Playboy Magazine, these were the top party schools for 2012:

1. University of Virginia
2. University of Southern California
3. University of Florida
4. University of Texas
5. University of Wisconsin
6. University of Georgia
7. Vanderbilt University
8. Tulane University
9. Texas Christian University
10. Ohio State University

Imagine it is just some elaborate Saturday Night Live skit in which you are grudgingly playing along.

—ANONYMOUS

THE FIRST FEW PARTIES OF THE YEAR, they'll let pretty much anyone in just to get themselves known for killer parties. After a few weeks, though, they start patrolling their parties by placing a few brothers in the driveway to tell the masses that "the house occupancy is full, but try back later." If you drop the name of a brother, though, they'll let you in. So at the first party of the year, I randomly met a guy named Steve and found out he was from Louisiana. So every time I went back, I told the guys in the driveway I knew "Steve from Louisiana," and it worked like a charm. I passed Steve from Louisiana's name on to whoever wanted to hang out at that frat.

—*ASHLEY LEAVELL*
BOSTON UNIVERSITY, SENIOR

• • • • • • • • •

DO NOT BELIEVE THE HYPE that Greek organizations feed you during your first semester in college. You will not find friends who will be there for you if you join a fraternity or sorority just as you get into college. These organizations try to get freshmen to join by saying that this is the best way to find friends. On the contrary, it is the best way to exclude yourself from people who can become your best friends, and to get a narrow view of college life. Before joining a Greek organization, find an organization that shares your interests, perhaps something where you can have a wide variety of friends.

—*D.*
MOORHEAD STATE UNIVERSITY, JUNIOR

BIG FRATERNITY/SORORITY SCHOOLS

- University of Florida

- University of Georgia

- University of Illinois

- University of Texas – Austin

- Syracuse University

BEFORE COLLEGE, I WAS VERY ANTI-SORORITY; I thought they were evil. But now, even though I'm not in a sorority, I live with sorority girls, and they're all my good friends. I go to lots of their functions and have a great time. It's not a big deal if you're not in a sorority. It's only a big deal the first few weeks of the year and then the five days of Rush. During Rush I just remind myself that I do have friends; they're just all busy this week. If you're not sure whether you want to join a fraternity or sorority, remember that you can still join and it doesn't have to be the top priority in your life. Join; just don't become president. Sororities and fraternities are a great way to make a big school seem smaller.

> —SUMMER J.
> UNIVERSITY OF VIRGINIA, SENIOR

BE SWEET AS PIE during your sorority pledge period and wait until after you're active to tell off the snots who were mean to you. Better yet, just steal their boyfriends.

> —LYNN LAMOUSIN
> LOUISIANA STATE UNIVERSITY, GRADUATE

RUSHING A FRATERNITY OR SORORITY is a great thing to do. Going through rush can be really annoying and time-consuming, but it doesn't last long and it has so many benefits. Even if you decide that being in one of these organizations isn't for you, just being a part of the process will open your eyes to a huge organization. You will also make some friends in your rush group.

—*ANNIE THOMAS*
UNIVERSITY OF MICHIGAN, SENIOR

18

Road Trip! Vacations & Studying Abroad

*F*ive *years from now, some of your best college memories may be of journeys you took off campus. Picture yourself on a beach, enjoying tropical drinks with your best friends from the dorm; driving cross-country with the windows down and the music turned up, creating your own personal montage of carefree adventure; sipping coffee in a Paris sidewalk café, flipping through an impressively intellectual text before your afternoon class at the Sorbonne. These students did all those things and more, and you can, too.*

DECIDEDLY COLLEGIATE AND BRO-TASTIC, first-year road trips are an absolute must. Bring at least one responsible guy/girl with you to make sure that everyone gets back alive.

—*J.V.*
THE COLLEGE OF WILLIAM & MARY, GRADUATE

BRING FRIENDS HOME FOR THE HOLIDAYS.

—*D.D.*
UNIVERSITY OF PENNSYLVANIA GRADUATE

HEADLINES
Best Advice and Top Tips

- Your school most likely has one, if not several, study abroad programs. Check them out.
- A random road trip can be an important part of your time in college. Just bring everyone back alive and out of legal trouble.
- Many students use Spring Break to travel to third-world countries and volunteer – it's better for the résumé than partying!

Advice to the guys: Go on a cruise for spring break. The odds are unbelievable! You will be amazed at the ratio.

—JIMMY LYNCH
AUBURN UNIVERSITY
GRADUATE

GO TO ITALY. Spend a semester there. I did, and it completely changed my outlook on life. Before I went, I was only interested in the American college existence: partying, getting by, attending football games. After I got back, I wanted to learn more, to be more.

—M.A.
FLORIDA STATE UNIVERSITY, GRADUATE

• • • • • • • •

MAKE SURE YOU GO SOMEWHERE FOR SPRING BREAK. I knew some guys who didn't go anywhere, and it's just not fun. If you go to school in Texas, like I did, you can go to Mexico for Spring Break. It's great. There's cheap alcohol and they let you do anything. My freshman year, I went to this really sketchy border town. We actually stayed in a motel on the U.S. side and then walked across a bridge and partied down, and stumbled back every night.

—KYLE
UNIVERSITY OF TEXAS, AUSTIN, GRADUATE

I WENT HOME FOR THE HOLIDAYS my freshman year, and I think it was a good thing, because it can just get really crazy. Everything is so new and so exciting and there are so many people that you feel like you're at camp for an extended period of time. It depends on what your home situation is like, but it's important to keep in touch with your parents; it helps remind you that you're actually here to do something. For me, keeping in touch with my parents kept a balanced view; you should explore, but keep your feet on the ground, too.

—*SHANNON*
STANFORD UNIVERSITY, SENIOR

THE LESS OFTEN YOU GO HOME your freshman year, the better. The more you're at school your freshman year, the more you're going to make friends and have people to hang out with after that. Your ties from home are going to break anyway. The sooner you do it, the better off you are.

—*BETHANY*
JAMES MADISON UNIVERSITY, SENIOR

DOESN'T FEEL LIKE SCHOOL

Where can you get that vacation feeling without leaving campus?

- Beach house—The Citadel (South Carolina)
- Wilderness cabin—Linfield College (Oregon)
- Research boat—Hawaii Pacific University
- 2 private beaches and a private dock with a fleet of sailboats—Mitchell College (Connecticut)
- 20-foot boat "for marine studies"—Muhlenberg College (Pennsylvania)
- 29,000-acre experimental forest—University of Montana

I WOULD RECOMMEND DRIVING your parents' van, with a nice bed in back, coast to coast, 3,000 miles. It doesn't take too long. I did that with my girlfriend. I learned to surf once I got to California. My parents didn't know I had taken the van until I was in another state. But when I called them, they said, "We've been waiting for you to do something like that." It was great.

—STEVE BAKER
COLUMBIA UNIVERSITY, SENIOR

. . . .

MY JUNIOR YEAR, I TOOK ADVANTAGE of the "terms abroad" program and lived in Ecuador for a year. It was a phenomenal opportunity to study abroad. Life had seemed sort of small before that experience.

—CALE GARAMANDI
UNIVERSITY OF CALIFORNIA AT BERKELEY, JUNIOR

. . . .

TAKE A FUN JOB IN THE SUMMER after your freshman year; you deserve the break. I couldn't stand the thought of being at home all summer, living with a curfew, so a friend and I went to Orlando for the summer and got a job at Disney World. We didn't make any money, after paying our apartment and expenses, but we met lots of people and had a good time.

—K.E.R.
FLORIDA STATE UNIVERSITY, GRADUATE

NO FINANCIAL BREAK

In a survey of 500 parents, 70 percent said they were unwilling to pay for their child's spring break.

I WENT ON A SEMESTER-LONG TRIP on a cruise ship. It's a program where professors from around the country come and teach everything from anthropology to music to economics. We went to 10 countries around the world. It's the most amazing opportunity ever. You get to learn about countries from a very non-Western point of view. I went to a wild game reserve in South Africa and visited the sand people who live on the outskirts. We learned about them and they sold us their wares. We went skydiving. We went to Carnival in Rio. When you're a freshman you should plan to do something like that; it had such an impact on me.

—MAYTAL AHARONY
GEORGE WASHINGTON UNIVERSITY, SENIOR

> When you see the world from a different perspective, you realize what you can be.
>
> —M.A.
> FLORIDA STATE UNIVERSITY GRADUATE

BEST WEEKEND GETAWAY—CAMPING. It's cheap, it's fun, and all your friends will want to join you. Get a map of state campgrounds; a great weekend of hiking, nature, romance and s'mores may be just an hour's drive away.

—WENDY W.
UNIVERSITY OF GEORGIA, GRADUATE

STUDY ABROAD

I studied abroad for a semester, in Santiago, Chile. It was a fantastic experience, breaking out of the Princeton bubble. Going out and meeting new people, seeing a new culture, and learning from a different perspective was absolutely integral to my collegiate experience. We went on weekend trips, and one weekend we went to the south of Chile to Patagonia. We climbed a volcano and went camping. It was awesome.

—JOSH
PRINCETON UNIVERSITY, SENIOR

EXPLORE THE WORLD

Internships, Study Abroad programs and Alternative Spring Breaks are just three of the amazing opportunities that are only available while you're in college. Explore them now. After you graduate and move on to graduate school or full-time employment, you probably won't have time to go on any form of Spring Break or Study Abroad programs, and internships are what helps you discover possible career fields.

General tips to help you to discover these opportunities:

1. Check out what your campus offers, starting with the Campus Activities office, the Career Center, and the International Education departments. If there are workshops on how to select a program, or how to make your application stand out – attend them.
2. Review your options and decide on a few to apply for.
3. If Letters of Recommendation are necessary, ask for them early on.

Internships: Are you interested in a specific career field, inside or outside your areas of study? An internship in this field is a great way to learn more about it, and do something that looks good on your (future) résumé. Some tips:

- Research the company or department for which you want to intern for. Spend some time thinking about what job experiences and skills you want to gain from the internship. That will help you during the interview.
- Don't expect to get paid for every internship; in fact, most of them are volunteer positions.

Study Abroad: This is a fun way to meet students from other colleges and spend an entire term, or even a year, with them in another country, while earning class credit. Many colleges offer them – even to students who don't attend the college. The University of California, for instance, currently offers over 250 program options in over 30 countries. (http://www.eap.ucop.edu). To get started:

- Select two or three similar programs that you may want to apply to. It will increase your odds over just applying to one foreign college, and you may only need to do minor tweaks on your application answers for each.
- These programs are competitive because spaces are limited. Apply multiple times if necessary. Also, check out any opportunities your college may have for you to gain comparable experience in Washington, D.C., which is a growing trend.
- Your cost for your term studying abroad will likely be the same (in terms of tuition). Living expenses may be higher, and you have to pay for your airfare. There are companies that run Study Abroad programs outside of the college realm. These are more expensive, and your credits may not always transfer.

Alternative Spring Break: This is exactly what it sounds like – something different from the usual partying. Instead, you can spend Spring Break helping feed the homeless in Los Angeles, rebuilding New Orleans post-Hurricane Katrina, planting trees in South America, etc.

- If your college doesn't have a formal Alternative Spring Break program, find someone who might help you start one. Even without a formal program, you can still organize something with your friends. Find ways to reduce costs, but know that you will have to pay out of pocket for your expenses.
- Talk to your campus newspaper. Raising awareness of your efforts might even bring in some donations that you can use to fund the experience.
- If you find a faculty member or staff person to help you coordinate this, you and your friends could use them as a source of letters of recommendation later on.

Talk to the staff on your campus who specialize in off-campus experiential opportunities for credit like Study Abroad first. You may also look into sites like these for other possibilities:
http://www.semesteratsea.org/
http://www.studyabroad.com/

Scott C. Silverman

THE *OTHER* SPRING BREAK

FOR SPRING BREAK I WENT TO EUROPE with my good friend Dave. We went to Switzerland and France with backpacks and thoroughly enjoyed getting to know the cities and each other. I think this was valuable because we are now greatly connected and also learned so much about the cities we explored. In particular, it was nice to be with a fellow student because this attracted other student travelers over the break.

> —GERALDINE SARAH COWPER
> CUNY/MACAULAY HONORS COLLEGE, SENIOR

I TOOK AN ALTERNATIVE SPRING BREAK to Honduras with a bunch of friends. We helped build latrines in an underdeveloped village. It was a great experience. At college there are amazing extracurricular service volunteer opportunities.

> —ELIZABETH ROTH
> UNIVERSITY OF PENNSYLVANIA, SENIOR

MANY OF MY FRIENDS HAVE BEEN TO CANCUN or did the "crazy" Spring Break thing. They've inevitably been disappointed. I found that leaving those weeks unplanned has been a big blessing. I've gotten in shape, and caught up on work and (what I miss most in college) sleep. That said, I've also gone to Liverpool, London, and Oxford for Spring Break when I was studying abroad. My girlfriend went with me. We're huge Beatles fans and we loved staying in hostels and visiting all the haunts and museums dedicated to that awesome band.

> —RON Y. KAGAN
> CUNY/MACAULAY HONORS COLLEGE, SENIOR

IF IT'S NOT YOUR THING TO DRINK A LOT and do all that stuff, you probably won't enjoy spring break. You only get four spring breaks while you're in college. If you don't enjoy partying all the time, you're not going to enjoy it in Mexico after you spent $1,000.

—JONATHAN COHEN
EMORY UNIVERSITY, SENIOR

" When you go to school overseas, you get a better perspective on the world. You don't see the world from an American point of view. It will help anybody. "

—MICHAEL LANDIS GOGEL
NEW YORK UNIVERSITY, SOPHOMORE

I GOT INVOLVED IN SERVICE WORK, traveling to other countries. I've been to Mexico and down south to North Carolina for Habitat for Humanity. That's defined my college career, my transformation. It gave me a better appreciation for my position in the world and at the same time for others in the world who don't have as much as I do. It's been an enlightening experience. But I've still had plenty of time to party.

—JONATHAN GIFTOS
BOSTON COLLEGE, SENIOR

SETTING AN EXAMPLE

One of the most memorable times I had in college was a road trip to New York City with about five pals, an idea hatched at 10 p.m., executed immediately, and celebrated in Central Park in the wee hours. We all flopped on the floor at a friend's place at Columbia University, partied some more with him, and woke up in a stupor. The highlight was a morn-

ing visit to the home of one of the pals, the only son of a working-class couple in Queens. In that cramped apartment, during the time it took to eat a carefully prepared breakfast, we observed in utter awe the incredible, unfettered love of a mother and father for their son. They were so proud of their boy. It wasn't so much in what they said, but the ambience, the pictures on the mantle, the beam in dad's eye, the doting by the mother. There was nothing overpowering or unbalanced or pushy about it; it was a natural pride and confidence in their son. For me, there have been few times when I was inspired by the human condition; this was one of them.

—R.S.
GEORGETOWN UNIVERSITY, GRADUATE

Consider

IF SOMEONE YOU KNOW OFFERS to have you stay with her over a break, take her up on it. One of the most interesting experiences I had was staying with the parents of a roommate or friend, and discovering what her life was like before I met her. It is really mind-expanding, and allows you to get to know someone in your life even better. You also have the added bonus of a personal tour guide to show you around. Nothing is more fun than rediscovering where you have lived for your whole life by showing your college friends all of the tourist destinations.

—AMY
PRINCETON UNIVERSITY, FRESHMAN

FOUR THINGS TO BRING ON A RANDOM ROAD TRIP

Look, we realize that part of the joy of a road trip is the lack of planning. One moment, you're sitting around with your friends at 3 a.m., and the stress of college is the topic of discussion. The next moment, you suddenly know just the way to rid yourself of stress: Road trip, right now, destination TBD.

We don't want to interfere with the spontaneity. But after you pocket your wallet and keys, if you happen to see any of the following items on your way out the door, grab them. (And, admittedly, if you take all five items, you're ruining the spontaneity.) Most of all, be careful and have fun in TBD!

1. **A sleeping bag and pillow.** Depending on how cold it is, the pillow might be the most important item here. Have you ever slept in a car without a pillow? In place of the sleeping bag, you can use a long-sleeved shirt.

2. **A Styrofoam cooler.** Aside from storing food and drink, have you ever considered all the things you can do with a Styrofoam cooler? Road trips are made for thinking about questions like this.

3. **A hat.** Not many people know this, but the hat was originally invented as a way to hide the fact that the wearer hadn't showered in days.

4. **A bobble-head Elvis Presley.** Or, whatever random figurine or toy you can find. Are you looking for a reason why you should bring something like this? We don't really have one.

The Editors

THE NOT-TOO-EARLY STUDY-ABROAD LIST

Even though you're only a freshman, it's not too early to start planning to study abroad, especially if you want to be away for a whole semester or year. Follow these steps, and you'll be (almost) on your way.

Find out:
- Where is your college's study abroad office?
- What programs are offered?
- How much do they cost?
- Is financial aid available?
- Is there a GPA requirement?

Think about:
- Why you want to study abroad.
- Where you want to go.
- What kinds of classes you want to take.
- When you should go (fall semester of junior year is a popular choice).
- Whether there are older students who can share their study-abroad wisdom with you.

Sketch out:
- A rough, four-year plan to cover all your course requirements.
- How you'll earn/save/beg/borrow the funds you'll need.

And while you're thinking about it, check your passport—it should be valid until one year *after* you plan to get back from your adventures abroad.

The Editors

STUDYING ABROAD WAS A FANTASTIC EXPERIENCE: learning the culture of the British people, learning so much about a different way of studying, a different school system, and a different language in England. It's a valuable opportunity and experience.

—C.W.
RHODES COLLEGE, SENIOR

• • • • • • • •

ONE OF THE BEST PARTS about college is visiting your friends that go to other schools. Visit when your football teams play each other. It's a whole new batch of girls, and it'll spice up your party life.

—ILAN GLUCK
UNIVERSITY OF MARYLAND, JUNIOR

TAKE A CHANCE ON ME

Put yourself out there and take chances when it comes to making friends. Everyone is in the same boat and just as nervous as you. My school gives everyone a "fall break" during October, something I wasn't used to in high school. At first it sounded like a long weekend. But as it drew nearer, it seemed like people were treating it more like a mini-spring break. I started to panic because, while I had friends, I didn't have any I considered close enough to travel with.

Fortunately, one of my friends in a similar position took a chance and invited me and three other girls to drive to St. Simons Island, Georgia for a short beach trip. Nervously, we all accepted and packed up the car one Friday afternoon. The awkwardness quickly faded away as we all sang songs at the top of our lungs the entire six hours to the beach. That trip turned into the most memorable experience of my freshman year and those four other girls are now my best friends. If you have a chance to take a trip with people you think might turn out to be good friends, take it! Trips are one of the best ways to bond and you'll share memories for the rest of your life.

—MERELISE HARTE ROUZER
GEORGIA INSTITUTE OF TECHNOLOGY, SOPHOMORE

I WENT TO NIGER FOR A SEMESTER. It was amazing. The academics are not a priority, but the cultural experience shifted my direction of what I want to get involved in.

—*MAYA MOORE*
GEORGETOWN UNIVERSITY, SENIOR

• • • • • • • •

PART OF COLLEGE is sculpting your beliefs and attitudes about the world. I'm a huge advocate for getting out there and seeing the real world; it's easy to stay caught up in the drama of classes, classmates, bad teachers, good or bad grades. My favorite so far is car tripping around the east coast with my buddy, who is a history major. We did the Freedom Trail in Boston, took a train into New York City and stayed overnight in a hostel where the minority of kids was speaking a language we could understand. We stopped in Salem, saw the Flume in New Hampshire, and our base was in Vermont. We learned a lot about ourselves, and the areas we needed to focus on in order to excel in the basics of getting along in life; how to read a map, stop to ask for directions, and take independence one step at a time.

—*AMANDA*
UNIVERSITY OF COLORADO AT COLORADO SPRINGS, SOPHOMORE

SEE THE WORLD

The number of U.S. college students studying abroad has more than tripled over the past 20 years. And, more of them are choosing off-the-beaten-track destinations such as India, Israel, Brazil and New Zealand over more traditional European countries.

SPRING IS IN THE AIR - HERE

Orbitz's three most popular spring break destinations are the party capitals of Orlando, Las Vegas and Cancun. If you're the type who prefers a mellower, less crowded atmosphere and a more affordable trip, try an outdoor alternative like hiking a segment of the Appalachian Trail.

IF YOUR FRIENDS GO TO BIG SCHOOLS that have huge annual weeks (Indiana's Little 500, Wisconsin's Halloween, Penn's Spring Fling, etc.), these provide good excuses for road trips to see them and have a great time at a different school. Music festivals are also fun.

—*MANNY*
GEORGE WASHINGTON UNIVERSITY, SENIOR

• • • • • • • •

CALL YOUR FRIENDS before you go on a road trip to see them. My friends and I went up to Providence. We were having a good time, and then we decided we wanted to go to Newport. When we were driving, it was pretty late at night, so my friend in Newport wouldn't pick up his phone. So we had to keep on driving. When we got to Connecticut, we tried to call my friend there, and he didn't pick up either. Then we passed New York City and none of our friends would pick up the phone. They were all asleep. We ended up down at the Jersey Shore at four in the morning, after five hours of driving from Providence.

—*THEODORE SCHIMENTI*
COLUMBIA UNIVERSITY, FRESHMAN

Family Ties: Keeping in Touch & Setting Boundaries

Leaving home was all about the big break, but now you've got to figure out how to live your life as both a member of your family and an independent adult. (Although if you're taking your laundry home every weekend, you won't get your "Independent Adult" merit badge just yet!) How can you stay close when you're far away? And how can you grow as a person without growing apart from your loved ones back home? It's a tricky balancing act that every freshman has to work out for him- or herself—but these stories will help.

IN THESE TIMES OF TECHNOLOGY, when people text faster than they walk, I would say a phone call or text every day back home should not be too difficult.

—KANU
  HUNTER COLLEGE, SOPHOMORE

WHEN YOUR PARENTS VISIT, JUST LET THEM BABY YOU.

—M.A.
  FLORIDA STATE UNIVERSITY GRADUATE

HEADLINES
Best Advice and Top Tips

- Surprise visits from the family are off limits!
- Scheduling a weekly phone call with your parents will help with homesickness.
- Don't tell your mom everything that goes on!
- Staying connected to your family can help get you through the stressful times.

SKYPE IS A REALLY AMAZING THING. You shouldn't Skype every night because you need to be spending time socially, but especially if you have little siblings - like my friend with a 5-year-old brother - it can really help you feel in touch to be using Skype regularly.

—*EMILY*
HARVARD COLLEGE, SENIOR

• • • • • • • • •

I'M CLOSE TO MY PARENTS. We talk on the phone every other night and my mom IM's me. In college it's important to have your parents in your life, because we may think that we're really mature and know everything, but a lot of times they give you really good advice. They've been there before. In college, your parents are finally honest with you. In high school, they're like, "I never drank." Then in college, they're like, "This one time, I did this. You never want to do that." They become more human and less authoritarian. They help you.

—*ALYSSA*
JAMES MADISON UNIVERSITY, SOPHOMORE

MAKE IT CLEAR TO PARENTS and grandparents that surprise visits are not a good idea, given how often you will be at the library.

—*D.D.*
UNIVERSITY OF PENNSYLVANIA, GRADUATE

• • • • • • • •

" Do a lot of things your mother would disapprove of. Tattoos, body piercing, spring break trips; as long as you can act like an adult, the sky's the limit. "

—*ANONYMOUS*
MISSISSIPPI STATE UNIVERSITY

• • • • • • • •

CALL YOUR PARENTS EVERY SINGLE WEEK, but you don't have to tell them everything. I call my mother on Sundays and talk to her for an hour and I'll catch her up with the things she will not be judgmental about. And the other stuff, I just don't tell her anymore. Pick and choose what you tell your parents.

—*CATE*
BROWN UNIVERSITY, JUNIOR

• • • • • • • •

I HATE TO ADMIT IT, but freshman year I learned that when my parents tell me something, they may actually be right, and I realized that I should start to listen to what they say, especially since they have much more life experience than I do.

—*STEPHANIE KLEINER*
UNIVERSITY OF DELAWARE, SENIOR

EMAIL TO MOM MADE EZ

Bet you didn't know, *Hundreds of Heads Books* also runs a side business called Super-EZ Emails. It's for people who "don't have time" to write an email to someone important - like you and that email you should be sending to your mother.

Don't worry – we have a Super-EZ Email ready to go. Fill in the blanks. Attach a picture of yourself (one in which you are not doing something that might concern your mom). Hit send. EZ!

"Hi Mom!

How are you? How's Dad? I miss you both, but college has been great so far.

This past weekend I did a lot of studying for an upcoming exam in (insert class title here). I also took some time to go to this really great party – I met a bunch of cool people and might have even gotten a date out of it. But I'm not rushing into anything – studies come first.

Oh, funny story: I did my laundry. That's the story. Isn't that funny?

Hey, can you send me and my dorm mates some (favorite homemade snack item)? I know it would be a big hit. And it will hold me over until I come home during break.

Well, gotta get back to studying. First, I think I might go for a jog with my friends.

I love you and Dad. Tell (insert sibling's name(s) here) I like them all right too, and I can't wait to tell them about college so far.

Love,
(insert your name)"

The Editors

I'M FROM L.A. and I have no family up here, so the transition from having a lot of family to not having anybody was tough. My mom used to call me twice a day—once at noon and once around 9 or 10 at night, just to check in on me, and say, "Where are you?" And I'd say, "I'm out." She'd be okay as long as I wasn't doing anything bad. When I think about it, it was a good thing that she gave me a call every day, even though sometimes it was an invasion.

—*EDUARDO CHOZA*
SAN FRANCISCO STATE UNIVERSITY, SOPHOMORE

* * * * * * * *

SET UP ONE NIGHT A WEEK when you call your parents. Then they're not calling you every day and you're not calling them every day; that's not healthy for anyone.

—*J.G.*
GEORGE WASHINGTON UNIVERSITY, SENIOR

* * * * * * * *

I HAVE REALLY CLOSE TIES with my family. I get along well with my parents and my little brother is my best friend. It was hard to say goodbye. I talk with them a lot. I call them on my cell phone every other day, and talk for 45 minutes to an hour. And I email my little brother.

—*CESAR*
YALE UNIVERSITY, FRESHMAN

* * * * * * * *

I NEVER GOT HOMESICK, but staying close to my parents and siblings definitely kept me sane over the course of freshman year.

—*PETE*
PRINCETON UNIVERSITY, SOPHOMORE

My parents get their two calls a week and that's about all they're going to get right now. It's the best way to do it.

—*WALTER*
UNIVERSITY OF MARYLAND—COLLEGE PARK SOPHOMORE

MY DAD IS KIND OF OLD-FASHIONED. Before I went to school he didn't even want me to have an ATM card. Then in the dorms, everyone had a mini-fridge. My dad said no to that, too. But I eventually won on both counts. College has changed so much that you should be patient with your parents, as they don't always understand the needs of today's freshmen. It might even be a good idea to give them a list of must-haves for freshmen: cell phones, computers, Internet, etc.

—A. ROSEN
UNIVERSITY OF FLORIDA, GRADUATE

• • • • • • • • •

ONCE I GOT TO COLLEGE, I curtailed all contact with home. I didn't call home as often as we agreed; sometimes I just wouldn't call home at all. My parents really worried. In retrospect I really regret that, because I put them through a lot of shit doing that. That's definitely a resolution for next year—to be more up on it when it comes to communication with back home.

—F.S.
STANFORD UNIVERSITY, SOPHOMORE

Go to school away from home and away from your parents. But let them into your life. Be friends with them.

—GINGER M. BRODTMAN
SPRING HILL COLLEGE GRADUATE

WHEN TO CALL MOM AND DAD

Kids shouldn't feel pressured to call their parents (or not call them at all). They should call them when they want to talk to them, even if that's five times in a day because it's a really exciting day. I was ready to move out of the house when I came to college, but that doesn't mean you can't talk to your parents just because you don't live with them.

—TOBIAS
HARVARD COLLEGE, FRESHMAN

It's good to share your experiences with your parents, but not all your experiences. Part of becoming your own person is having your own secrets and your own personal business. But if you share with your parents the things that fascinate you about growing up and being an adult, then that strengthens your bond. And they remember that they were kids once, too; they remember how it was.

—*Shelby Noel Harrington*
University of California at Santa Barbara, Freshman

" Whenever you think about old friends or family, call them or write them right then. If you put it off you'll get preoccupied with a million other things and never get to it. "

—*Aubrey Walker*
Santa Barbara City College, Sophomore

You've got to be honest with your parents. You've got to break them in. If you do bad stuff, you've got to let them know; they're going to find out anyway, so you might as well be honest about it. If you tell them the way it is, they'll get used to it.

—*Beth*
Diablo Valley College, Freshman

GRANDMA KNOWS BEST

It was the second half of my freshman year and I had my first hangover. My friends and I were at a concert and we were all drinking. I couldn't tell exactly what I drank and how much, but I tried anything and everything. It's all about discovering what you like and what you don't like, right? The next morning when I woke up, before I even opened my eyes, my head was throbbing. I hadn't eaten anything and my stomach and I were definitely not on speaking terms. I called my grandmother and asked her if she had ever experienced a hangover. She said, "Yes." I then told her I was having one. She laughed and came over to my apartment to comfort me. It's funny; I was 18 and thought I knew it all, but once I got my first hangover, whom did I go running to? My grandmother! Keep close ties with your family as you may need them at any time.

—Stephanie M. McKnight
Frostburg State University, Senior

My relationship with my parents has improved a lot over the phone versus in person.

—Chana Weiner
Barnard College
Sophomore

IF YOU GO HOME FOR THE SUMMER, make sure you go on vacation. I had to take trips by myself because I cannot be around my parents all the time. I realize they are real people and not all their habits are ones I want to live with.

—S.
University of California at Santa Barbara, Freshman

• • • • • • • •

ASK FOR CARE PACKAGES. I loved receiving cookies and photos every now and then, and this lets your parents remain part of your life even if you are far away.

—Amy
Princeton University, Freshman

I TALK TO MY PARENTS A LOT AT NIGHT. Last night was the season premiere of a show. I used to watch with my dad a lot, so I called him before and after. And besides that, I talk to them twice a week just to catch up and see how it's going. It was my little brother's birthday and I wished him a happy birthday.

—MATT MONACO
GEORGE WASHINGTON UNIVERSITY, FRESHMAN

. . . .

BY MID-SEMESTER I WAS extremely homesick. I suddenly realized that my life was never going to be the same. I called home a lot and talked to my parents all the time. My dad emailed me every single day, and he always said, "P.S. Take your vitamins, go to church, and pray." Talking to them really helped me.

—A.G.H.
UNIVERSITY OF VIRGINIA, SENIOR

. . . .

YOUR PARENTS WILL LET GO of a lot once you leave for college, but swearing (especially f-bombs) when you're home on visits won't be well received.

—D.D.
UNIVERSITY OF PENNSYLVANIA, GRADUATE

. . . .

I WENT TO COLLEGE PLANNING on staying in close contact with all my "friends" in high school – all 200 of them. I had to learn that being a social person did not mean I had to talk to everyone I was friends with in high school on a regular basis. With my true friends, I found the best thing to do was send an encouraging or "just saying hi" text message or email to those I really cared about when I didn't have time to have a long conversation.

—MERELISE HARTE ROUZER
GEORGIA INSTITUTE OF TECHNOLOGY, SOPHOMORE

Only tell your parents a fourth of what's really going on. They're on a need-to-know basis.

—J.G.
FLORIDA STATE UNIVERSITY GRADUATE

FACEBOOK AND YOUR PARENTS

FACEBOOK IS A VERY IMPORTANT tool in college – even if your mom has signed up. However, if you are concerned with your mom checking your wall posts and other information, you can easily block her from viewing your profile in its entirety by changing the privacy settings. That way, you can continue flirting with that hot person in your psychology class without worrying about your parents.

—*KANU*
HUNTER COLLEGE, SOPHOMORE

• • • • • • • • •

WHEN I GET OUT OF AN EXAM, I sometimes post on Facebook from my phone about how "rough" it was or how I never want to go back to school again, to vent from stress. By the time I check my Facebook page later that day, I find all kinds of responses from my dad, mom, stepmom, brothers, sisters, cousins etc., reassuring me that all is not lost, or making sassy comments. It's a different way of doing things. It's made me want to keep a lot more under wraps regarding school and schoolwork, but at the same time it is good to get some encouragement when you know that the next economics exam is going to kick your butt.

—*AMANDA*
UNIVERSITY OF COLORADO AT COLORADO SPRINGS, SOPHOMORE

• • • • • • • • •

FACEBOOK CAN BE A DANGEROUS THING now that everyone from pre-teens to parents to job interviewers can use it. Most college students have cleaned up their Facebook pages a great deal since so many more people have access to it. People have also started protecting their profiles more carefully with safety features. Of course, there are still those who post pictures of blatant underage drinking on their profiles. But the chances are, they will learn their lesson later on when applying for a job, a committee, etc.

—*MERELISE HARTE ROUZER*
GEORGIA INSTITUTE OF TECHNOLOGY, SOPHOMORE

NEVER BE FACEBOOK FRIENDS WITH YOUR PARENTS. NEVER. It's just not a good idea, because, without fail, at some point in time, there will be something posted on your Facebook, be it a comment or a picture of a status or whatever, that you will NOT WANT YOUR PARENTS TO SEE. And if you're friends with them, they'll see it. And then ask you about it. And then you're screwed.

—*SETH*
OGLETHORPE UNIVERSITY, FRESHMAN

I DON'T THINK MANY COLLEGE STUDENTS are affected by their parents being on Facebook. Most parents understand that their child lives alone in a college town and is going to have a beer every once and a while. Personally, I like my parents being on Facebook so they can see what I've been up to at school.

—*ILAN GLUCK*
UNIVERSITY OF MARYLAND, JUNIOR

FACEBOOK IS JUST ANOTHER WAY parents can keep up with their children's lives in college, and they have a right to do so. Most parents leave loving and supporting messages on their child's pages, with no intention of prying into their personal lives.

—*JONATHAN LIU*
UNIVERSITY OF TENNESSEE - KNOXVILLE, FRESHMAN

IF YOU WANT TO KEEP YOUR PARENTS and family members at arm's length on Facebook, put them on limited profile. Parents like to see your Facebook because there are pictures on there. They want to see what you are doing, that you are okay and making friends. If you are concerned with them getting too up close and personal with your Facebook, pick a couple of pictures to send to them every once in a while.

—*ANNIE THOMAS*
UNIVERSITY OF MICHIGAN, SENIOR

BOTH OF MY PARENTS ARE ON FACEBOOK, and Facebook keeps telling me I should be friends with them. I refuse to do so, and my parents completely get it. It is not because I don't love my parents, but rather because Facebook is something I use to keep in touch with my friends in ways that I don't need my parents to see. I don't tell them everything all the time (which does drive them nuts), but Facebook is just another extension of that.

—*BARRY LANGER*
OGLETHORPE UNIVERSITY, JUNIOR

WITH FACEBOOK, I try to make sure that whenever someone tags me in a picture or posts something on my wall, I ask myself, "Is it okay for my mom to see this?" I know a lot of people do not really use that rationale for Facebook.

—*G.L.*
GEORGE WASHINGTON UNIVERSITY, SENIOR

I AM REALLY CLOSE WITH MY PARENTS, so I talk to them at least once a day. A good time to make these calls is walking to and from class. This way, you have enough time to fill your parents in – but if you don't want to get into a long conversation you have an easy out.

—*ANNIE THOMAS*
UNIVERSITY OF MICHIGAN, SENIOR

JUST MAKE SURE TO KEEP in touch with your parents. It makes it easier when problems arise or you make drastic changes in your plans for the future.

—*MANNY*
GEORGE WASHINGTON UNIVERSITY, SENIOR

HOMESICKNESS

Homesickness is the number one stressor for college students because of the temporary loss many people experience when they leave home. Adapting to this temporary loss involves four basic tasks: accepting the reality that you are away from family, friends, pets, etc.; experiencing the pain (crying, sadness, and loneliness); adjusting to a new environment, and withdrawing and reinvesting emotional energy.

Participating as fully as possible in the activities sponsored by the First Year Experience, Living/Learning Floors and other college organizations, can help with the anxiety, fear, and discomfort that may result from the transition to college. And don't overlook the power of friends helping friends; this requires trust and willingness to really listen to your friend and then allowing the friend to listen to you. Many times we try to "cheer up" our friend – but this has the effect of minimizing, or discounting, the importance of the person's feelings. It's not helpful to say, "Next week, month, or year, you'll forget about all this."

If we are miserable we can move through it in a healthy manner if we are allowed to express our misery and sit for a while and reflect. We soon get tired and figure out a way to do something different to improve our own situation. Before you even think about it, you will call home less frequently, stay on campus on the weekends instead of going home, attend sporting events to meet new friends, and invite friends from home to visit your campus. Remember, there are people on campus who can help you through the homesickness process: your resident adviser, professor, staff, and counseling center, to name just a few. You will be welcomed by all no matter how you feel, while at the same time finding your "niche" at your college/university.

Dr. Clarice Ford
Associate Vice Chancellor of Student Services
University of Illinois Springfield

TO WAIVE OR NOT TO WAIVE?

It will happen either at an orientation program for families, or when your parents call the college to check on you. They will be told about the Family Educational Rights and Privacy Act* (FERPA), and about something called a FERPA/confidentiality waiver. Your grades, attendance, class behavior, even the names of the classes you're taking – none of this can be disclosed to your parents or anyone else without a waiver. Since your parents may ask you to sign one, you should think about what your answer will be.

Should you sign a confidentiality waiver? First, understand that colleges usually require a separate waiver for each department. If you have a bunch of complicated loans and scholarships that your family is involved with, you may want to give the financial services office clearance to talk to your parents.

But is it a good idea to authorize your professors to share information? As a general rule, professors do not want to discuss your work with your parents; they want to deal directly with you. Respect this. If you find yourself having a conflict with a professor over grades, course content, or anything else, use your parents as a sounding board but keep the official conversation between you and your professor. If you're not able to reach a resolution, a college mentor such as an academic adviser or student dean can help.

Is it a good idea to authorize your academic adviser to share information? Depending on the level of involvement your parents are seeking, your academic adviser may be able to assist them even without a confidentiality waiver on file. She can discuss typical freshman experiences, recommend college resources, and demystify the rules for good standing and probation. This background information will allow your parents to make informed and constructive suggestions when you share your college experiences with them.

There are, however, some situations when granting your academic adviser more freedom to share information can benefit you. As you make the transition from high school to college, you may feel you're not ready to go from an environment of total parental supervision to total independence all at once. You may recognize that you have a tendency to procrastinate in your work, or to avoid revealing difficulties to your family. If that's the case, consider allowing your adviser to have the occasional discussion with you *and* your parents during the first semester. You can put an end date on your waiver, after which time your information will become confidential once again.

Frances Northcutt

* *To learn more about the Family Educational Rights and Privacy Act, visit www2.ed.gov/policy/gen/guid/fpco/ferpa/index.html*

ONE THING I TRY TO DO IN TERMS of talking with my parents is to keep a set "talk schedule." I tend to talk to my parents over the phone about three times per week. I'll call my dad every Sunday to rehash about the weekend in sports. I'll call my mom on Monday when I have a free hour between classes. If you can set up an informal schedule, that makes it much easier to keep in contact. Your parents will know when you're calling and will be eager to speak to you. This also avoids any calls at unwanted times.

—ANDREW OSTROWSKY
PENNSYLVANIA STATE UNIVERSITY, JUNIOR

MY PARENTS UNDERSTAND that this is my college experience and that I am legitimately doing my own thing. Some parents that I know of are not quite as understanding, and it mostly seems like an inability to tell your parents, "This is my time. Let me have it. They're my mistakes to make, not yours. It's my turn." Whether or not you're actually making mistakes, parents need to understand that you can be on your own without them.

—*BARRY LANGER*
OGLETHORPE UNIVERSITY, JUNIOR

. . . .

Become easy
to reach.

—*REYNER*
OLIN COLLEGE
FRESHMAN

IF YOU DON'T CALL HOME at least once a week, parents will get antsy. And for good reason. If you don't call home at least once a week, you have done something in that time frame that you know would make them uncomfortable. Parents are smarter than you will give them credit for, mainly because they've smothered you for 18 years.

—*J.V.*
THE COLLEGE OF WILLIAM & MARY, GRADUATE

More Wisdom: Good Stuff That Doesn't Fit Anywhere Else

Looking back on their first year of college, whether from a distance of ten years or ten weeks, our respondents often waxed philosophical—especially those who'd taken Philosophy 101. Like a lot of good advice, their observations just didn't fit neatly into those earlier chapters, but they were way too important to ignore. As you read their thoughts, consider how you might look back on your freshman year of college. Will it be everything you hoped? How will you make it the best it can be?

BE ADVENTUROUS. Be open to doing things outside of your comfort zone.

—*J.V.*
THE COLLEGE OF WILLIAM & MARY, GRADUATE

DON'T TAKE YOURSELF SO SERIOUSLY.

—*TREVOR*
AMHERST COLLEGE GRADUATE

IF YOU DON'T HAVE AN OPENNESS to the situation, you're going to have trouble. You're going to meet people of different backgrounds and beliefs, some people that have been coddled and some people that haven't. You need an openness to learn and an openness to accept. If you don't have that, you won't do very well. If you do, your experience will be a lot better.

—*ZACH FRIEND*
UNIVERSITY OF CALIFORNIA AT SANTA CRUZ, GRADUATE

• • • • • • • •

MY FIRST DAY OF CLASS, a department chair said something that stuck with me. He said, "It's possible to go through four years of college unscathed by education. It's a tragedy if that happens." He went on to say that college is about challenging all of your preconceived notions; from your personal values to your religious values to your social values to your political values. If you have a real college experience, it should all be challenged. If you don't have the courage to face that, you're not getting as much out of college as you could. Be prepared to be challenged.

—*MICHAEL A. FEKULA*
UNIVERSITY OF MARYLAND, GRADUATE

• • • • • • • •

IF YOU'RE NOT CAREFUL, the first year of college will be the most unhealthy year of your entire life. The food is bad for you, you're probably not exercising as much as you were in high school, you drink tons of caffeine and even more alcohol, and you don't sleep. Freshman year, try to remember to sleep more and exercise more. That way you'll be a fully functioning human being. Sometimes it's hard to pass up parties, but remember that there will be other nights and other funny stories. Choose your night.

—*SUMMER J.*
UNIVERSITY OF VIRGINIA, SENIOR

KNOW WHAT YOU WANT TO DO when you go to college. I didn't know and I didn't care. I didn't go to many classes; I just spent my time meeting people and going to parties. I did everything you weren't supposed to do: I signed up for hard classes, I didn't go to them, and I went out every night. When I was 18, I acted a lot younger.

—*A.G.S.*
UNIVERSITY OF TENNESSEE, DID NOT GRADUATE

• • • • • • • •

IT'S HARD TO REMEMBER back to freshman year. There's a lesson there: It will pass, good and bad.

—*LINDSEY SHULTZ*
CARNEGIE MELLON UNIVERSITY, SENIOR

• • • • • • • •

Don't set your mind on anything the first year. Explore. That's what it's about.

—*M.M.*
NEW YORK UNIVERSITY, SENIOR

Have an open mind and try to see everything. Not everything will be your thing, but there is something that you'll find.

—*ANONYMOUS*
UNIVERSITY OF PENNSYLVANIA, FRESHMAN

• • • • • • • •

I THOUGHT THAT COLLEGE would be what you learn in the classroom. But the real wealth of information is not from your professors: It's from the other people you meet and the experiences you have.

—*RENE*
DUKE UNIVERSITY, GRADUATE

STUDENT TEACHERS

Here's the best piece of advice I think I got in four years: At the end of my freshman year, I set up a meeting with a professor who had befriended me. I had been considering taking more classes over the summer to get ahead towards my degree (yes, I was a little nerd) and so I asked, "Is the quality of the courses the same as during the year? Do the same professors teach during the summer?" He said, "The professors are the same, but the courses are not as good." He paused for a second to enjoy the look of confusion on my face. "It's the students that are generally worse. During the summer, there are a lot of high school students, trying to put something on their résumé. You learn from your peers more than from the professor, you know."

My professor's advice was excellent—the people I met at college were so exceptional and taught me so much, everything from literature to physics.

—*NOAH HELMAN*
HARVARD COLLEGE, GRADUATE

KNOW WHICH CLASSES TO SKIP, and which classes not to skip. This is really a key point, because some professors don't care one way or another if you show up for class. All they care about is your test and homework performance. There are other professors who are sticklers for attendance, and even if you are an A student you can end up with a C, because of poor attendance.

—*TONYA BANKS*
MIAMI UNIVERSITY, GRADUATE

I WAS NEVER A FRESHMAN. When asked, I was an "undergrad," or for those not into the whole brevity thing, I was "finishing up my lower-division classes," or "in my second semester." Did this help me? Yes and no. If you are around other freshmen, you don't really have to do it; they don't need to be impressed. It works fairly well on upper-division students, though. If you tell one of them that you are a freshman, they immediately sort of shy away from you. So, use euphemisms, but use discretion, too.

> —KARLA SAIA
> SAN DIEGO STATE UNIVERSITY, JUNIOR

SLEEP EARLY AND OFTEN—Don't stay up till 2 a.m. because you'll never get up for your 8 a.m. class. **EAT EARLY AND OFTEN**—Don't skip breakfast, and eat three meals a day.

DRINK—but not too early and not too often.

> —C.B.

ANYTHING RANDOM IS BAD. Don't allow them to pick a random roommate for you; find one and request him. Don't go into a random dorm or room; pick your own. Same thing with the meal plan; do your due diligence and find out what the options are or you will be unhappy with the choices made for you. This is true for life as well as college. Don't be a sheep: Take charge.

> —ANGEL NYA
> CARNEGIE MELLON UNIVERSITY, SOPHOMORE

The iPhone has hundreds of cool game applications that make classes go by a lot faster.

> —ILAN GLUCK
> UNIVERSITY OF
> MARYLAND, JUNIOR

FORM HABITS THAT WILL TRANSLATE into career traits after your schooling is complete. This does not have to be stressful. It can be simplified:

1) Find a place that's just yours where you can study comfortably.
2) Get up early a few days a week and walk, jog, or practice something physical.
3) Do something at least one day a week that's for someone else—visit a facility where you can volunteer (not with a bunch of friends; just you).
4) Write in a journal. Give yourself time to reflect and see things through someone else's eyes.

If you get into these habits, it will carry you not only through your first year, but also through your whole college career. You'll amaze yourself at how consistent you can be. And the carryover of these habits will frame your post-school life for  success, no matter what you choose to do.

—*TREVOR*
AMHERST COLLEGE, GRADUATE

> Never be lazy. College only happens once and it's not long enough, so take advantage of it.
>
> —*KERRY*
> *GEORGETOWN UNIVERSITY GRADUATE*

COLLEGE CHANGES YOU

The college experience helped me become a leader in so many ways. I came out of high school, shy like no other, unsure of myself, quite insecure. College allowed me to find out who I am, my potential to be someone great, and put my insecurities out at the curb. I am able to voice my opinion, speak in public places, and lead a group without feeling unsure of myself. College is what you make it!

—*VIVIAN ORIAKU*
UNIVERSITY OF MIAMI, GRADUATE

MY FRESHMAN YEAR WAS GOOD, BAD, everything you could possibly imagine. The bad parts were adjusting, then readjusting, then readjusting again to leaving home and being on your own and making your life work. There was a lot to be exposed to really fast.

—*J.P.G.*
UNIVERSITY OF PENNSYLVANIA, SOPHOMORE

" Have your fun, but realize you're here to get an education (and, hopefully, a degree!) Make it all worthwhile— academics and social life. "

—*KHALIL SULLIVAN*
PRINCETON UNIVERSITY, JUNIOR

AN IMPORTANT RECOMMENDATION

When you ask for a letter of recommendation, ask at least two weeks in advance, and try to give four weeks' notice, or more… seriously! Sometimes a professor may not be able to respond to your email quickly, or they may *want* to write a letter but then forget to do it. Once you get someone to agree, occasional gentle reminders may be in order. You probably need to send the individual your résumé and a description of what you're applying for - and potentially meet with them to discuss details before they agree to write that letter for you.

Scott C. Silverman

Everyone searches for an identity their freshman year; that's one of your biggest struggles.

—RYAN A. BROWN
UNIVERSITY OF
NORTH CAROLINA
AT CHAPEL HILL
GRADUATE

WHAT I NEGLECTED MY FRESHMAN YEAR was taking advice from professors. In high school, I always felt like my teachers didn't know what they were talking about. But the professors really do know what they're talking about, and not just in their fields. When they give you advice, listen to it. I didn't take the advice of people who could've helped me. Most freshmen have this attitude: "I got to college, so why do I need you now?" Your pride and self-confidence get in the way of re-evaluating the situation you're in. That's what it comes down to. You've got to shed your attitude; it really gets in the way.

　　—ZAK AMCHISLAVSKY
　　　GEORGETOWN UNIVERSITY, SENIOR

• • • • • • • •

FRESHMAN YEAR WAS NOT an endurance test—it was a friggin' celebration!

　　—L.
　　　DUKE UNIVERSITY, GRADUATE

COLLEGE FOOTBALL'S CONTRIBUTIONS TO MANKIND

1. Gatorade was named for the University of Florida (football) Gators, for whom it was developed in 1965. Coach Ray Graves's Florida team—powered by the potion concocted by a UF med-school professor—came from behind to defeat heavily favored Louisiana State in 102-degree heat, and a legend was born.

2. The football huddle originated at Gallaudet University, a liberal arts college for the deaf, when the football team found that opposing teams were reading their signed messages and intercepting plays.

IF YOU GO TO SCHOOL IN A BIG CITY, you have to be more careful. Watch out for your surroundings. If you have to take a route where you might have trouble, stay away from it. Take the long way. There's nothing more important than your life.

> —*B.L.*
> *JOHN JAY COLLEGE OF CRIMINAL JUSTICE, GRADUATE*

• • • • • • • •

" You can graduate with decent grades, you can do nothing and just get four years older, or you can suck the marrow out of your university and garner all the knowledge, academic and other, that comes your way. The choice and your future are in your hands. "

> —*ADAM*
> *ELON UNIVERSITY, SOPHOMORE*

• • • • • • • •

PART OF BEING A FRESHMAN is about being away from parents and doing stupid things. Doing stupid things is the best way to learn.

> —*CAITLIN BERBERICH*
> *UNIVERSITY OF GEORGIA, GRADUATE*

SHOULD I STAY OR SHOULD I GO? IS TRANSFER THE ANSWER?

So you're already at a four-year institution and maybe you're thinking of transferring to another college or university. Before you decide, make sure you're doing this for the right reasons. Remember that the grass is not always greener on the other side. Some students who end up transferring, like their new university - and some do not. Here are some suggestions:

If you really feel that the institution you're in is not the best fit for you, or you're not completely happy, you have only two responsible choices: adapt and make it work, or explore transfer options.

Don't transfer solely because you are homesick, the classes are too difficult or you're having problems with your roommate – or to run from or pursue a specific relationship. You can deal with any of these in less drastic ways...visit home, challenge yourself in your classes, ask your RA for tips for dealing with your roommate, etc. If you transfer only because you hope one aspect of the experience is better, you may find other things at the new place that you don't like as much.

Transferring to a new university is tough, and can be harder than starting college in the first place. Everything will work somewhat differently than what you've already gotten used to. You'll need to establish new networks of friends and peers – with students who have already made friendships and had common experiences, learn about new course requirements, find new student organizations, etc. Many transfer students end up taking 5 years or more to graduate, because inevitably the transfer process sets them back a few terms.

Of course, there are some valid reasons to transfer… Check any of these that apply:

- **A major that doesn't exist on your campus.** If you want to pursue a program of study that isn't offered at your school, you don't have a lot of options. However, don't get hung up on the specific major, because as long as you take the right classes, you can pursue any career or graduate program. That said, if you want to specialize in underwater basket weaving, and only two schools in the country teach that, you owe it to yourself to check out those programs.

- **A specific professor with whom you want to study or work.** Well, you can't very well get that person to switch to *your* university. However, you may have equally renowned faculty in your major with your current institution.
- **A financial incentive.** This could be because of a new scholarship, or because you were recruited as an athlete. But be sure also to check out the scholarships for students that continue on at your institution; you may be surprised at what you find there, or by doing a web search for scholarships.
- **Family obligations.** If your family needs you at home to take care of a relative or to help out with another matter, you may be better off taking a temporary leave of absence from college. Transferring to be close to home may not solve your problem because you still will not be able to focus on your classes.

In any case, before you apply to transfer, see your academic adviser to discuss the process...who knows, there may even be a reason to stay at your university that you haven't thought of yet.

If you do decide to transfer - talk to the admissions office and academic adviser of the college and major you want to transfer to, to make sure that you meet all of their requirements. You'll also have to think about living arrangements...if you've signed a lease near the school you're leaving, you'll have to break it. You may have a hard time finding housing at your new institution. Once you transfer, make sure you go to the transfer orientation, which will help you transition to your new university.

Remember, think twice before you transfer...but if you go that route, make sure it's for the right reasons. The last thing you want is to get buyer's remorse once you transfer and not be able to come back.

Scott C. Silverman

DON'T TALK BAD ABOUT ANYONE. My dad told me that when I was in high school and I stuck with it. No one has a bad thing to say about you if you don't say bad things about them. If they do, you realize they're not worth your time.

—*CASEY*
GEORGETOWN UNIVERSITY, SENIOR

. . . .

" Make a plan. Write out everything you have to do, every day. Follow that plan and stick with it. Don't let anything get in the way of taking care of that plan. It's like a schedule. Write down everything that you have to do, and get it done. Social things, everything. "

—*BRIAN*
JAMES MADISON UNIVERSITY, JUNIOR

. . . .

COLLEGE IS DIVERSE. Be open to new experiences. Don't judge people on whether or not they get wasted on the weekends. That's just one aspect of a person.

—*ERIC MCINTOSH*
UNIVERSITY OF NORTH CAROLINA AT CHAPEL HILL, JUNIOR

I'M FROM NEW YORK and I went to a very rural, small, homogeneous southern school my freshman year. It was a bit of a culture shock. I was in classes with white, upper-middle-class kids and that was it. On your tour they say it's diverse, but I don't know what their definition of that is; it's not the New York definition. I didn't realize how much it would affect me, not having access to plays and restaurants and jazz clubs. You had to really travel if you wanted to do anything that would stimulate you. I knew by November that it was not where I wanted to spend my college life. People make you think your decision to pick a college is the end-all of your entire life. So find a place that looks interesting, and figure out what's important to you before you check out a college. Don't be influenced by a beautiful campus or the nice people in your tour. Expect that you're going to spend four years there, but know that if you don't, it's not jail; you can transfer. College is about *you*, not the school.

—HANNAH SMITH
HARVARD UNIVERSITY, JUNIOR

• • • • • • • •

REMEMBER, EVERYONE ELSE IS IN THE SAME BOAT as you. College is your first taste of freedom, but it comes with a lot of responsibility. No freshman has it all figured out, so if you find people that act like they do, they're drunk or lying.

—ANONYMOUS
UNION COLLEGE

• • • • • • • •

FIND A GROUP ON CAMPUS that interests you, so you don't feel that the school is so huge.

—STEPHANIE
UNIVERSITY OF PENNSYLVANIA, SENIOR

I learned that college is like a big high school. It's just older people, who take being immature to another level.

—M.G.
VALDOSTA STATE UNIVERSITY, SENIOR

I SURVIVED MY FRESHMAN YEAR

Cursed with an annoying stammer, I always scrupulously avoided doing anything at all in front of an audience. But in my first week as a freshman I was forced to come face-to-face with "the stammer."

In a business management course, we were asked to debate issues given to us by our lecturers. My group was given the ridiculous proposition that "welfare benefits assist unemployment" and told to argue against it. Maintaining my treasured high school stance of protected anonymity, I offered a few ideas to my group while stead-fastly refusing to be the spokesperson for the group.

However, our dear teachers were not to be fobbed off with such an approach. They started firing questions at *all* the participants.

I waited for my turn to come. When it did, I opened my mouth to answer and . . . nothing. Zilch. I writhed and wriggled, and still nothing.

I prayed hard that the earth would open and swallow me up. I knew that I'd blown it for the rest of my college life, and all in the first week.

And then, suddenly, it came: "This form of intolerance and precon-ceived notions is the same that the proposers of this motion are suggesting for the unemployed."

There was total silence, then applause. I had bowled them over with an outrageous display of demagoguery. Within the month, I was a candidate for the Student Representative Council. Within the year, I was conducting workshops and making speeches before thousands. Lots of screaming, plenty of demagoguery and no end of guilt-tripping. A political career was born; I had survived my freshman year.

—*Phil Carmel*
University College–Salford (England), Graduate

DON'T BE AFRAID TO USE THE HEALTH CENTER, for both medical and mental problems. It's cheap, it's confidential, and it really can help if you get the blues.

—*ANONYMOUS*
UNIVERSITY OF GEORGIA, GRADUATE

• • • • • • • •

" I recommend taking a year off before starting college. It gives a fantastic perspective on why you need to be sitting in classes day after day. "

—*LEAH PRICE*
GEORGETOWN UNIVERSITY, SOPHOMORE

• • • • • • • •

I WAS EXPOSED TO A LOT OF THE SCARY SIDES of people that I hadn't come so close to before. Like the time some guys beat up and killed a raccoon outside my dorm. Or the time a dorm mate expressed to me that she often felt like committing suicide, and I felt like there was nothing I could do to help her, except let her know that a lot of people around her really cared about her.

—*K. HARMA*
WESTERN WASHINGTON UNIVERSITY, GRADUATE

THE BEST YEAR OF YOUR LIFE

The experience of leaving my freshman year of college is among the most memorable times of my life, along with graduating from high school. Coming to college, I was scared shitless and had no idea how I was going to survive. In May, the heat hit me hard as I was packing up my life into a few duffel bags and sweeping out the room that witnessed my first attempts at independence. I peeled off the walls the pictures of people I once saw every day and swore always to be best friends with, who became people I only talked to once in a while on IM. It sounds sad, but my high school friends and I had gone our separate ways and discovered new lives with people we once called strangers. With these strangers I now had inside jokes, crazy blurry memories, and new pictures to plaster on my wall. Not to say that college is always amazing: the food sucks, your roommate will smell, your professor can be an asshole, there are morning classes, and the guy you can't believe you hooked up with will live down the hall all semester long. It's what makes college college. With all the bad, there is the good. With all your worries and all your fears, freshman year won't suck that bad—it might even be the best year of your life.

—KAREN
STATE UNIVERSITY OF NEW YORK AT NEW PALTZ, SOPHOMORE

THE HARDEST PART OF MY FRESHMAN YEAR was to let go of my former morals, friends, and hobbies in order to develop and grow. I was so afraid that in letting go of these things I was going to lose myself.

—ANNIE VERNA
UNIVERSITY OF NORTH CAROLINA AT GREENSBORO
SOPHOMORE

A BIRD OF PEACE

I don't remember much about sophomore year microeconomics, but one class stands out vividly in my memory. The only people who ever spoke in lecture were the teacher and the five nerds sitting up front, while the other 75 of us sat as close as possible to the door and sent each other obnoxious Facebook messages. I happened to tune in for a few minutes on this fateful day when the teacher (I'll never remember his name, but he signed all his emails "Peace, Josh") posed a question I decided I knew the answer to. Peace Josh, surprised to see a new hand raised in the crowd, called on me immediately.

I began to utter what I'm sure were supposed to be words, but instead issued a variety of meaningless syllables/noises, every second growing increasingly conscious that more and more faces were turning to look at me. Eventually I decided that no coherent English sentences were going to come out of my mouth, so I trailed off, turned beet red, and started staring at the floor. At this point my jerk friends all started to clap softly, so I snapped my head up and flipped them a giant bird. What I *hadn't* noticed was that Peace Josh was attempting to respond to my nonsense and was looking me dead in the eye as he spoke, so it now appeared I was giving him the finger in front of the entire class.

How did this affect me in the long run? Other than never hearing the end of this story from my friends - not much. I did learn a lesson though, which is to speak up early and speak up often, even in a large lecture. If you stay silent for too long, voicing an answer will seem insurmountably daunting by the end of the semester.

—CAITLIN
GEORGETOWN UNIVERSITY, GRADUATE

I TOOK A GAP YEAR before college and I think more people should do it. But only do it if you have something to do – don't just bum around on your parents' couch. That's not going to add a lot of value to your life. I had two jobs during that time and the experience of working hard and having those jobs has given me a lot of confidence coming to college. It's also way less scary to graduate because I know I can live by myself and cook for myself and pay my bills and find an apartment. If I could do it when I was 18 I can do it now!

Taking a gap year is great because you know you're going to college after - it's very low risk. You can do whatever you want to do; use the time to do what YOU want to do. Also it's great because you're 21 a year before everyone else in your class!

—*CATIE*
HARVARD COLLEGE, SENIOR

• • • • • • • •

ALL THE TROUBLE I GOT INTO, all the bad things that came from college, came from the social gatherings. All the good things came from people I met in the classrooms.

—*J.H.*
WIDENER UNIVERSITY, GRADUATE

APPENDICES

THE ESSENTIAL FRESHMAN FILL-IN LIST

Some of these answers you'll find in your new-student orientation pack or handbook, or on the college website. The rest you'll have to discover for yourself—sort of like a first-semester treasure hunt!

Places
Best study spot _____
Best computer lab _____
Best coffee _____
Best late-night food _____
Best inexpensive date location _____

People
For help with rules and requirements _____
For help dealing with stress _____
For answers about student activities _____
For late-night philosophical discussions _____
For fun and laughs _____

Activities
To do when you're homesick _____
To do when you're stressed out _____
To do when you need to be healthier _____
To do when you want to meet new people _____

To do when you want to avoid the people you already know _____
_____

Useful websites

College Connection Scholarships: www.collegescholarships.com

Scholarships.com: www.scholarships.com

College Board scholarship search: apps.collegeboard.com/cbsearch_ss/welcome.jsp

College Board AP credit policy info: collegesearch.collegeboard.com/apcreditpolicy/index.jsp

Hundreds of Heads: www.hundredsofheads.com

International Baccalaureate FAQ: www.ibo.org/ibna/parents_students/dpstudents.cfm

American Medical Student Association: www.amsa.org

Music and Entertainment Industry Student Association: www.meisa.org

American Psychological Association, resources for students interested in studying psychology: www.apa.org/students

The Roosevelt Institution, "The Nation's First Student Think Tank": rooseveltinstitution.org

FAFSA (Free Application for Federal Student Aid): www.fafsa.ed.gov

Volunteer Match: www.volunteermatch.org

Idealist.org, "Action without Borders": www.idealist.org

Student Environmental Action Coalition: www.seac.org

Campus Climate Challenge: climatechallenge.org

CampusActivism.org, "Tools for Activists": www.campusactivism.org

ULifeline, "An online resource center for college student mental health and emotional well-being.": www.ulifeline.org/main/Home.html

LdPride.net, "Information about learning styles and Multiple Intelligence (MI is helpful for everyone, but especially for people with learning disabilities and attention deficit disorder." www.ldpride.net

"Healthy Minds. Healthy Lives.", from the American Psychiatric Association: healthyminds.org

CREDITS/SOURCES

p. 10: http://greenliving.about.com/gi/o.htm?zi=1/XJ&zTi=1&sdn=greenliving&cdn=homegarde
n&tm=135&f=20&su=p284.13.342.ip_&tt=3&bt=0&bts=0&zu=http%3A//www.bikeleague.org/

p. 22: *The Princeton Review*: http://www.princetonreview.com/schoollist.aspx

p. 35: http://www.knox.edu/about-knox/we-are-knox/our-traditions.html

p. 62: *The Princeton Review*: http://www.princetonreview.com/schoollist.aspx

p. 77: http://en.wikipedia.org/wiki/Streaking

p. 83: Wall Street Journal, Aug. 14, 2012 http://online.wsj.com/article/SB10000872396390444
04270457758766234527568.html

p. 83: National Retail Federation, July 19, 2012 http://www.nrf.com/modules.
php?name=News&op=viewlive&sp_id=1405

p. 85: *The College Board College Handbook 2004*. Copyright © 2003 by College Board. All
rights reserved. Reproduced with permission.www.collegeboard.com; http://www.collegex-
press.com/lists/list/colleges-most-like-hogwarts/1460/

p. 118: http://www.usatoday.com/story/news/nation/2012/11/12/record-number-of-
international-students-enrolled-in-colleges/1698531/

p. 122: www.streetdirectory.com/travel_guide/111319/sleep_disorders/sleep_deprivation_
and_the_problems_it_causes.html

p. 137: *The New York Times*, Nov. 2, 2012 - http://www.nytimes.com/2012/11/04/education/
edlife/choosing-one-college-major-out-of-hundreds.html?emc=eta1

p. 152: www.usnews.com/health/family-health/sleep/articles/2008/06/09/college-kids-and-
sleep-4-tips.html

p. 182: http://www.nytimes.com/2010/07/06/education/06cheat.html

p. 194: http://www.huffingtonpost.com/2010/10/12/10-weird-extracurricular-_n_759401.
html#s148833&title=Campus_People_Watchers

p. 205: *The College Board College Handbook 2004*. Copyright © 2003 by College Board.
All rights reserved. Reproduced with permission.www.collegeboard.com.

p. 237: http://gigaom.com/apple/mac-101-10-essential-tips-for-bringing-a-mac-to-college/

p. 239: http://gigaom.com/apple/mac-101-10-essential-tips-for-bringing-a-mac-to-college/

p. 243: Hobson's College View Survey; www.collegeview.com

p. 243: *Sallie Mae*, "How Undergraduate Students Use Credit Cards: Sallie Mae's National
Study of Usage Rates and Trends 2009", www.credit.com/press/statistics/student-creditand-
debt-statistics.html

p. 259: http://www.nytimes.com/2013/01/15/education/parents-financial-support-linked-to-
college-grades.html?emc=eta1

p. 272: http://www.princetonreview.com/schoollist.aspx

p. 273: Medical News Today,http://www.medicalnewstoday.com/articles/236994.php

p. 292: www.hackcollege.com/blog/2009/6/23/mix-your-own-laundry-detergent-mom-tip.html

p. 317: http://collegeprowler.com/rankings/guys/top-hottest-guys/

p. 331: http://collegeprowler.com/rankings/girls/top-hottest-girls/

p. 346: National Survey on Drug Use and Health, cited at http://healthland.time.
com/2012/09/28/college-binge-drinking-how-bad-is-the-problem-really/

p. 352: www.usatoday.com/news/education/2009-03-11-college-drinking_N.htm

p. 366: See, e.g., http://www.snopes.com/language/literary/seuss.asp

p. 367: http://www.playboy.com/playground/view/top-10-party-schools

p. 369: http://collegeprowler.com/rankings/greek-life/top-where-greek-life-rules/

p. 373: *The College Board College Handbook 2004*. Copyright © 2003 by College Board.
All rights reserved. Reproduced with permission. www.collegeboard.com.

p. 374: http://alcoholism.about.com/cs/college/a/aa020318a.htm

p. 384: http://www.iie.org/en/Who-We-Are/News-and-Events/Press-Center/Press-
Releases/2011/2011-11-14-Open-Doors-Study-Abroad

p. 385: http://www.hotelnewsresource.com/article52846Survey_Reveals_Majority_of_
Spring_Travelers_ Staying_Away_from_College_Spring_Break_Towns_And_Spending_
Under_____on_Getaways.html

p. 410: http://www.research.ufl.edu/publications/explore/v08n1/gatorade.html;
http://www.kelloggconferencehotel.com/gallaudet-university/index.php

ADVICE FROM:

Albany State University
American Repertory Theater at Harvard
American University
Amherst College
Anderson University
Auburn University
Barnard College
Baylor University
Biola University
Bloomsburg University
Boston College
Boston University
Bowdoin College
Bowling Green State University
Brown University
Bryn Mawr College
Cal Poly San Luis Obispo
California State University
California State University–Fullerton
Calvin College
Carnegie Mellon University
Central Bible College
Claremont McKenna College
Clemson University
Colby College
College of San Mateo
Columbia University
Cornell College
Cornell University
CUNY/Macaulay Honors College
Curtis Institute of Music
DeSales University
Diablo Valley College
Duke University
Elon University
Emory University
Florida A&M University
Florida State University
Foothill College
Franklin and Marshall College
Frostburg State University
George Washington University
Georgetown University
Georgia Institute of Technology
Georgia Southern University
Georgia State University
Hamilton College

Harvard College
Harvard University
Howard University
Hunter College
Illinois Wesleyan University
Indiana University
James Madison University
John Jay College of Criminal Justice
Johns Hopkins University
Kean University
Kenyon College
Kingsborough Community College
Kutztown University
Los Medanos College
Louisiana State University
Massachusetts Institute of Technology
Marist College
McGill University
Miami University
Michigan Technological University
Mississippi State University
Missouri State University
Montclair State University
Minnesota State University Moorhead
Mount Holyoke College
Newbury College (MA)
New York University
North Carolina State University
Northern Illinois University
Northwestern University
Oberlin College
Oglethorpe University
Olin College
Oxford College
Parsons School of Design
Pennsylvania State University
Pomona College
Princeton University
Purdue University
Queens University
Rhodes College
Rice University
Riverside Community College
Rutgers University
San Diego State University
San Francisco State University
San Jose State University

Santa Barbara City College
Santa Clara University
Sonoma State University
Spring Hill College
St. John's University
St. Joseph's (PA)
Stanford University
State University of New York at Albany
State University of New York at Binghamton
State University of New York at Geneseo
State University of New York at New Paltz
Suffolk University
Syracuse University
Temple University
Texas State University
The College of William & Mary
The Jewish Theological Seminary
Trinity University
Tufts University
Union College
United States Military Academy at West Point
University College–Salford (England)
University of Arizona
University of California at Berkeley
University of California at Davis
University of California at Irvine
University of California at Santa Barbara
University of California at Santa Cruz
University of Colorado
University of Delaware
University of Florida
University of Georgia
University of Illinois
University of Maryland
University of Maryland–College Park
University of Miami
University of Michigan

University of Missouri
University of Nebraska
University of New Hampshire
University of North Carolina
University of North Carolina at Chapel Hill
University of North Carolina at Greensboro
University of Notre Dame
University of Oregon
University of Pennsylvania
University of Rhode Island
University of Rochester
University of South Florida
University of Tennessee at Knoxville
University of Tennessee at Martin
University of Texas
University of Texas at Austin
University of Toronto
University of Tulsa
University of Virginia
University of West Georgia
University of Wisconsin at Madison
Valdosta State University
Vanderbilt University
Villa Julie College
Villanova University
Wake Forest University
Washington and Lee University
Wellesley College
Wesleyan University
Western Illinois University
Western Washington University
Westfield State College
Widener University
Williams College
Xavier University
Yale University
Youngstown State University

SPECIAL THANKS

Thanks to our intrepid "headhunters" for going out to find so many respondents from around the country with interesting advice to share:

Jamie Allen   Lisa Powell
Helen Bond   Beshaleba Rodell
Cindy Ferraino   Kerry Rogers
Brandi Fowler   Staci Siegel
Chelsee Lowe   Annie Stone
Andrea Nackenson   Andrea Syrtash
Adam Pollock   Beth Turney

Thanks, too, to our Chief Headhunter, Jamie Allen, editorial advisor Anne Kostick, and production editor Gayle Green. And thanks to our assistant, Miri Greidi, for her yeoman's work at keeping us all organized. The real credit for this book, of course, goes to all the people whose experiences and collective wisdom make up this guide. There are too many of you to thank individually, but you know who you are.

CHECK OUT THESE OTHER BOOKS FROM HUNDREDS OF HEADS®

HOW TO GET A's IN COLLEGE: Hundreds of Student-Tested Tips (300 pages, $14.95)

ISBN-10: 1-933512-08-3
ISBN-13: 978-1-933-512-08-2

Hundreds of successful college students and grads share their wisdom, tips, and advice on how to get top grades, find the right major, manage your time, stay motivated, avoid stress, seek out the best teachers and courses, and graduate – happily – at the top of the class. Special Editor Frances Northcutt is an academic advisor in the Honors Program at Hunter College in the City University of New York.

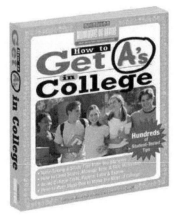

By intertwining practical advice on service and volunteerism with real-life stories of personal transformation, this book is the perfect companion for people who want to be inspired and informed and to take action to change their lives and their world. Edited by Michelle Nunn, Co-founder and CEO of Hands On Network.

BE THE CHANGE! CHANGE THE WORLD. CHANGE YOURSELF.
(336 pages, $14.95)
ISBN-10: 1-933512-00-8
ISBN-13: 978-1933512-00-6

"This is a wonderful and inspiring book."
—WALTER ISAACSON CEO, ASPEN INSTITUTE

"This is a book that could change your life … It's almost magic and it could happen to everyone. Go!"
—JIM LEHRER, ANCHOR, PBS' NEWSHOUR WITH JIM LEHRER

Need a job? An apartment? Insurance? A plan to pay for it all, without going into debt? Know how to cook and iron? And what ever happened to the weekend keg party? It seems like only yesterday that you were tossing your graduation cap in the air. Now, you're confronted with challenging real-world questions. There's

LIFE AFTER COLLEGE: THE NEW GRADUATE'S GUIDE
(428 pages, $16.95)
ISBN-13: 978-1933-512-907

no need to stress. Here's help. *Life After College* is an orientation guide to be- coming a successful, semi-mature adult. Special Editor Nadia Bilchik is a CNN anchor, author, keynote speaker, media trainer, and communications consultant.

Featured on the Today Show and in *USA Today!*

"… the perfect gift for the newly minted college graduates on your list."
—THE (CHARLESTON, SC) POST AND COURIER

ABOUT THE CONTRIBUTORS

BRENT J. BELL, PH.D., is an associate professor of outdoor education at the University of New Hampshire in Durham, NH. He researches student transition to college using outdoor and adventure based programs. Before coming to UNH, Brent designed the Adventure Bound Program at New England College (1991-1996), then directed the First-year Outdoor Program at Harvard University (1999-2005). Brent is the organizer of the Outdoor Orientation Program Symposium (www.outdoororientation.com). You can reach Brent at bbell@unh.edu.

LEE DESSER is Student Services Advisor at UC Berkeley. Lee earned a Master's of Education from the University of Southern California (USC). She has worked in career services at USC, Mount St. Mary's College, and UC Berkeley. Lee writes on higher education issues and has a passion for improving student services and advocating for students. Feel free to reach her at lmdesser@gmail.com.

DR. CLARICE FORD is the founder of Pass the P's Please (Pass the Knowledge). She is as an educational leader, consultant, author, minister, and speaker. Ford holds a doctorate degree in Educational Leadership from Fielding University and a Master's Degree in Multicultural/ Diversity Education from Antioch University. She has facilitated workshops on working with college students in religious and secular organizations nationwide, student and academic affairs, and diversity. As a result of her work, Dr. Ford speaks regularly at educational institutions and civic functions in the U.S. and abroad, and at spiritual conferences. Dr. Ford is the Associate Vice Chancellor of Student Services at a state institution in Illinois.

PAMELA M. GOLUBSKI, PH.D., is the Director of Training, Implementation and Standardization at Brightside Academy Inc. and has 16 years of experience in the areas of student academic and career advising, mentoring, specialized programming, teaching, training, onboarding, first-year experience, accreditation, and assessment in higher education. Currently, she is an Associate Editor for the International Journal of Adult Vocational Education and Technology.

DR. CASSANDRA C. GREEN, Director of the Academic Support Center at Delaware State University, leads a professional staff in providing academic support services for all DSU students. She enjoys teaching first-year courses that emphasize learning strategies and study skills. Her expertise and work is in Peer Educator support and training. Her professional workshops have included the following topics: practicing effective metacognitive and study skills; issues in diversity; students with learning disabilities; and effective communication/helping skills. Dr. Green has a B.A. in Psychology and an M.A. in Counseling from Indiana University of Pennsylvania, and an Ed.D. in Education from Wilmington University. She can be reached at cgreen@desu.edu.

THOMAS J. GRITES serves as assistant provost at The Richard Stockton College of New Jersey. He has been directly involved in the academic advising process in higher education for almost 40 years. He has served as a consultant, program evaluator, and faculty development workshop leader to more than 100 different campuses. He was instrumental in forming the National Academic Advising Association (NACADA) and held the position of president for two terms. Grites has authored more than 60 journal articles, position statements, book chapters, program evaluations, consultant reports, and has delivered over 80 conference presentations. He co-edited the second edition of *Academic Advising: A Comprehensive Handbook* and has co-authored an orientation textbook for transfer students, *Transfer Student Companion.* He is the Lead Editor of a 2012 NACADA monograph on advising transfer students. He earned his bachelor's and master's degrees from Illinois State University and completed his doctoral work at the University of Maryland. Both institutions honored Grites with Distinguished Alumni awards, and he was inducted into the College of Education Hall of Fame at Illinois State. You can reach Tom at: gritest@stockton.edu.

DOUGLAS HASTY is the First Year Experience Librarian with Florida International University Libraries in Miami. He has been with the university since 1990, first as the Interlibrary Loan Librarian, then Head of Access Services Department, and most recently as the FYE Librarian. Douglas earned his B.A. in History from Guilford College in Greensboro, NC, and his MLS at the University of North Carolina – Greensboro. He is active in a number of ALA groups and divisions.See http://douglashasty.com, and you can contact Douglas at hastyd@fiu.edu.

CHRISTINE KIRK-KUWAYE, PH.D., has worked in higher education for over 30 years, as an academic advisor, instructor in English and American Studies, and as a faculty in student affairs where she taught leadership courses. She and several colleagues publish collegewisdom.com, a blog for those who want to help students get the most out of their college experience. She has an M.A. in English and a Ph.D. in American Studies from the University of Hawaii at Manoa. She can be reached at kirkkuwaye.chris@gmail.com.

JIM LABATE has been the Writing Specialist in The Writing and Research Center at Hudson Valley Community College (HVCC) in Troy, New York, since 2000. He earned his bachelor's degree in English from Siena College in Loudonville, New York, and his master's degree, also in English, from The College of Saint Rose in Albany, New York. Jim worked as a high-school English teacher for 10 years and as a technical writer for 11 years before arriving at HVCC. Jim has also written four novellas: *Let's Go, Gaels; Mickey Mantle Day in Amsterdam; Things I Threw in the River, and My Teacher's Password* – see www.mohawkriverpress.com. You can reach Jim at j.labate@hvcc.edu.

JUSTIN LONG received his Bachelors of Science in Education and Masters of Science in College Student Personnel at The University of Southern Mississippi. He served as a Resident Assistant for two years and a Hall Director for three years. He currently works at The University of Southern Mississippi in the Department of Residence Life as Associate Director for Residence Education & Student Relations.

Whether it's art reviews, corporate communications, or her latest project, *Your Little Black Facebook,* **ELIZABETH LOVETT** infuses her artistic and creative background into everything. Her international background spanning London, Southeast Asia, and the deep South gives her a unique vantage point from which she observes emerging social trends. Lovett currently lives in Atlanta with her equally adventurous husband and much less adventurous beagle.

EDWIN B. MAYES, M.Ed., is the Director of First Year Experience and Family Programs at Case Western Reserve University. Mayes has 22 years of experience in Higher Education with a wealth of knowledge both in Student Affairs and Academic Affairs developing and implementing new programs to improve student retention and meeting the needs of students in their transition from high school to college. Mayes has served administrative roles at Earlham College, Wittenberg University, University of Colorado-Boulder, the University of Michigan and Wright State University. See http://case.edu/provost/enrollmentmgmt/ for information about First Year Experience and Family Programs, and http://firstyear.cas.edu/, which is aimed at Case's first-year incoming students. Edwin can be reached at Edwin.mayes@case.edu.

ANGIE MOCK'S varied career has taken her from CPA, to CEO of a hotel management company, to communications consultant, to relationship expert and co-author of *Your Little Black Facebook.* The common theme throughout her career has been her interest in people and their interactions: her colleagues, her friends and family, and the world at large. She has been interviewed by several media outlets on this subject, and she's always learning more. She lives with her husband and three children in San Antonio, Texas.

People and their stories hold no end of fascination for **ROBERT RHU.** A professional speaker and co-author of *Your Little Black Facebook* by day, after hours, his focus shifts to his music. An accomplished singer/songwriter, Rhu's music is a vehicle for connecting with audiences and telling his story. Rhu currently resides in Boulder, Colorado, where he wakes up every morning, looks at the mountains and is happy to be there.

DAVID ROTHMAN grew up in the New York City area. He received his Master's degree in TESOL from the University of Wisconsin in 1994. He also studied social policy as an international student at the University of Lund in Sweden. As a professional educator in English as a Second Language, he has taught abroad as a head instructor in Prague, Czech Republic and in the department of tourism at The University of Seville in Spain. He has coauthored a series of reading textbooks with Dr. Jilani Warsi, *Read to Succeed* and *Read to Achieve*, and has published multiple works of fiction. Currently, he is a full-time faculty member in the Department of Academic Literacy at Queensborough Community College, the City University of New York. David can be reached at drothman@qcc.cuny.edu.

PEYVAND MIRZADEH SILVERMAN, DVM, is a veterinarian with the South East Area Animal Control Authority in Downey, CA. She earned her DVM degree at Western University of Health Sciences in Pomona, CA in 2011. She moved to the US from Tehran in 2001 to pursue her dream to become a veterinarian. Her main goals as a shelter veterinarian are to promote responsible pet ownership and to increase the number of animals adopted from the shelters. As she was growing up in Iran, she always had a fondness for animals, fostering strays and adopting any animal that needed her help. Being a veterinarian is a true passion and calling for her. Together with her husband (Special Editor) Scott Silverman, she also takes care of Tina, Troy, Greg, Blackie, and occasional fosters. Her other hobbies include painting, traveling, cooking, hiking and swimming. She can be reached at pmirzadeh@westernu.edu.

TATUM SOO KIM, M.S.Ed., is the Director of Academic Services for New York University's Division of Programs in Business. In this role, she spearheads the administration of student services across admissions, registration, academic advisement, and student support services. In previous roles with NYU since 2005, Ms. Soo Kim directed the advisement process for both undergraduate and graduate students, supporting program development and curriculum requirements. Previously with Marymount Manhattan College in New York, Ms. Soo Kim served as Assistant to the Vice President for Student Affairs and Enrollment Management. Ms. Soo Kim holds an M.S.Ed. with a focus on Higher Education Administration from Baruch College of the City University of New York, and a B.A. in Psychology from Marymount Manhattan College. She has also taken coursework in Quality Assurance in Higher Education Administration from NYU, and is currently working toward a Doctorate of Philosophy in Organizational Leadership from the Chicago School of Professional Psychology. She can be reached at t.sookim@nyu.edu.

JILANI WARSI earned his Ph.D. in applied linguistics at Boston University. He has taught English as a Second Language courses at Salem State, Fisher, and Newbury Colleges; in Framingham StateCollege's overseas programs in Trinidad and Tobago, Guyana, and Bolivia; and in the Institute for English Language Programs (IEL) at Harvard University. He recently published, with colleague David Rothman, a content-based reading textbook series entitled *Read to Succeed* and *Read to Achieve*. Dr. Warsi is an Associate Professor in the Department of Academic Literacy at Queensborough Community College, the City University of New York.

DR. MICHELLE T. WILLIAMS is dedicated to empowerment through education. She has developed retention and support programs for academically at-risk, first generation, and minority students at the high school and college levels. Her expertise lies in the development and implementation of mentor training frameworks to be used in educational settings. She is currently researching/developing mentoring frameworks that enhance social and cultural capital. She is also a mentor to several students. Dr. Williams earned both her undergraduate and graduate degrees from Temple University. She graduated from Saint Joseph's University with her Doctorate in Educational Leadership, and was awarded the Rashford Award for Outstanding Dissertation. You can reach her at drmtwilliams@gmail.com.

ABOUT THE SPECIAL EDITORS

SCOTT C. SILVERMAN, ED.D., is the Associate Director of Student Affairs in the University Honors department at the University of California, Riverside, his alma mater. His professional career includes prior work coordinating new student orientation and first-year programming, advising student organizations and planning campus activities at UC Riverside, where he earned a B.S. and M.S. in Environmental Science.

In 2007, Scott earned an Ed.D. in Higher Education Administration from the University of Southern California. His doctoral research on Facebook and other online social networks, was chosen for the Outstanding Research Award by the National Orientation Directors Association (NODA) in 2008. Scott continues to be involved in NODA, serving on the Board of Directors and as an Associate Editor of the Journal of College Orientation and Transition, among other roles.

Throughout his tenure as a student, he was a heavily involved student leader and activist, having roles in multiple student organizations, student government, peer mentoring, and in community activities, including non-profit work. In addition to establishing two Non-Profit Organizations, Scott served as Vice President of Campus Internal Affairs, Academic Affairs Director and Senator for the Associated Students, then Graduate Division Liaison and Vice President of Academic Affairs of the Graduate Student Association, and as chair of the Chancellor's Student Services Fee Advisory Committee, just to name a few. Scott continues to be involved as an alumni volunteer, and through staff activities, including a 2010-2011 term as President of Staff Assembly.

Scott enjoys attending campus and community events with friends and family, and when the occasion arises, decking himself out in face paint and school colors on campus. He loves speaking on other college campuses as well, though he may not have your school colors in his face paint repertoire. Scott recently got married to the love of his life, Peyvand, a licensed veterinarian, and they live together in Pasadena with an assortment of pets. Follow him on Twitter @ ScottCSilverman.

FRANCES NORTHCUTT, ED.M., remembers that it was her work-study job at the Wesleyan University campus post office that first inspired her to seek a career in student affairs. She loved working at the post office window, where she explained all the complicated postage options to students, faculty, and staff, and made sure that care packages were delivered promptly. During her senior year, she made the move from the post office to the registrar's office. She also helped to start a peer advising program.

After completing her B.A. with honors in English, Fran struck out for the West Coast and became an academic advisor and admissions reader at the University of California, Berkeley. Later, she advised students and taught college skills courses at the University of the Sciences in Philadelphia. At night, she studied at Temple University and earned a master's degree in Higher Education Administration. Fran has presented at conferences of the National Academic Advising Association and was selected as the Outstanding Advisor (Primary Role) for the Mid-Atlantic region in 2006. Most recently, she has been an honors adviser and admissions reader for the Macaulay Honors College of the City University of New York. Fran lives in Manhattan with her husband and daughter.

ABOUT THE SERIES CREATORS

MARK BERNSTEIN graduated from the Wharton School of the University of Pennsylvania and later from NYU School of Law. Since college he helped launch CNN.com, helped start the nation's leading volunteerism not-for-profit and has still stayed friends with many friends from freshman year. While at Penn, Mark survived by starting a business that provided freshmen with "survival kits" consisting of unhealthy food purchased by parents, who were coping with the absence of their kids.

YADIN KAUFMANN graduated from Princeton University, and later from Harvard Law School and the Harvard Graduate School of Arts and Sciences. Since college he's been helping entrepreneurs start technology companies, and started a non-profit organization. While at Princeton, he was involved in journalism and started a student agency to publish a book he wrote. He survived his freshman year by chugging Hershey's syrup, straight up. Yadin and his wife Lori – whom he met during her freshman year! – wrote *The Boston Ice Cream Lover's Guide*.